Expert's Guide To Men's Tailoring

Patterns for different body shapes

Expert's Guide To Men's Tailoring

Patterns for different body shapes

Sven Jungclaus

Bibliografische Information der Deutschen Nationalbibliothek:
Die Deutsche Nationalbibliothek verzeichnet diese Publikation
in der Deutschen Nationalbibliografie; detaillierte bibliografische
Daten sind im Internet über www.dnb.de abrufbar.

© 2022 Sven Jungclaus
Cover and Illustrations by S. Samayeva

Herstellung und Verlag:

BoD – Books on Demand, Norderstedt
ISBN 9783756850297

All rights reserved. It is not permitted to save,
copy or otherwise reproduce this book or any part of it
in any form whatsoever, whether for private or educational use,
without the prior written consent of the copyright holder.

Contents

7	Preface
8	Body shapes
11	Taking measurements

Patterns for men with a belly

18	Under-belly pants for belly figures
28	Over-belly pants for belly figures
38	Single-breasted vest for belly figures
50	Shirt for belly figures
60	Shirt's sleeve for belly figures
64	Shirt's collar for belly figures
66	Single-breasted jacket for belly figures
80	Jacket's sleeve for belly figures
86	Collar for the single-breasted jacket

Patterns for Bodybuilder

88	Pants for extra muscular thighs
98	Alteration of a regular trouser pattern
100	Single-breasted vest for the bodybuilder
112	Shirt for the bodybuilder
122	Shirt's sleeve for the bodybuilder
-	Shirt's collar, see p. 64
126	Single-breasted jacket for the bodybuilder
140	Jacket's sleeve for the bodybuilder
146	Collar for the single-breasted jacket for the bodybuilder

More patterns

149	Pants for the straight body shape
150	Single-breasted jacket for a straight body shape
152	Vest for a straight body shape
153	Pants for strong hips
154	Single-breasted jacket for strong hips
156	Vest for strong hips

Appendix

158	Measurement table for belly figures
159	Abbreviations
160	Biography
161	Book recommendation
164	Index

Every person is different
Instead of forcing the customer into a norm, as it happens in the clothing industry with its ready-to-wear sizes, bespoke tailoring adapts to the people. Each body is individual and unique. Of course, a master tailor also categorizes the customer's body shape, but just in order to then develop the best possible personal pattern. In all variants of drawing a pattern, there are almost infinite possibilities in many places to adapt the pattern and set it up for the customer.

Any body shape is normal
There are no extraordinary body shapes in bespoke tailoring. There is also no 'norm' that should be particularly emphasized since every customer brings their challenges. But with a bit of practice in pattern drawing and conscientiousness in fitting and processing, each body can be dressed optimally.

Assistance by the pro
In this book, the proven step-by-step instructions ensure that even less experienced pattern designers can work out the ideal fit for men with trained muscles or a pronounced belly to make jackets, pants, etc. - based on individual body measurements.
Master tailor Sven Jungclaus has refined his know-how over the years in a practical way and is now passing on this knowledge in a way that is easy to understand. For starters, it is advisable to follow the instructions with the given measurements precisely to learn and internalize the processes. Then, once this knowledge has been consolidated, nothing stands in the way of a pattern with your measurements.

Have fun discovering different body shapes!

The body shapes

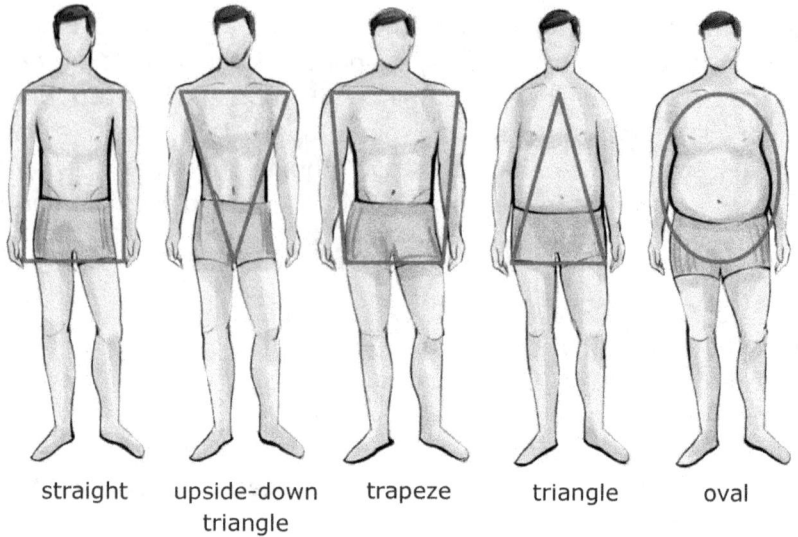

straight   upside-down   trapeze   triangle   oval
            triangle

Different body shapes
Although there are many different body shapes, they can be summarized in five basic shapes:

- the straight shape
- the upside-down triangle
- the trapeze
- the triangle
- the circle or the oval

The straight shape
The entire physique is relatively straight. This corresponds to the 'norm' in ready-to-wear clothing. Of course, we all know this norm does not exist, but it seems that most people are reached here. The shoulders are standard, and the hips are about the same width as the shoulders. The waist is, in proportion, not particularly small.
Of course, this 'norm' is available in any size (width) as well as in long or short. The clothing sizes here would be between 46 and 64 (the 'normal' German size), short between 23 and 32 (half the 'normal' German size) and long between 98 and 128 (twice the 'normal' German size). You can find this pattern for straight body shapes starting on page 149. More patterns can be found in the book 'Modern men's tailoring', see page 161.

The upside-down triangle
No ready-to-wear suit will fit this customer. There are a few things to consider here. The shoulders are broad and trained, and the chest muscles are pronounced. On the other hand, the waist and hips are relatively narrow and slim. You can choose the standard pattern for the trousers, but you should be aware that the thighs can be very strong (page 98). The jacket requires a special pattern and processing. A chest dart under the lapel should be used here. You should also pay special attention to the pressing process (ironing into shape).

The trapeze
This type is a mixture between the straight shape and the upside-down triangle. With the pattern, it is usually adequate to add a chest dart under the lapel (pages 132/133) and draw the jacket a little narrower at the waist and hips. The 'standard' pattern usually works for trousers.

The triangle
Even with this body shape, you can usually follow the 'standard' pattern. The hips are simply drawn wider. Likewise, the trousers will be a bit wider but still correspond to the 'standard' design. A dart or a second pleat may be required at the waistband seam of the front trousers. The patterns for wide hips can be found starting from page 153.

The circle or the oval
For this group of customers, the patterns are significantly different than the 'standard' ones. The basic principles are retained here, but you can work without the waist dart most of the time. Instead, a belly dart is worked in so that the jacket or waistcoat is not too wide and 'fluttering' below the belly. When it comes to pants, you have to decide whether the waistband goes over the belly and is held in place with suspenders or it runs under the belly, where a belt is usually adequate.
You can find the clothing sizes of the belly figures on page 158.

Taking measurements

Instructions for taking measurements

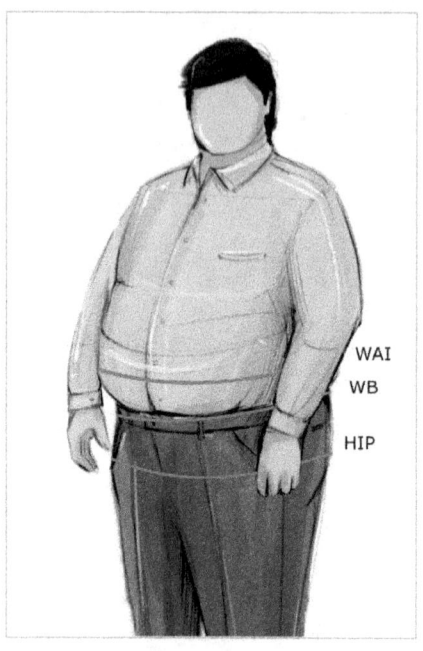

Waistline (*WAI*)
The waistline is measured exactly around the waist, just above the hipbone. Here a waist measuring tape is fixed to determine more measurements.

Waistband (*WB*)
The waistband is measured at the height of the desired position, exactly where the waistband of the pants should sit. This is very individual for each client.

HIP
The hip width, or seat, is measured horizontally around the strongest point of the buttocks.

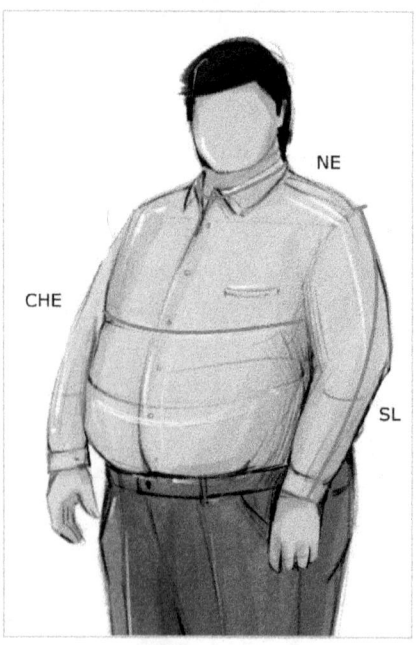

Neck (*NE*)
When measuring the neck, care must be taken that the tape measure is not set too high. The circumference is measured at the base of the neck (on the skin), directly above the collarbone. It helps to keep two fingers between the tape measure and neck not to measure too narrow.

Chest (*CHE*)
When measuring the chest, the tape measure will be placed around the strongest chest point, then passed under the arms and slightly higher at the back.

Sleeve length (*SL*)
Measure the sleeve length from the shoulder bone over a slightly bent elbow to the wrist.

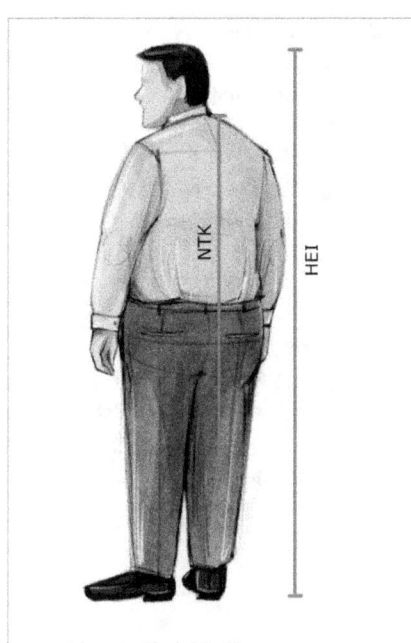

Height (*HEI*)

Mostly, the customer knows his height. However, if you do not trust this information, it is measured from the top of the head to the sole of the foot, preferably without shoes. Otherwise, simply subtract the heel height.

Nape to knee (*NTK*)

The nape-to-knee is measured from the 7th cervical vertebra along the mid-back across the seat to the knee.

Note

The 7th cervical vertebra is the vertebra protruding slightly at the back of the neck. In the pattern construction: it is called the cervical-vertebra-point **CVP**.

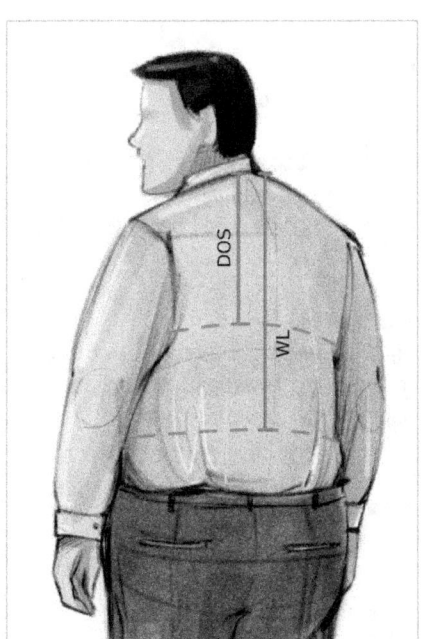

Depth of Scye / Depth of armhole (*DOS*)

To measure the depth of scye, push a piece of cardboard under the customer's arm and measure from the 7th cervical vertebra along the middle of the back to the upper edge of the cardboard.

Nape to waistline / Waist length (*WL*)

The length of the waist is measured from the 7th cervical vertebra along the middle of the back to the tape measure fixed at the waist.

Instructions for taking measurements

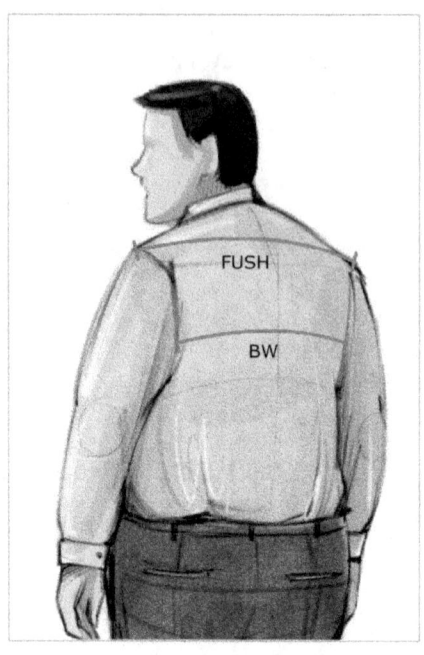

Full shoulder width (*FUSH*)
The entire shoulder width is measured from the left shoulder bone across the back to the right shoulder bone.

Back width / across back (*BW*)
It is measured across the back in a relaxed position, from the left to the right arm.

Note
The taken measurements should be used in the pattern instead of the calculated ones with clients that deviate from the 'standard' clothing sizes (broad shoulders, strong back, etc.). The calculated measurements are more used for the theory of proportions.

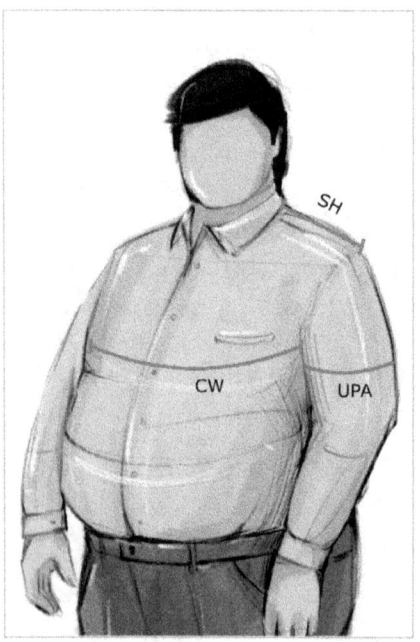

Shoulder width (*SH*)
The shoulder width is measured from the neckline to the shoulder bone.

Chest width / across chest (*CW*)
The chest width is measured across the strongest breast point from the left to the right arm.

Upper arm (*UPA*)
For strong biceps, this measure should be read necessarily. It is measured around the strongest point of the upper arm.

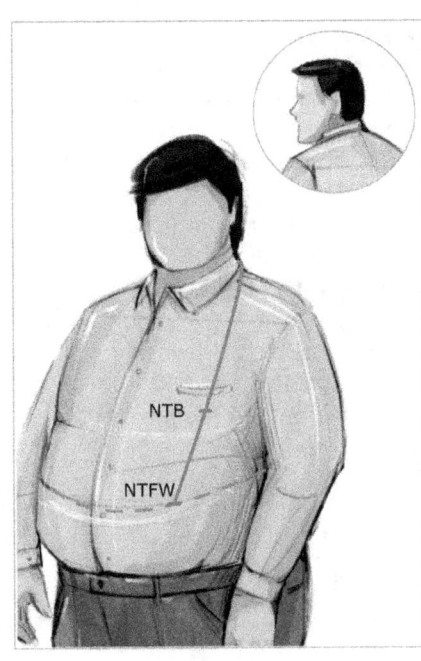

Nape to breast (*NTB*)

The nape to breast/chest is measured from the 7th cervical vertebra over the shoulder toward the front to the point of the breast. To draw a pattern, you will need the depth of breast *DOB* measurement.
For this, subtract the back neckline (*DOB* = *NTB* - back neckline). Pay attention to the seam allowances at the shoulders of the jacket and coat.

Nape to front waist (*NTFW*)

The nape-to-front-waist is measured from the 7th cervical vertebra over the shoulder across the breast point to the tape measure fixed at the waist. To draw a pattern, you will need the front-waist-length **FWL**. For this measure, just subtract the back neckline (*FWL* = *NTFW* - back neckline). Pay attention to the seam allowances.

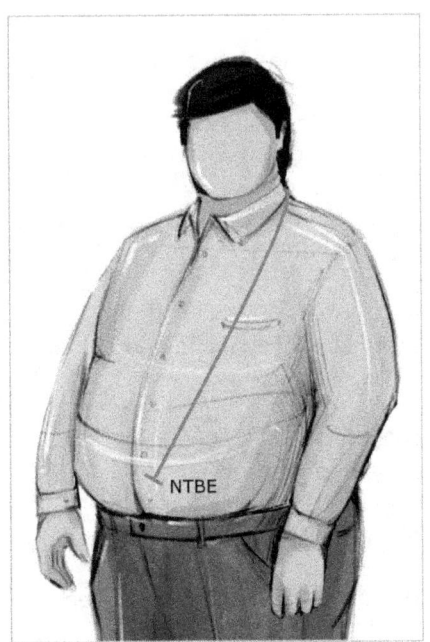

Nape to belly (*NTBE*)

The nape to belly is measured from the 7th cervical vertebra (see explanation on page 13), over the shoulder forwards, to the strongest point on the belly. Since there are different belly shapes, such as the high belly, pointed belly or hanging belly, this measurement is essential for a perfect fit.

Note

The measurements nape-to-front-waist *NTFW* and nape-to-belly *NTBE* are not the same.

Instructions for taking measurements

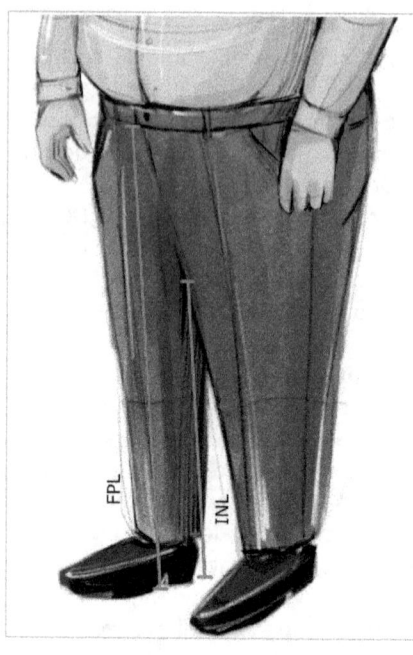

Inside leg (*INL*)

To measure the inside leg, have the customer pull up the pants into the crotch. Then it is easy to determine the measurement on the inside of the leg from the crotch to the floor. (If the customer wears shoes, the heel height is subtracted.)

Front pants length (*FPL*)

First, fix a tape measure at the point where the waistband should sit. Now the front length of the pants is measured from the waistband seam down to the floor. (If the customer wears shoes, the heel height is subtracted.)

Note

The *FPL*, and also the trouser fly are noticeably short at underbelly trousers.

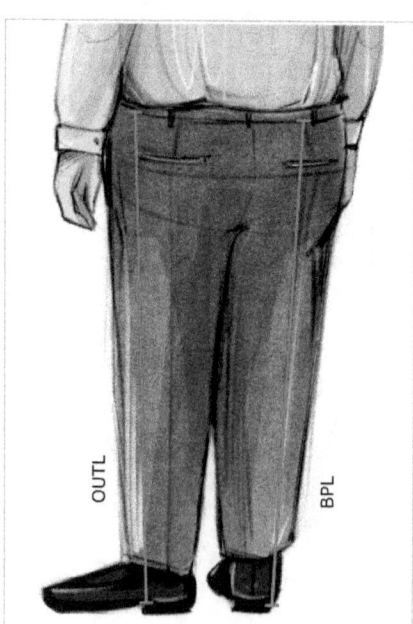

Outside leg (*OUTL*)

First, fix the tape measure at the point where the trousers' waistband should sit. Now the outside leg can be measured on the side from the waistband seam down to the floor.
(If the customer is wearing shoes, measure to the top of the heel.)

Rise

The difference between *OUTL* and *INL* results in the rise.

Back pants' length (*BPL*)

First, fix the tape measure at the point where the waistband should sit. Now the back pants' length is measured from the waistband seam to the floor.
(If the customer is wearing shoes, measure to the top of the heel.)

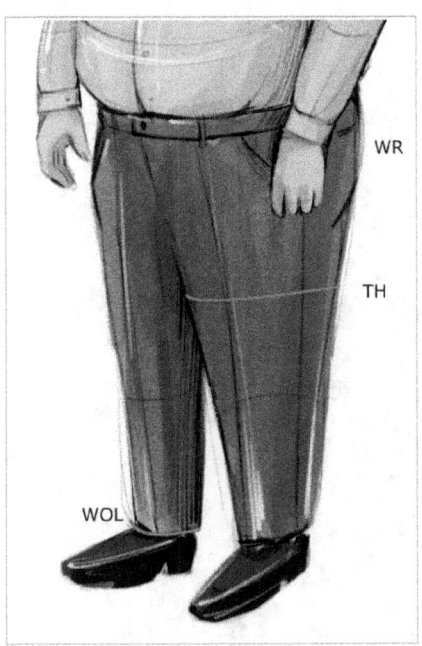

Wrist (*WR*)

The circumference is measured at the wrist, directly at the base of the hand. It helps to slide two fingers between the tape measure and the wrist to avoid measuring too tight.

Width of thigh (*TH*)

The thigh circumference is measured around the strongest point of the thigh, about 10 cm below the crotch.

Width of length (*WOL*)

The hem circumference is measured at the bottom of the trouser's hem according tov the customer's requirements.

Manual for the under-belly pants

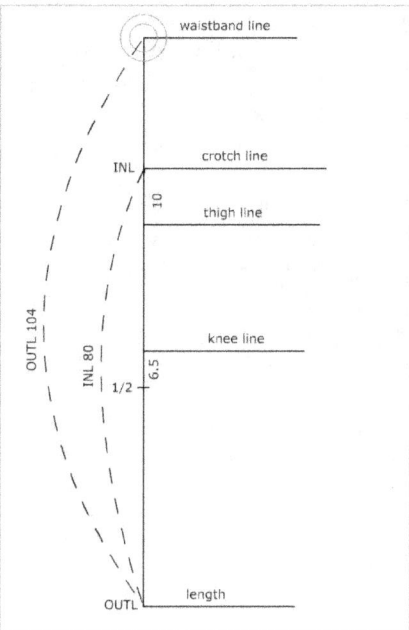

The measurements and further information can be found on page 25.

Start basic structure of front pattern
- draw a 90° angle
- the horizontal line is the waistband-line
- from starting point: mark down outside-leg *OUTL* 104 cm and square right, this line is the length *LG*
- from *LG*: mark up inside-leg *INL* 80 cm and square right; this line is the crotch-line
- from *LG*: mark up 1/2 *INL* + 6.5 cm and square right; this line is the knee-line
- from *INL*: mark down approx. 10 cm and square right for the thigh-line

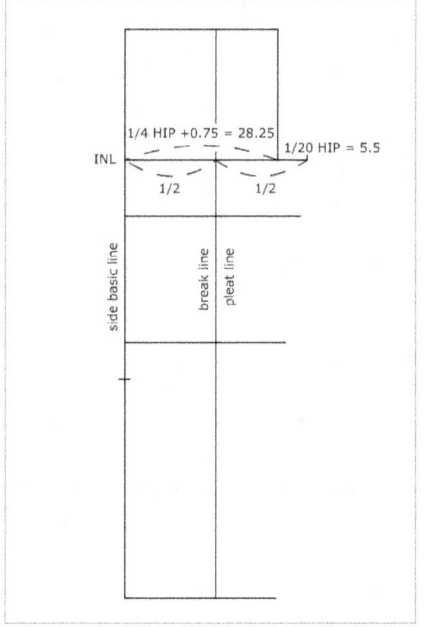

Basic structure
- on crotch-line from side-basic-line: mark to the right 1/4 hip-width *HIP* 27.5 + 0.75 (1/4 depth of pleat at the break line) = 28.25 cm and square up
- from this point: mark to the right 1/20 *HIP* = 5.5 cm
- on crotch-line: halve the hole section and square up and down; this line is the break-line or pleat-line
(see also page 27)
(the break line is also known as pleat line or crease line)

With or without pleat
- you will find more information about the depth of the pleat on page 20, picture 2
- if you draw the pants without pleats, the measurement of 1/4 *HIP* on the crotch-line will be suitable

The under-belly pants

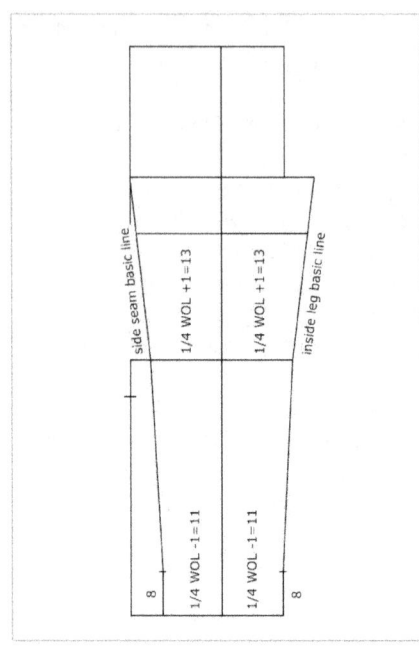

Width of length WOL
- on *LG*-line from break-line: mark to each side, 1/4 width of leg *WOL* - 1 = 11 cm, square up and mark 8 cm

Knee-width
- on knee-line from break-line: mark to each side 1/4 *WOL* + 1 = 13 cm
- connect the points at the knee-line with the points at the length
- connect the points at the knee-line with the points at the crotch-line

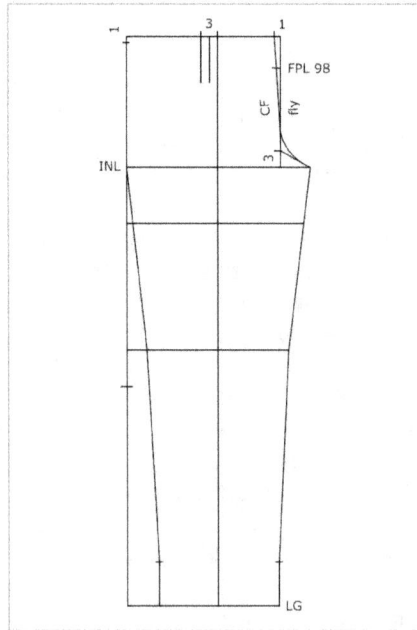

The fly - center front CF
- on fly-line from crotch-line: mark up 3 cm and connect with right point on crotch-line
- on waistband-line from fly-line: mark to the left approx. 1 cm and connect with previous point at center-front *CF*
- shape lower fly seam

- from *LG* to the top of the fly: mark up front-pants-length *FPL* 98 cm

The pleat
- on waistband-line from break-line: mark to the left 3 cm (2 x 1.5 cm) and square down
- on side seam from waistband-line: mark down approx. 1 cm

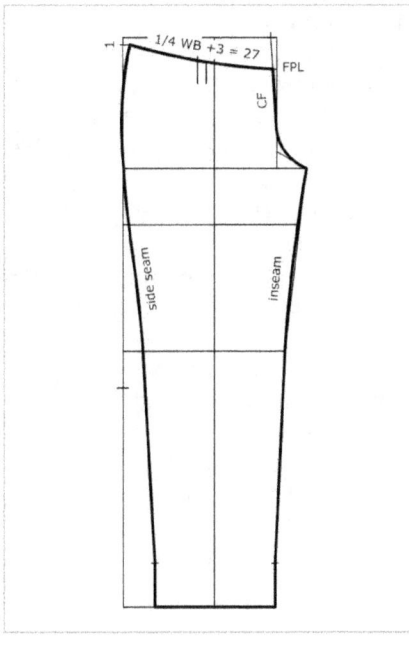

Waistband-line
- on side seam from 1-cm-point: draw curved line to crossing point of *CF/FPL*
- on waistband-line from *CF*: mark to the left 1/4 waistband *WB* + 3 (for the pleat) = 27 cm (this measurement should not extend beyond the side-seam-basic-line)

Finish the front-pattern
- shape side seam and inseam nicely

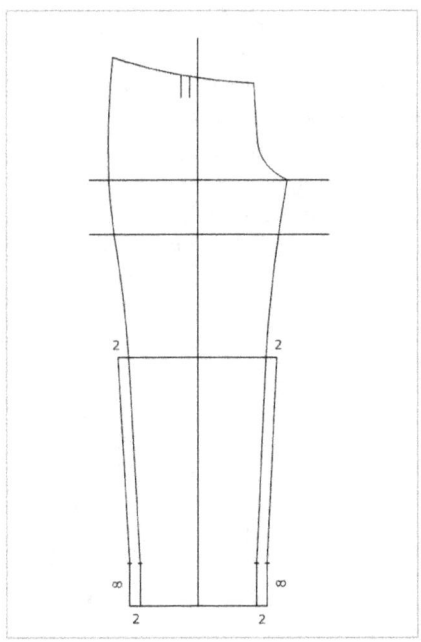

Back pattern
Cut out the front pattern and use it as a basis. Then, place it on a new piece of pattern paper.

- extend all lines (waistband-line, thigh-line, knee-line, length and break-line)
- on *LG*-line from the front pattern: mark 2 cm to each side, square up and mark 8 cm
- on kneeline from the front pattern: mark 2 cm to each side
- connect the points at the kneeline with the lower points

The under-belly pants

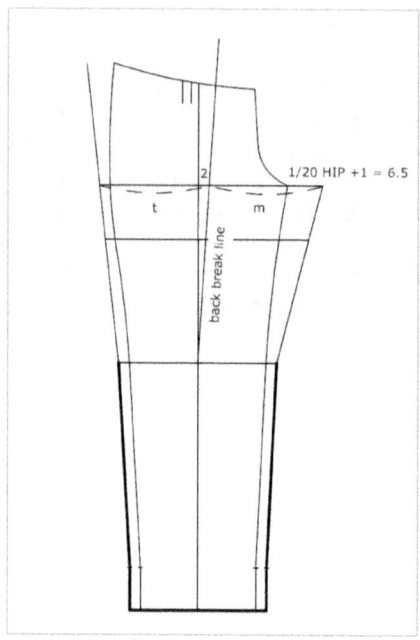

Width of back pants
- on crotch-line from front-break-line: mark to the right approx. 2 cm
- at the crossing of the front-break-line and knee-line: draw up a line through the previous 2-cm-point
- this line is the re-placed back-break-line
- on the crotch-line from the tip of the front trousers: mark to the right 1/20 HIP + 1 = 6.5 cm
- on crotch-line: measure M the entire distance from the tip of the back trousers to the new back-break-line and transfer T to the left
- finish inseam-basic-line and side-seam-basic-line as shown

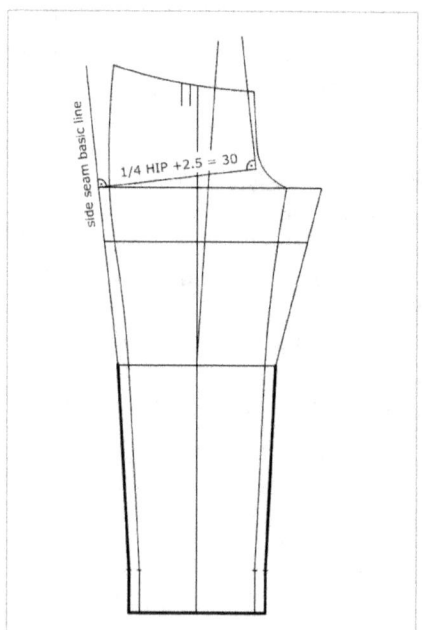

The inclination of the seat seam
- at the crossing of crotch-line and side-seam-basic-line of the back pants: square upward to the right
- on that line from side-seam-basic-line: mark to the right 1/4 HIP + 2.5 fullness = 30 cm and square up
- pierce this point with the tip of the pencil to transfer it to the lower paper

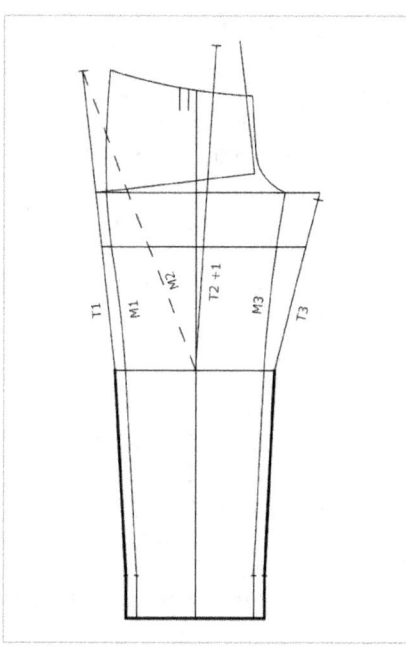

Back pants length *BPL*
- measure the length of the side-seam-basic-line at the front pants from the knee point up *M1* = 56 cm and transfer it to the side-seam-basic-line of the back pants *T1*
- from the crossing front-break-line/knee-line: measure up to the side-seam-basic-line of the back pants *M2* = 60 cm and transfer it + 1 cm to the back-break-line *T2* + 1 = 61 cm
- measure here from the top to the length *LG* and compare with the measurement *BPL* (see page 16)
- measure the length of the inseam-basic-line of the front pants from the knee-point up *M3* = 33.5 cm and transfer it to the back pants *T3*

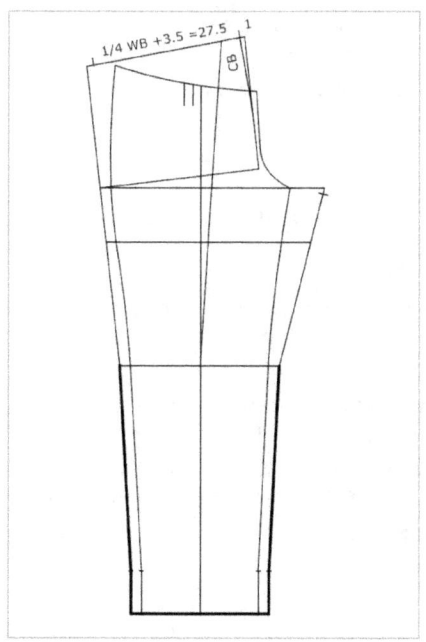

Width of waistband at back trousers
- connect the top points for the waistband of the back pants
- from right point on waistband-line: mark to the left approx. 1 cm for center back *CB*
- from the center back *CB*: mark to the left 1/4 waistband *WB* + 3.5 cm (for darts) = 27.5 cm
- this measure should not go beyond the side-seam-basic-line, otherwise decrease the darts
- if only one dart is required due to a smaller difference between the waistband and the hip, then the fullness at the back-waistband is also calculated just with one dart
- remove the front pants pattern and retrace all lines below, shape inseam and side seam (see picture on next page)

The under-belly pants

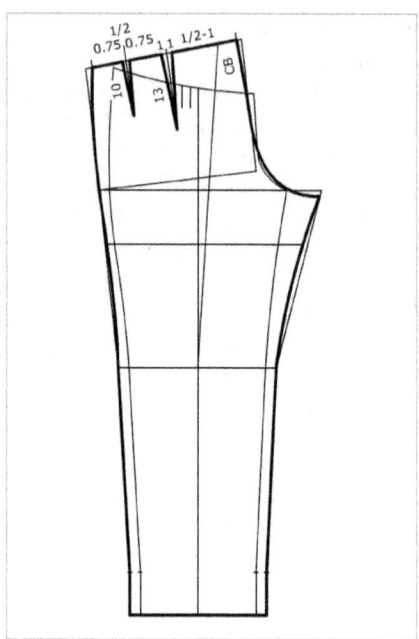

Darts at the back pants

Dart 1
- at waistband from *CB*: mark to the left 1/2 - 1 cm of the entire length of the back-waistband (including fullness for darts) and square down
- the dart length is approx. 13 cm
- the 1/2 dart is about 1 cm on both sides (it depends on the difference between hips and waistband)

Dart 2
(the quantity of darts depends on the difference between hips and waistband)
- halve the distance between side seam and 1st dart and square down
- the dart length is approx. 10 cm
- the 1/2 dart is about 0.75 cm
- the width for both darts is approx. 3.5 cm in total

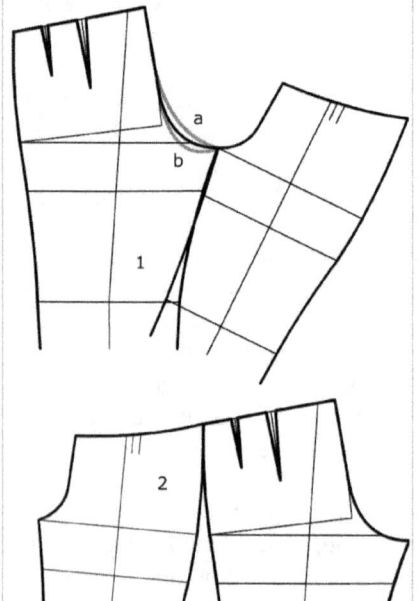

1. Shaping the seat-seam
- put the inseam of the front pants to the inseam of the back pants and shape the seat-seam

Note
Make sure that the curve of the seat-seam is not too flat (a) and definitely not too deep (b).
Otherwise, the back pants will be too tight at the butt.

2. Controlling the waistband-line
- put the side seam of the front pattern to the side seam of the back pattern, control the shape of the waistband-line and level out if necessary

Cutting
- cut front pants 2 x
- cut back pants 2 x

Instructions
- all measures are in cm
- all seams are without seam allowances
- the lower parts of the front and back pants' breakline serve as the grainline

Fullness
At the waistband, the measure should fit exactly. The fullness at the 1/2 hips should be about 2.5 cm + 1/4 of the pleat-measure.
This fullness is already considered in the calculation.

Measurements for the pants

			1/2	1/4
Waistband	(WB)	96	48	24
Hips	(HIP)	110	55	27.5
Outside leg	(OUTL)	104		
Front pants length	(FPL)	98		
Back pants length	(BPL)	108		
Inside leg	(INL)	80		
Width of length	(WOL)	48	24	12

Seam allowances

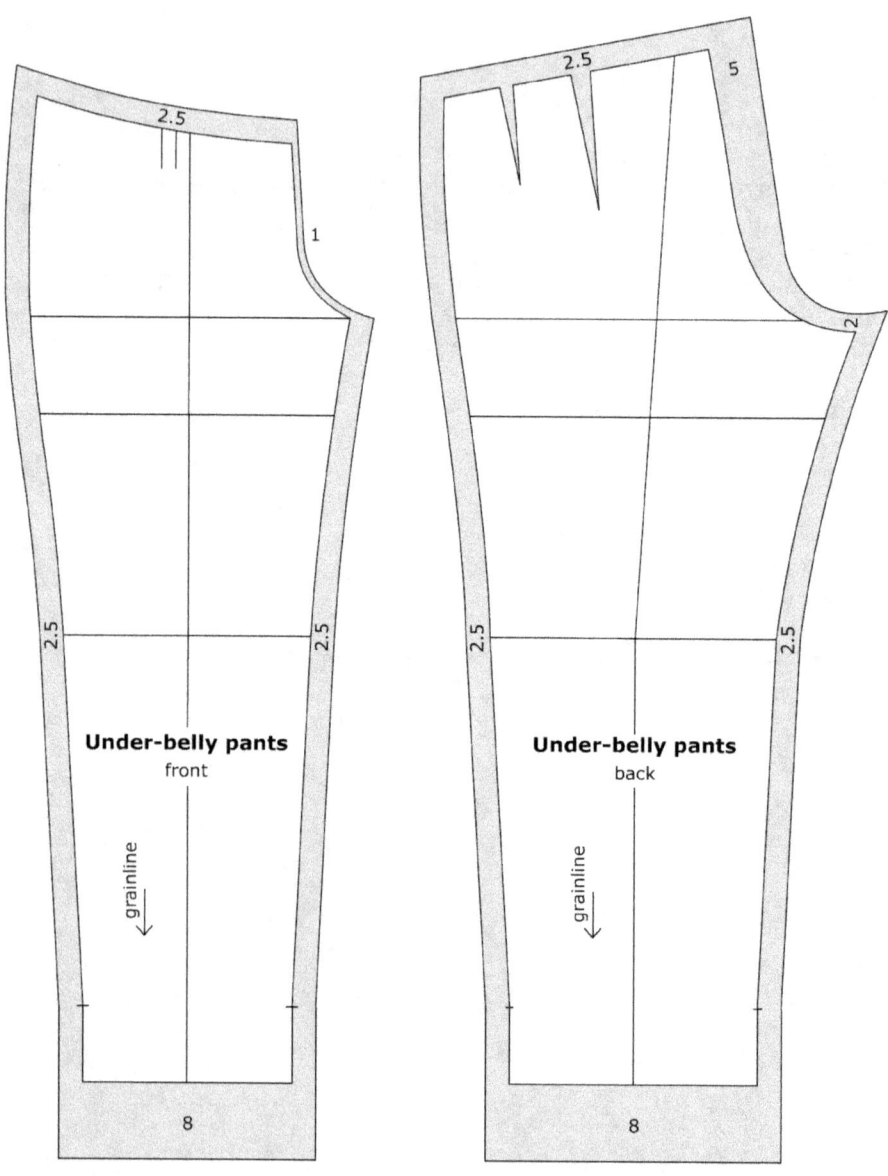

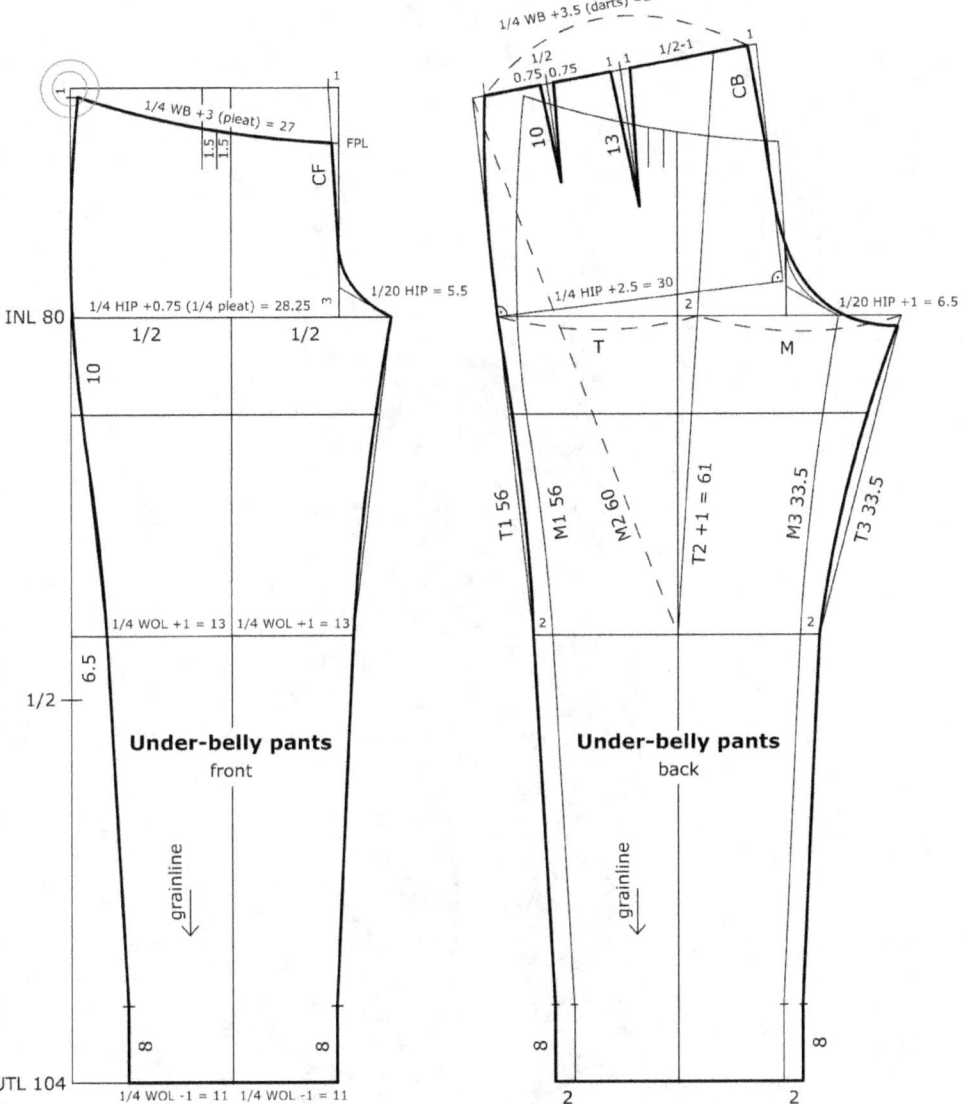

Manual for the over-belly pants

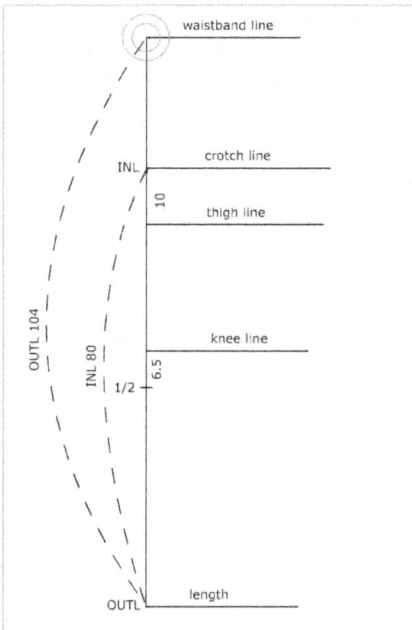

The measurements and further information can be found on page 35.

Start basic structure of front pattern

- draw a 90° angle
- the horizontal line is the waistband-line
- from starting point: mark down outside-leg *OUTL* 104 cm and square right; this line is the length *LG*
- from *LG*: mark up inside-leg *INL* 80 cm and square right; this line is the crotch-line
- from *LG*: mark up 1/2 *INL* + 6.5 cm and square right; this line is the knee-line
- from *INL*: mark down approx. 10 cm and square right for the thigh-line

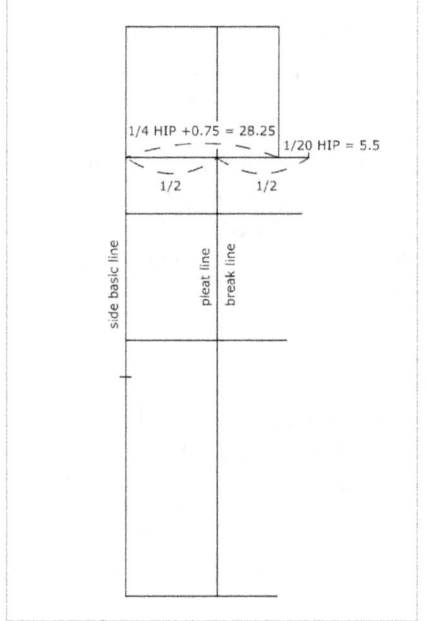

Basic structure

- on crotch-line from side-basic-line: mark to the right 1/4 hip-width *HIP* 27.5 + 0.75 (1/4 depth of pleat at the break line) = 28.25 cm and square up (the break line is also known as pleat line or crease line)
- from this point: mark to the right 1/20 *HIP* = 5.5 cm
- on crotch-line: halve the hole section and square up and down; this line is the break-line or pleat-line (see also page 37)

With or without pleat

- you will find more information about the depth of the pleat on page 30, picture 2
- if you draw the pants without pleats, the measurement of 1/4 *HIP* on the crotch-line will be suitable

29

The over-belly pants

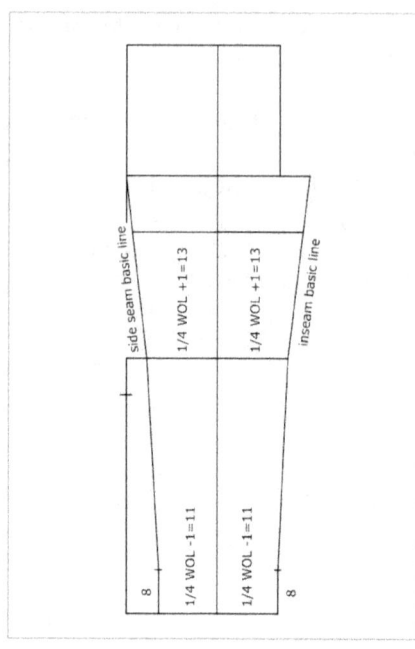

Width of length WOL
- on *LG*-line from break-line: mark to each side 1/4 width of leg *WOL* - 1 = 11 cm, square up and mark 8 cm

Knee-width
- on knee-line from break-line: mark to each side 1/4 *WOL* + 1 = 13 cm
- connect the points at the knee-line with the points on the length
- connect the points at the knee-line with the points at the crotch-line

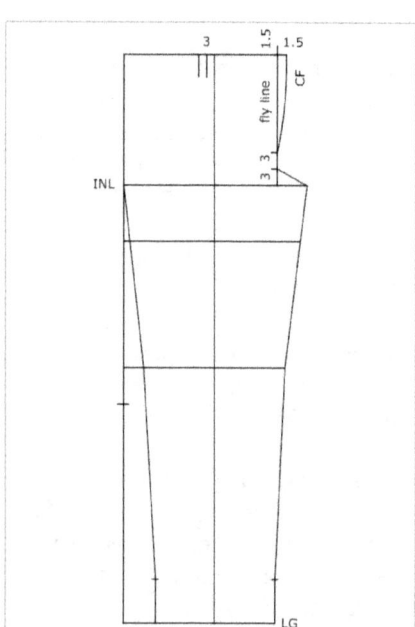

The fly - center front *CF*
- on fly-line from crotch-line: mark up 3 cm and connect with right point on crotch-line
- on fly-line from previous point: mark up 3 cm
- on waistband-line from fly-line: mark to the right belly-difference *BD* = 1/4 *WB* - 1/4 *HIP* = 1.5 cm
- on fly-line from waistband-line: mark up *BD* 1.5 cm
- shape fly seam at *CF*

The pleat
- on waistband-line from break-line: mark to the left 3 cm (2 x 1.5 cm) and square down

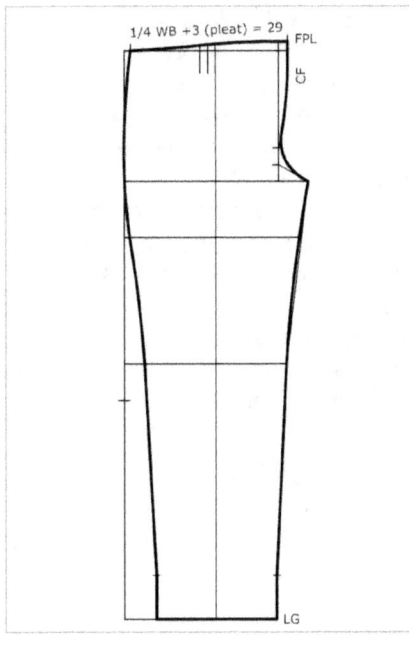

Waistband-line
- on waistband-line from *CF*:
  mark to the left 1/2 waistband *WB* + 3 cm
  (for the pleat) = 29 cm
  (this measurement should not
  extend beyond the side-seam-basic-line)
- shape waistband-line nicley
- draw *CF* nicely shaped
- from *LG* to *CF* at waistband-line:
  control the measurement front-pants-
  length *FPL* 105 cm

Finish the front-pattern
- shape side seam and inseam nicely

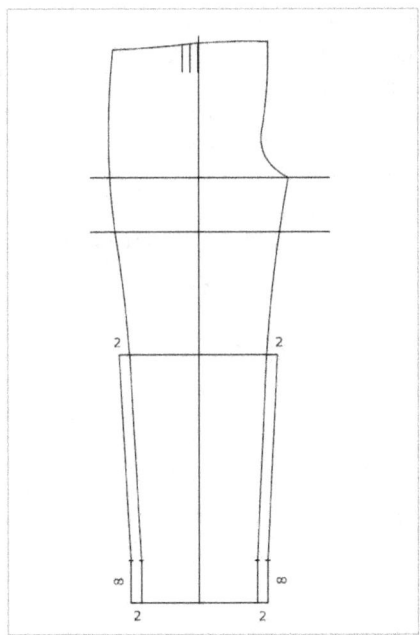

Back pattern
Cut out the front pattern and use it as a basis. Then, place it on a new piece of pattern paper.

- extend all lines (waistband-line, thigh-line, knee-line, length and break-line)
- on *LG*-line from the front pattern:
  mark 2 cm to each side, square up
  and mark 8 cm
- on knee-line from the front pattern:
  mark 2 cm to each side
- connect the points at the knee-line with the lower points

The over-belly pants

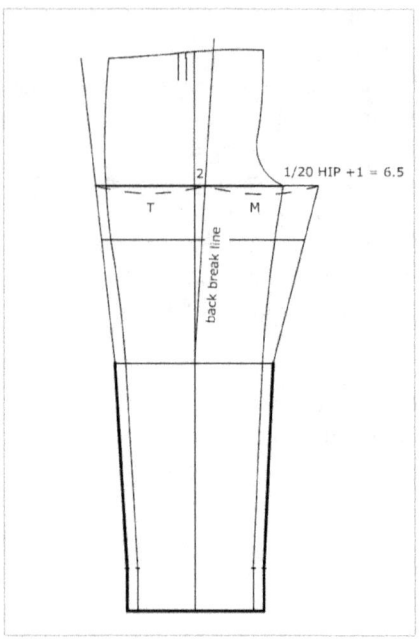

Width of back pants
- on crotch-line from front-break-line: mark to the right approx. 2 cm
- at the crossing of the front-break-line and knee-line: draw up a line through the previous 2-cm-point
- this line is the re-placed back-break-line
- on the crotch-line from the tip of the front trousers: mark to the right 1/20 *HIP* + 1 = 6.5 cm
- on crotch-line: measure *M* the entire distance from the tip of the back trousers to the new back-break-line and transfer *T* to the left
- finish inseam-basic-line and side-seam-basic-line as shown

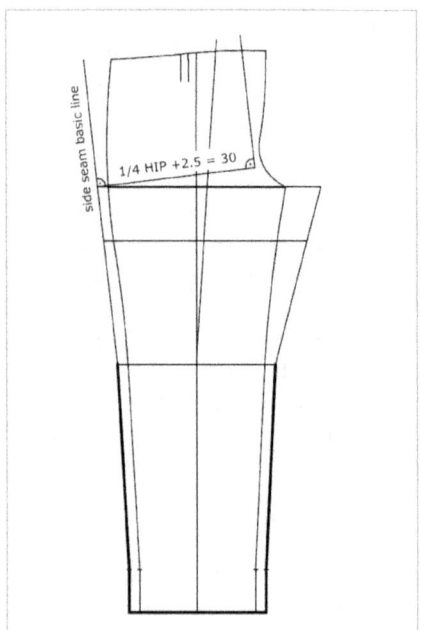

The inclination of the seat seam
- at the crossing of crotch-line and side-seam-basic-line of the back pants: square upward to the right
- on that line from side-seam-basic-line: mark to the right 1/4 *HIP* + 2.5 fullness = 30 cm and square up
- pierce this point with the tip of the pencil to transfer it to the lower paper

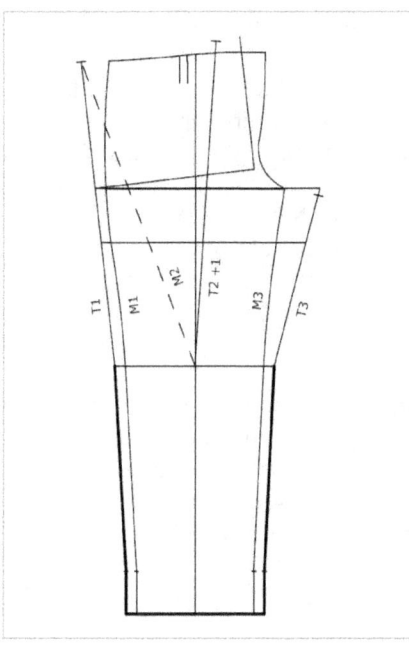

Back pants length *BPL*
- measure the length of the side-seam-basic-line at the front pants from the knee point up *M1* = 56 cm and transfer it to the side-seam-basic-line of the back pants *T1*
- from the crossing front-break-line/knee-line: measure up to the side-seam-basic-line of the back pants *M2* = 60 cm and transfer it + 1 cm to the back-break-line *T2* + 1 = 61 cm
- measure here from the top to the length *LG* and compare this measure with the taken measurement *BPL* (see page 16)
- measure the length of the inseam-basic-line of the front pants from the knee-point up *M3* = 33.5 cm and transfer it to the back pants *T3*

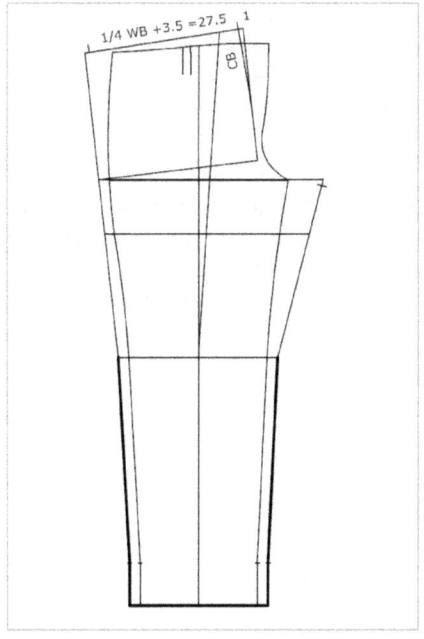

Width of waistband at back trousers
- connect the top points for the waistband of the back pants
- from right point on waistband-line: mark to the left approx. 1 cm
- from the center back *CB*: mark to the left 1/4 waistband *WB* + 3.5 cm (for darts) = 27.5 cm
- this measure should not go beyond the side seam, otherwise decrease the darts
- if only one dart is required due to a smaller difference between the waistband and the hip, then the fullness at the back-waistband is also calculated just with one dart
- remove the front pants pattern and retrace all lines below shape inseam and side seam (see picture on next page)

The over-belly pants

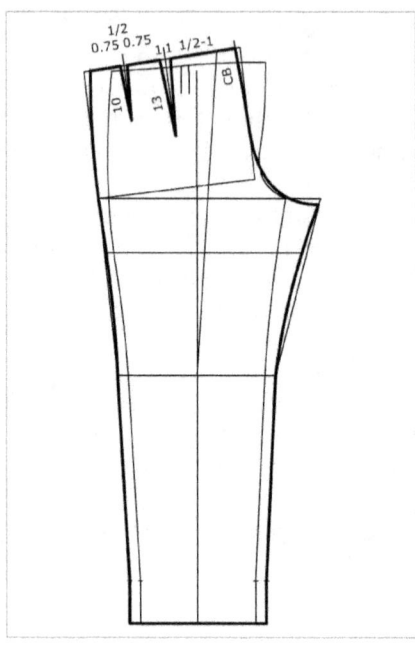

Darts at the back pants

Dart 1
- at waistband from *CB*: mark to the left 1/2 - 1 cm of the entire length of the back-waistband (including fullness for darts) and square down
- the dart length is approx. 13 cm
- the 1/2 dart is about 1 cm on both sides (it depends on the difference between hips and waistband)

Dart 2
(the quantity of darts depends on the difference between hips and waistband)
- halve the distance between side seam and 1st dart and square down
- the dart length is approx. 10 cm
- the 1/2 dart is about 0.75 cm
- the width for both darts is approx. 3.5 cm in total

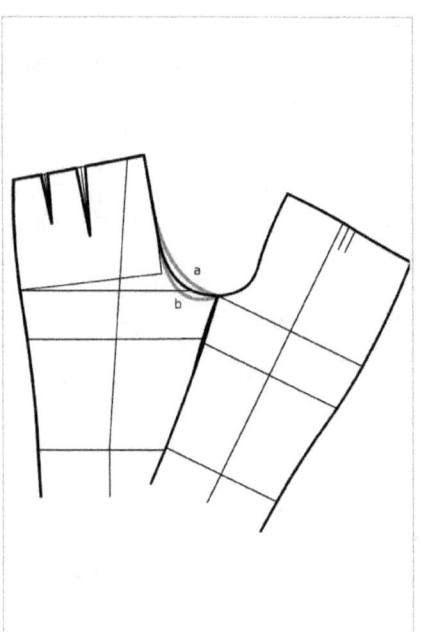

Shaping the seat-seam
- put the inseam of the front pants to the inseam of the back pants and shape the seat-seam

Note
Make sure that the curve of the seat-seam is not too flat (a) and definitely not too deep (b).
Otherwise, the back pants will be to tight at the butt.

Cutting
- cut front pants 2 x
- cut back pants 2 x

Instructions
- all measures are in cm
- all seams are without seam allowances
- the lower parts of the front and back pants' breakline serve as the grainline

Fullness
At the waistband, the measure should fit exactly. The fullness at the 1/2 hips should be about 2.5 cm + 1/4 of the pleat-measure.
This fullness is already considered in the calculation.

Measurements for the pants

		1/2	1/4
Waistband	(WB)	104 | 52	26
Hips	(HIP)	110 | 55	27.5
Outside leg	(OUTL)	104	
Front pants length	(FPL)	105	
Back pants length	(BPL)	108	
Inside leg	(INL)	80	
Width of length	(WOL)	48 | 24	12

Calculated measurements
belly-difference   (BD)   1/4 WB - 1/4 HIP = 1.5 cm

Seam allowances

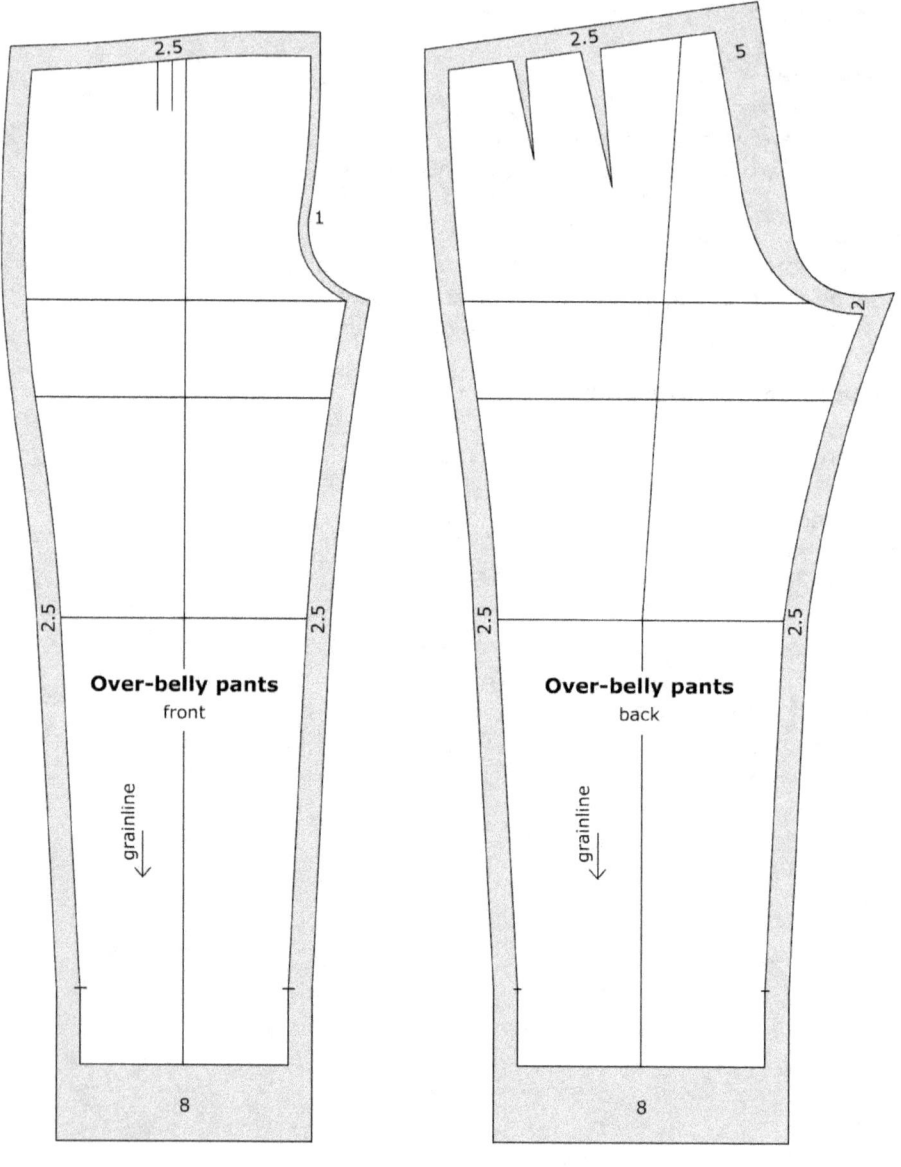

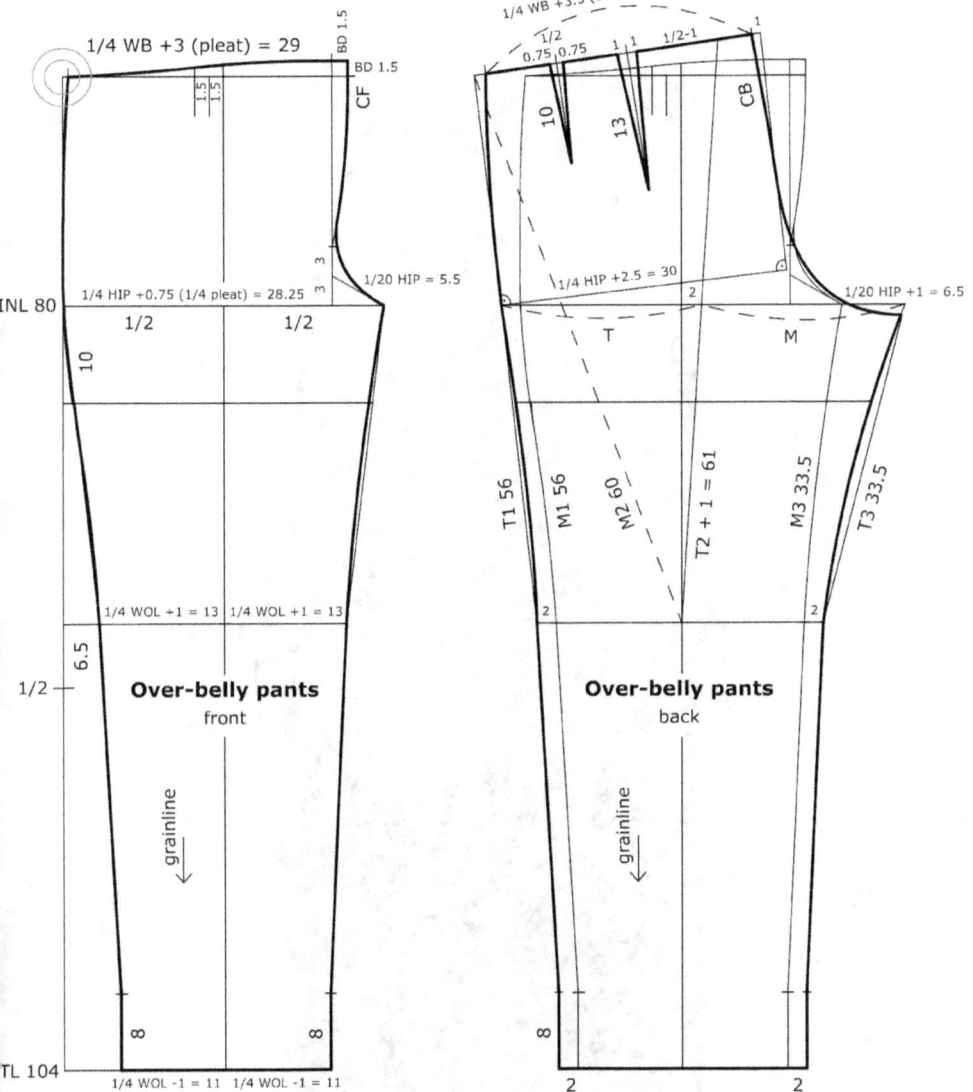

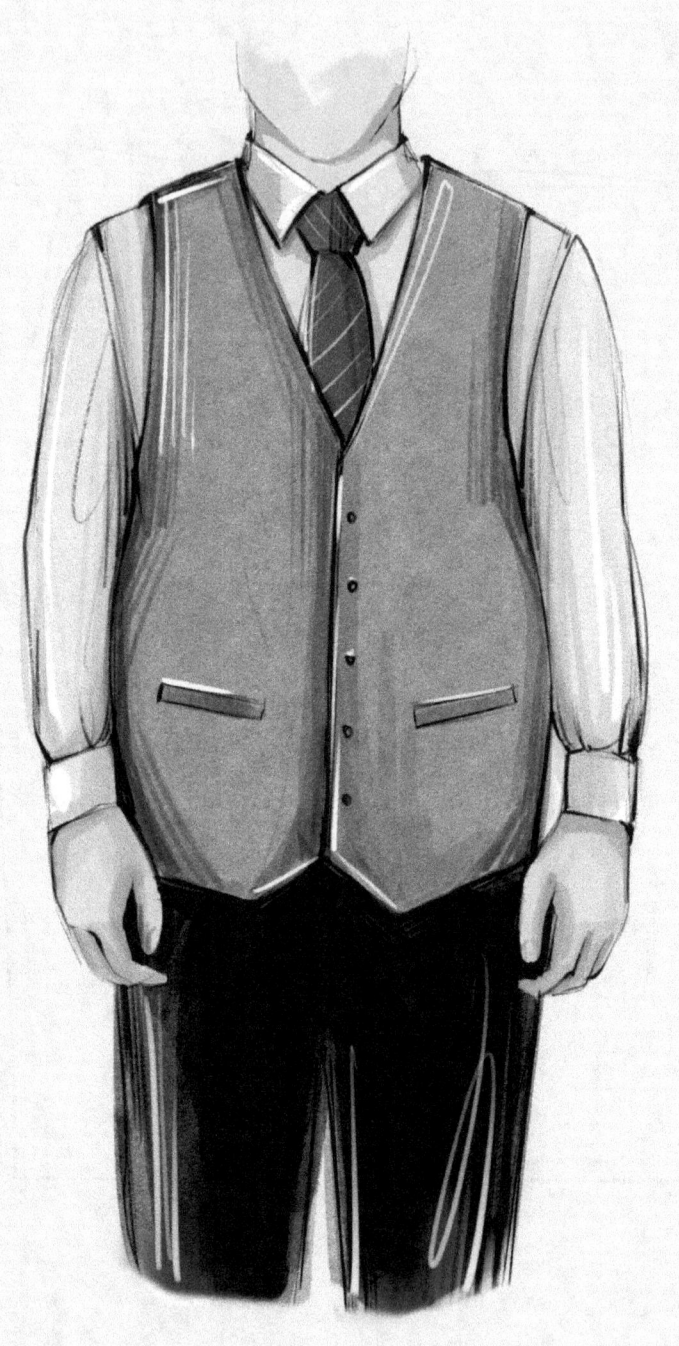

Manual for a single-breasted vest for the belly

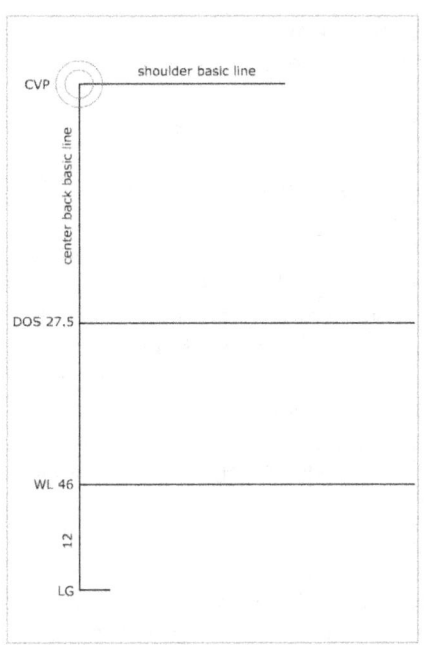

The measurements and further information can be found on page 46.

Start
- draw a 90° angle
- vertical line is the center-back-basic-line
- horizontal line is the shoulder-basic-line
- on center-back-basic-line from 7th cervical-vertebra-point *CVP*:
  mark down depth-of-scye *DOS* = 1/16 *HEI* + 1/8 *CHE* + 1 = 27.5 cm and square right (chest-line)
- on center-back-basic-line from *CVP*:
  mark down waist-length *WL* = 1/4 *HEI* + 1 = 46 cm and square right (waistline)
- on center-back-basic-line from *WL*:
  mark down approx. 12 cm and square right

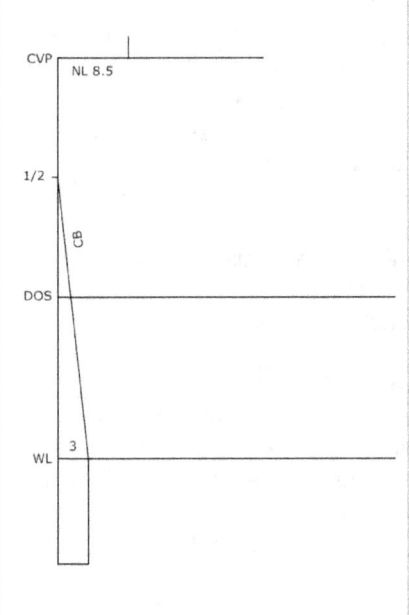

Center-back-seam
- on center-back-basic-line: halve the line between *CVP* and *DOS*
- on *WL*-line from center-back-basic-line: mark to the right 3 cm and square down
- connect this point with previous 1/2-point
- this line will become the center-back *CB*

Length of the waistcoat
- when drawing the length, make sure that the waistcoat covers the trousers' waistband

Neckline, shoulder
- on shoulder-basic-line from *CVP*:
  mark to the right neckline
  NL = 1/6 *NE* + 1 = 8.5 cm and square up

The single-breasted vest for the belly

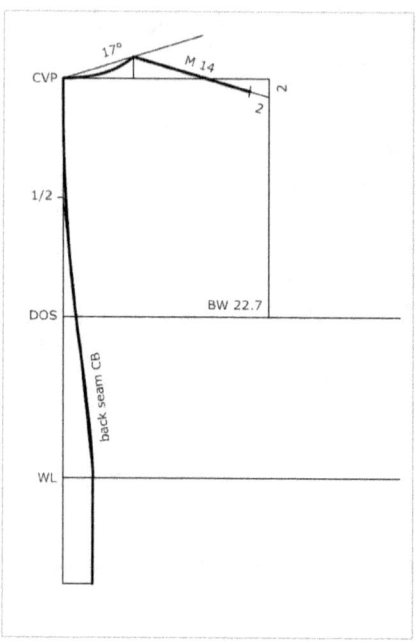

Center-back-seam
- shape seam at center-back CB

Shoulder
- on chest-line from seam at *CB*: mark to the right back-width $BW = 1/10\ CHE + 10.5 = 22.7$ cm and square up
- at *CVP*: create a 17° angle to the right up
- on *BW*-line from shoulder-basic-line: mark down 2 cm and connect this point with previous point at neckline
- mark shoulder seam from *BW*-line 2 cm narrower and measure this line M = approx. 14 cm
  (you will need this for the front shoulder)
- shape back-neckline

Note
The shoulder can be drawn broader or narrower, just as you wish for your design.

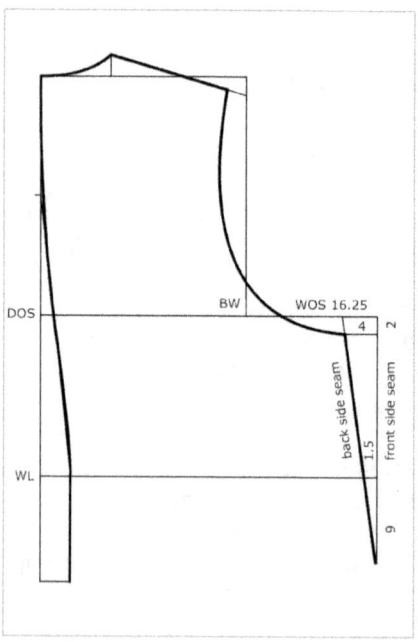

Side seam
- on chest-line from *BW*-line: mark to the right width-of-scye $WOS\ 1/8\ CHE + 1 = 16.25$ cm and square down
- on *DOS*-line from front-side-seam: mark to the left 4 cm
- on front side seam from *WL*-line: mark down approx. 9 cm
- on *WL*-line from front-side-seam: mark to the left 1.5 cm
- finish back-side-seam

Armhole
- at side seam from chest-line: mark down 2 cm
- this armhole enlargement is to give the wearer more room for moving his arms
- shape back armhole nicely

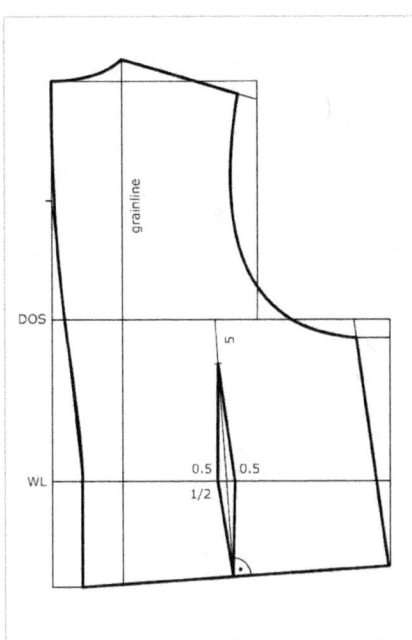

Hem
- connect lower point at *CB* with lower point at side seam

Dart
- at the back: halve *WL*-line
- from hem: square up through previous point
- on dart-line from chest-line: mark down 5 cm
- mark depth of the dart with 0.5 cm each
- the depth of the dart depends on the shaping at the back waist
- finish dart as shown

Grainline
- draw a line parallel to the center-back-basic-line

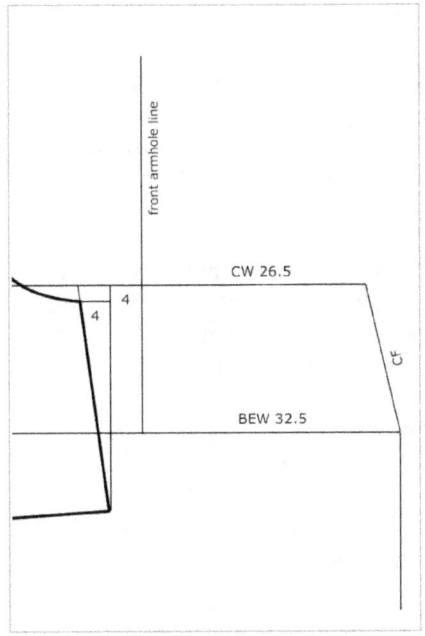

Basic front frame
- extend chest-line and *WL*-line to the right
- on chest-line from side seam: mark to the right 4 cm (this is the amount that has been subtracted from the width-of-scye *WOS* at the back armhole) and square up and down; this is the front-armhole-line
- from here on chest-line: mark to the right chest-width *CW* = 1/4 *CHE* - 4 = 26.5 cm
- on *WL*-line from front-armhole-line: mark to the right *BEW* belly-width = 1/4 *WAI* = 32.5 cm and square down
- connect *CW*-point and *BEW*-point; this line is the center-front *CF*

Note
The chest-line is called *DOS*-line or *BW*-line at the back and *CW*-line at the front.

The single-breasted vest for the belly

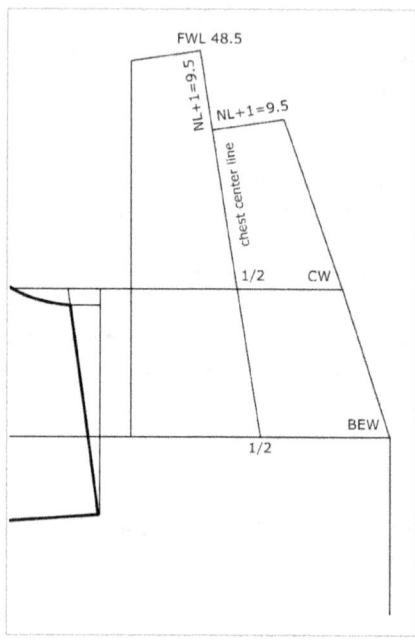

Shoulder
- halve distance on *CW*-line
- halve distance on *BEW*-line
- connect both previous points
- on chest-center-line from *WL*-line: mark up front-waist-lenght *FWL* = nape-to-front-waist *NTFW* - 10 (back neckline) = 48.5 cm and square left; this is the shoulder-basic-line

Neckline
- on chest-center-line from shoulder-basic-line: mark down front neckline *NL* = (1/6 *NE* + 1) + 1 = 9.5 cm square right and mark *NL* + 1 = 9.5 cm
- connect this point with *CF* on chest-line

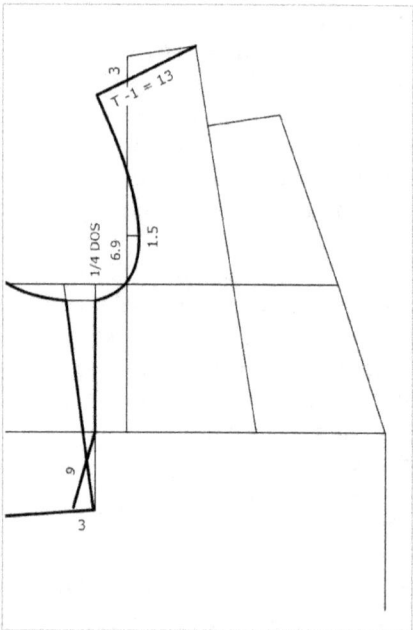

Shoulder
- at front-armhole-line from shoulder-basic-line: mark down 3 cm
- connect this point with point at neckline and transfer *T* the measure from back-shoulder - 1 cm = 13 cm

Armhole
- on front-armhole-line from chest-line: mark up 1/4 *DOS* = 6.9 cm, square right and mark approx. 1.5 cm
- shape front armhole nicely

Side seam
- on back lenght (hem) from back-side-seam: mark to the left 3 cm and connect this point with front-side-seam on *WL*-line
- on previous line: mark 9 cm

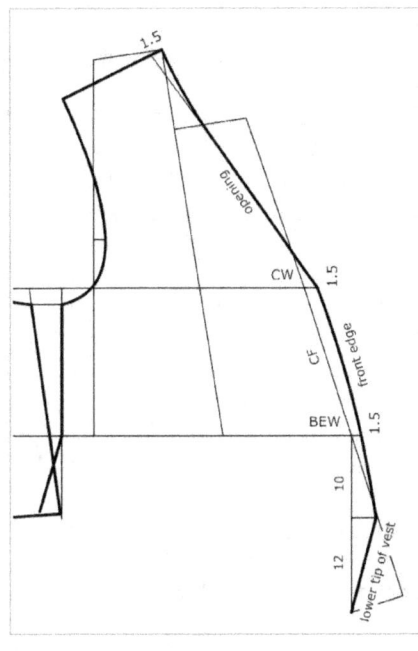

Opening

- at shoulder tip: mark to the left 1.5 cm
- on *CW*-line from *CF*: mark to the right 1.5 cm
- on *BEW*-line from *CF*: mark to the right 1.5 cm
- connect 1.5-cm-point at shoulder with front edge on *CW*-line
- shape opening by hollowing it slightly

Tip of vest

- on *CF* from *WL*-line: mark down 10 cm and square right
- from previous point: mark down 12 cm
- on *CF* from *BEW*-line: extend line downward and square left
- shape front edge slightly curved
- finish the lower tip of the vest at the lower front edge

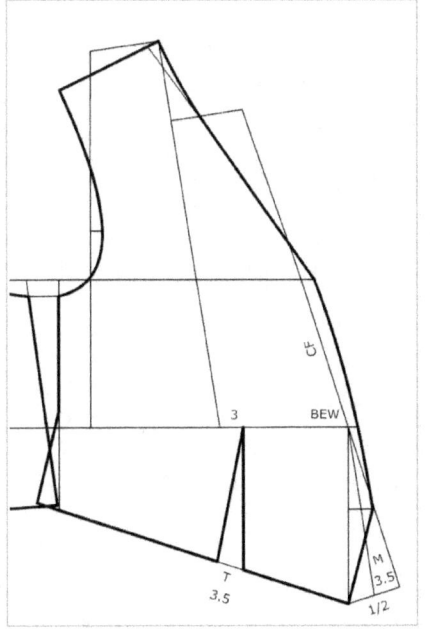

Tip of vest

- on 90° line from extended *CF*: halve the distance and measure one halve
  $M = 3.5$ cm

Length (hem)

- connect lower front side seam with lower tip of the vest

Belly dart

- on *WL*-line from chest-center-line: mark to the right 3 cm and square down
- on hem-line from previous line: transfer to the left, the measured distance at lower tip of the vest $T = 3.5$ cm
- connect previous point with 3-cm-point on *BEW*-line

The single-breasted vest for the belly

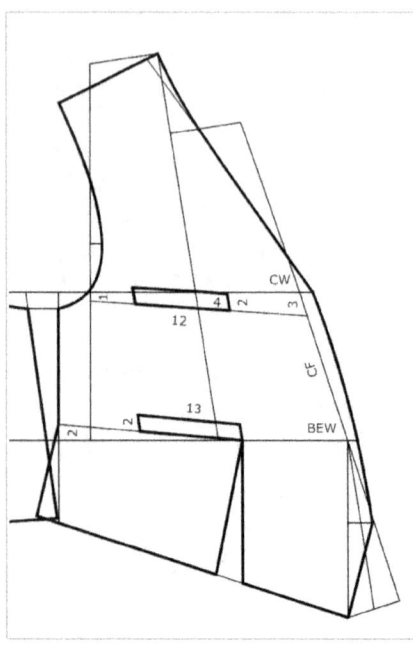

Chest pocket
- at front-armhole-line from chest-line: mark down 1 cm
- at *CF* from chest-line: mark down 3 cm
- connect both points
- from chest-center-line: mark to the right 4 cm and square down parallel to the chest-center-line
- mark height of welt with approx. 2 cm
- mark pocket-opening with approx. 12 cm

Waist pocket
- at front-armhole-line from *WL*-line: mark up 2 cm
- connect previous point with tip of belly-dart
- mark height of welt with approx. 2 cm parallel to the chest-center-line
- mark pocket-opening with approx. 13 cm

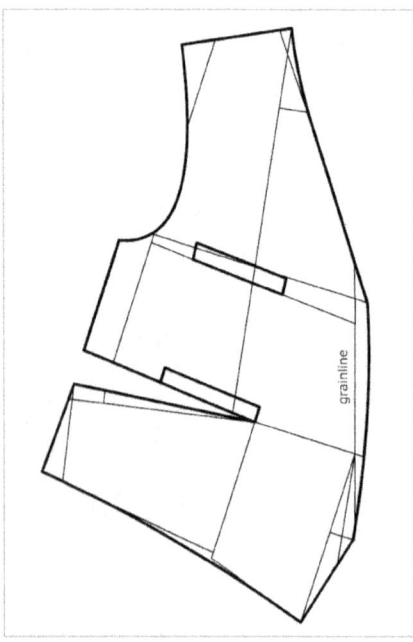

Relocate belly-dart
- cut open the line at the pocket and put together the belly-dart

Length (hem)
- re-balance the hem-line

Grainline
- the center front *CF* serves as a grainline reference

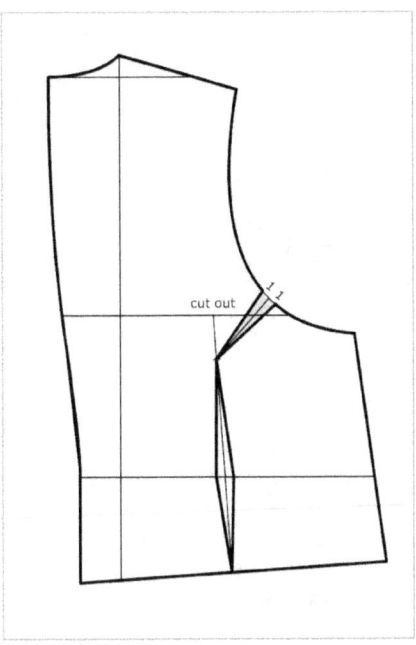

Narrow armhole

When the pattern is finished, the back pattern is cut out and the back armhole will be narrowed (reshaped).

- from armhole: draw a 90° angle toward the dart
- mark about 1 cm on each side
- cut out this amount and join together
- this opens the back-dart and the back gets a better fit at the armhole and around the scapula

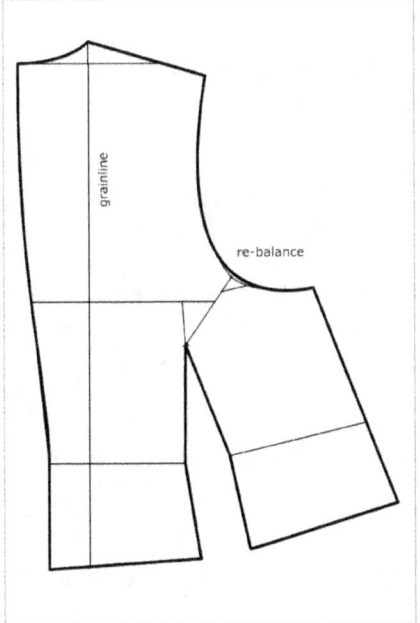

Re-balance the armhole

- the shape of the armhole should be well-balanced after joining together (see also large pattern on page 47)

Cutting
- cut front 2 x
- cut back 2 x (plus 2 x for the lining)

Instructions
- all measures are in cm
- all seams are without seam allowances

Taken measurements

		1/2	1/4	1/8	1/16
Height	(HEI)	180	90	45	22.5	11.25
Chest	(CHE)	122	61	30.5	15.25
Waist	(WAI)	130	65	32.5	
Neck	(NE)	45			
Nape to front waist	(NTFW)	58.5			

Calculated measurements

Depth of scye	(DOS)	= 1/16 HEI + 1/8 CHE + 1 = 27.5 cm
Waist length	(WL)	= 1/4 HEI + 1 = 46 cm
Neckline	(NL)	= 1/6 NE + 1 = 8.5 cm
Back width	(BW)	= 1/10 CHE + 10.5 = 22.7 cm
Width of scye	(WOS)	= 1/8 CHE + 1 = 16.25 cm
Chest width	(CW)	= 1/4 CHE - 4 = 26.5 cm
Belly width	(BEW)	= 1/4 WAI = 32.5 cm
Front waist length	(FWL)	= NTFW - 10 (back neckline) = 48.5 cm

For clients that deviate from the 'norm' (broad shoulders, strong back, etc.), the taken measurements should be used instead of the calculated ones.

Control
Compare chest and waist with the taken measurements. The fullness at the 1/2 chest and the 1/2 waist should be about 4.5 cm for each and is already considered in the calculation.
When drawing the length of the waistcoat, make sure that it covers the trousers' waistband (height of the waistline). If in doubt, measure from the 7th cervical vertebra to the back of the waistband to determine the desired length.

Grainline
In the front part, the center front *CF* serves as a grainline reference; in the back part, the line marked parallel to the center-back-basic-line is doing this job.

Double-breasted vest
Instructions for the double-breasted waistcoat can be found in our book 'Modern Men's Tailoring' (see p. 161).

Seam allowances

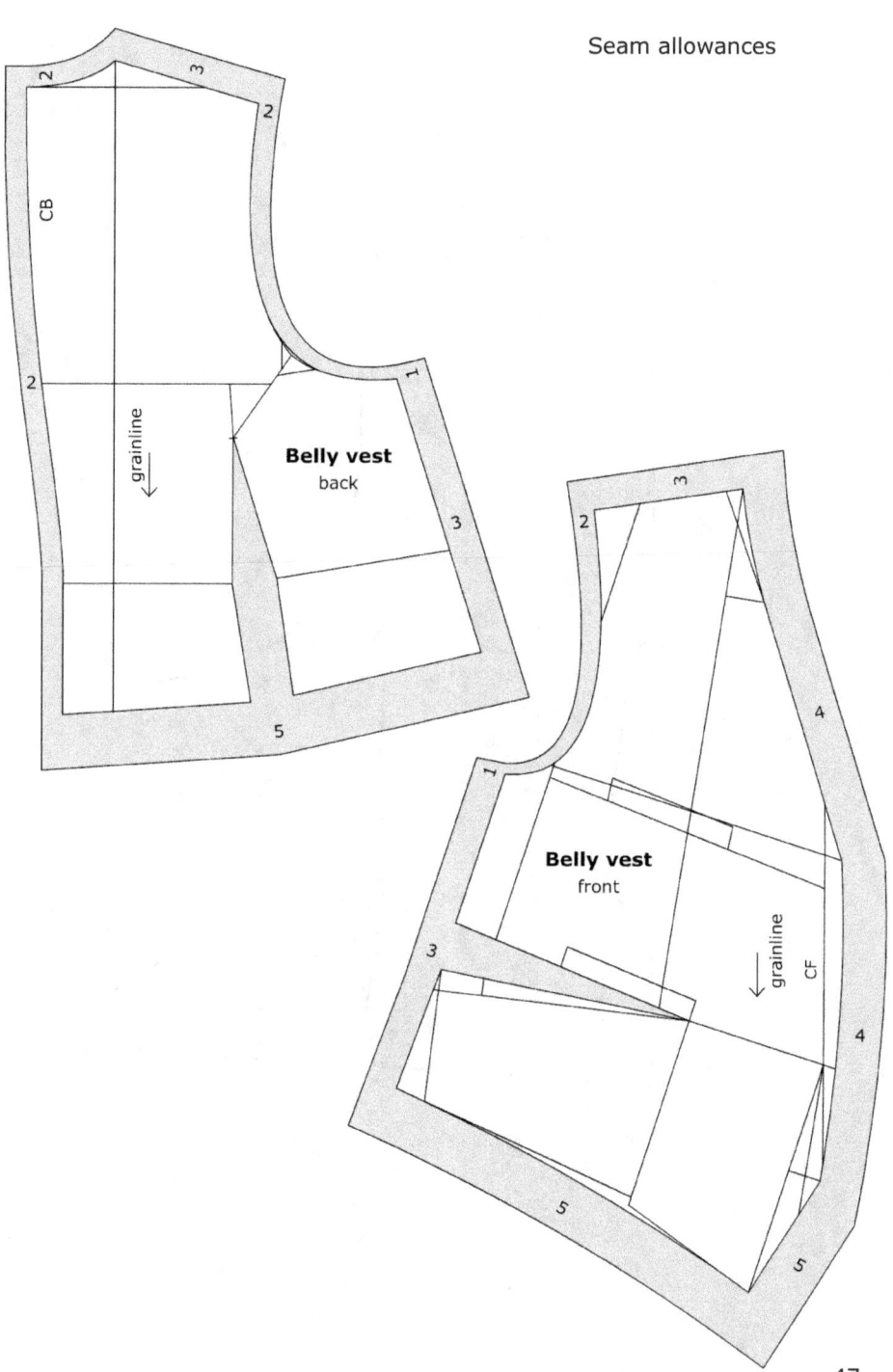

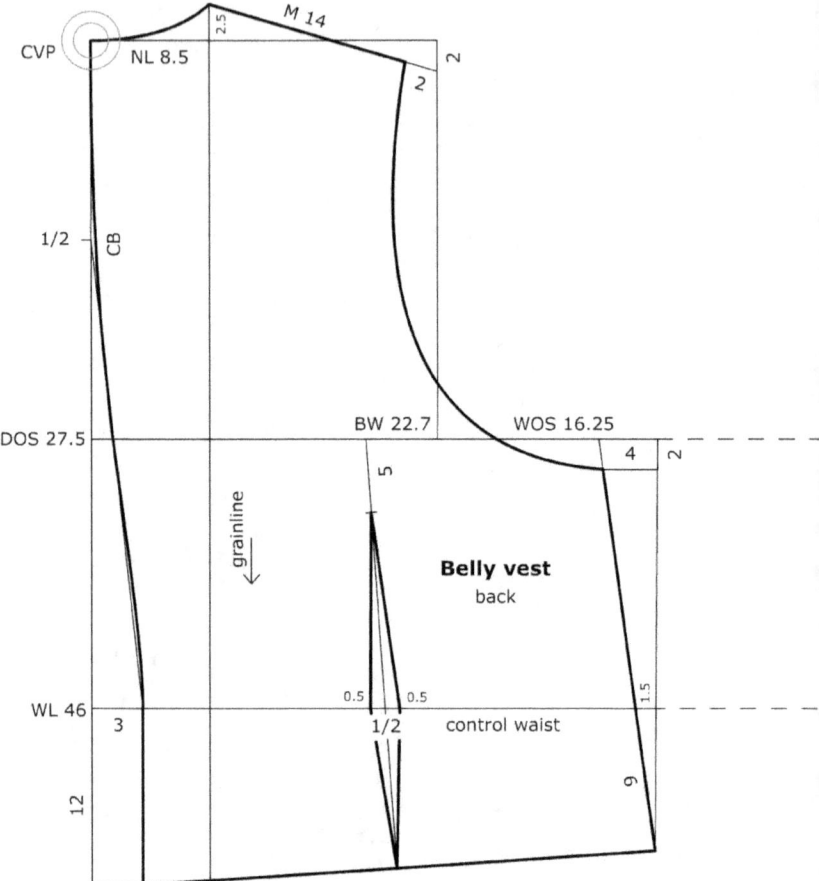

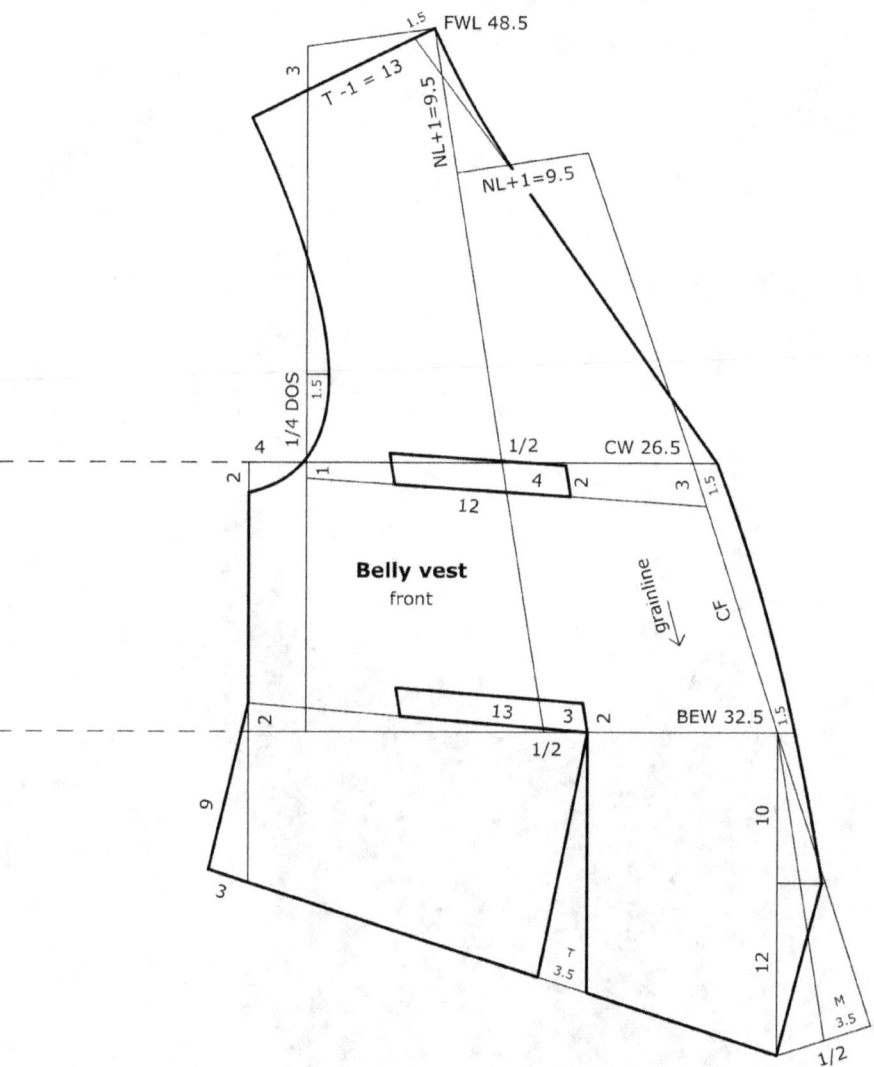

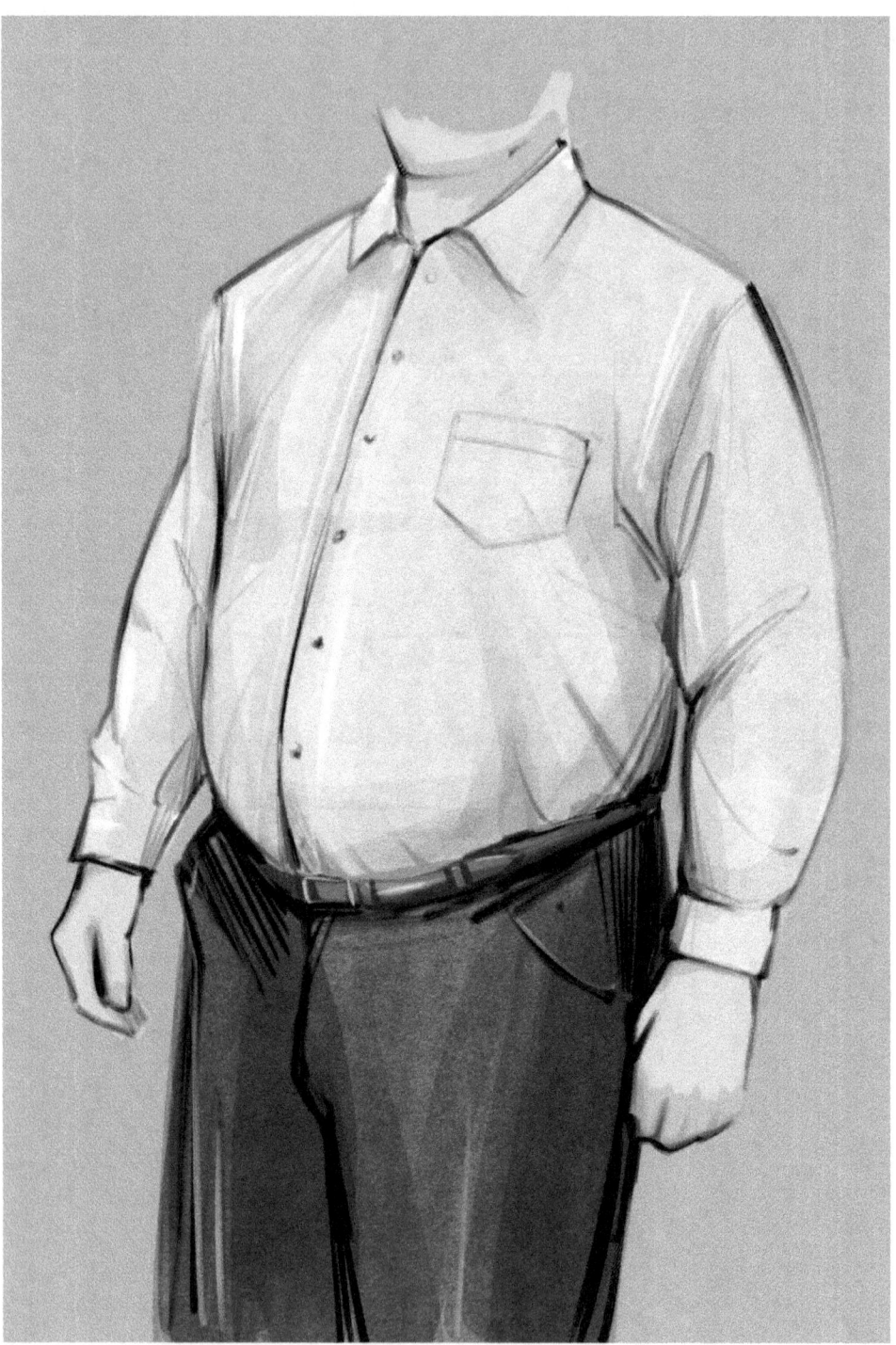

Manual for the belly shirt

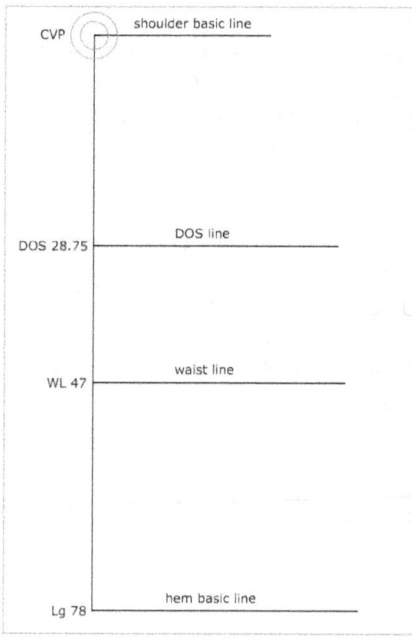

For measurements, see page 55.

Start
- draw a 90° angle
- on vertical line from the 7th cervical-vertebra-point *CVP*: mark down depth-of-scye $DOS = 1/16\ HEI + 1/8\ CHE + 2 = 28.75$ cm and square right (chest-line)
- on vertical line from *CVP*: mark down waist-length $WL = 1/4\ HEI + 2 = 47$ cm and square right (waist-line)
- on vertical line from *CVP*: mark down length $LG = 1/2\ HEI - 12 = 78$ cm and square right (hem-basic-line)
- compare the length with your favourite shirt

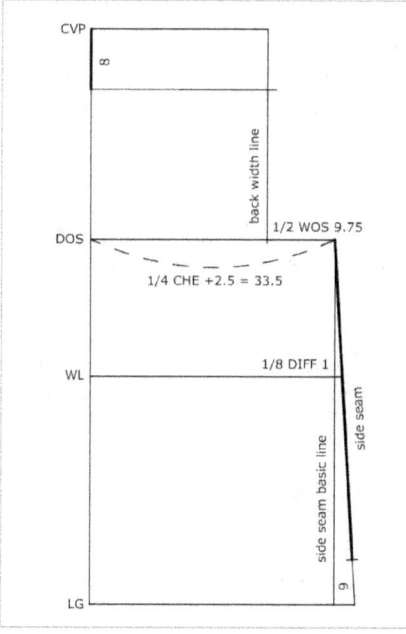

Chest width
- on *DOS*-line: mark to the right $1/4\ CHE + 2.5 = 33.5$ cm and square down

Back width
- on *DOS*-line: mark to the left 1/2 width-of-scye $WOS = (1/8\ CHE + 4) \div 2 = 9.75$ cm and square up

Side seam
- on *WL*-line from side-seam-basic-line: mark to the right approx. 1/8 difference $DIFF = 1$ cm and draw side seam
- on side seam from *LG*-line mark up approx. 9 cm

Yoke
- on vertical line from *CVP*: mark down 8 cm and square right

51

The shirt for the belly

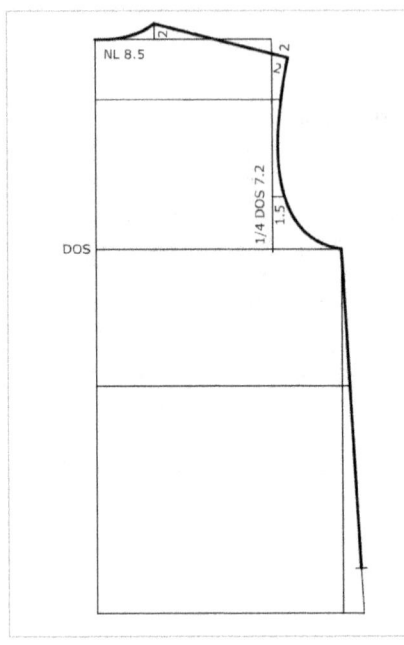

Back neckline
- from *CVP* on shoulder-basic-line: mark to the right neckline *NL* = 1/6 *NE* + 1 = 8.5 cm, square up and mark 2 cm
- shape neckline nicely

Shoulder
- from shoulder-basic-line on back-width-line: mark down 2 cm
- from upper point at neck draw shoulder-seam through previous point
- on shoulder-seam from *BW*-line: extend to the right by 2 cm

Back armhole
- on back-width-line: mark up 1/4 *DOS* = 7.2 cm, square right and mark 1.5 cm
- shape armhole nicely

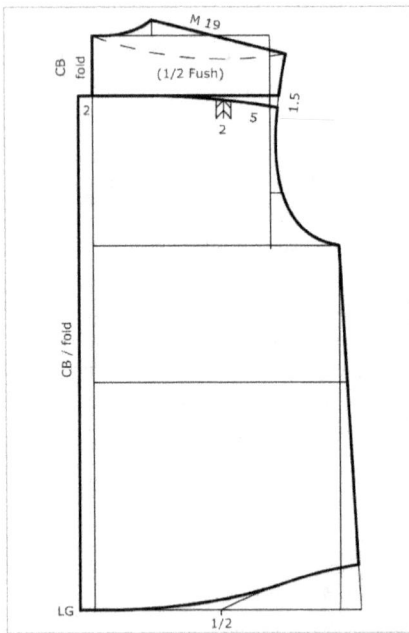

Shoulder
- for broad shoulders, use the measure 1/2 *FUSH* from the *CVP* point to the shoulder
- measure width of shoulder seam *M* = approx. 12.5 cm

Yoke
- at back-armhole from yoke-line: mark down 1.5 cm and shape seam nicely

Fold
- on seam of yoke from *BW*-line: mark to the left approx. 5 cm and mark width of fold by 2 cm
- at yoke-line: extend to the left by 2 cm and square down

Hem
- halve hem-basic-line and shape hem nicely

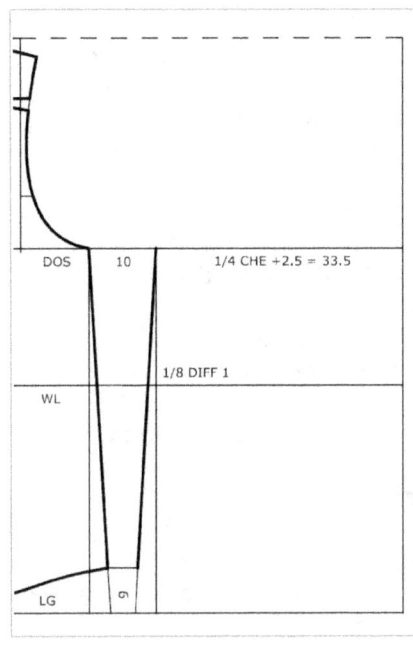

Basic frame front piece
- extend shoulder-basic-line, *DOS*-line, *WL*-line and hem-basic-line

Side seam
- on *DOS*-line from back side seam: mark to the right approx. 10 cm (to get enough distance to the back) and square down
- on *WL*-line from side-seam-basic-line: mark to the left approx. 1/8 difference *DIFF* = 1 cm and draw side seam
- on side seam from *LG*-line mark up approx. 9 cm

Chest
- on chest-line from side-seam: mark to the right 1/4 *CHE* + 2.5 = 33.5 cm and square up and down

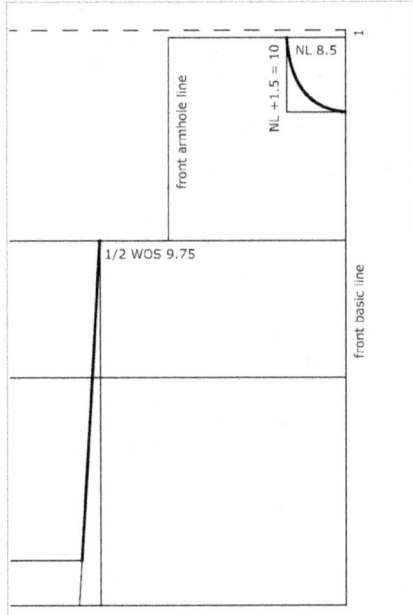

Chest width / front armhole width
- on chest-line from side seam: mark to the right 1/2 width-of-scye *WOS* (1/8 *CHE* + 4) ÷ 2 = 9.75 cm and square up; this line is the front-armhole-line

Front neck
- on front-basic-line from the extended back shoulder-basic-line: mark down approx. 1 cm and square left
- on previous line from front-basic-line: mark to the left *NL* = 1/6 *NE* + 1 = 8.5 cm and square down
- on previous line: mark down *NL* + 1.5 = 10 cm and square left
- shape front neckline

The shirt for the belly

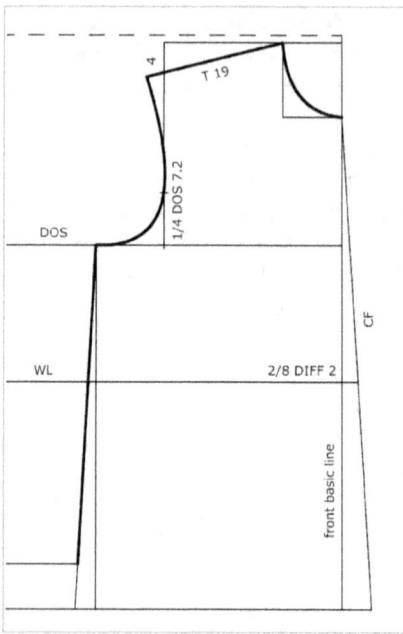

Front shoulder
- on front-armhole-line from shoulder-basic-line: mark down 4 cm, draw shoulder seam and transfer width-of-back $T = 19$ cm

Front armhole
- on front-armhole-line from *DOS*-line: mark up 1/4 *DOS* = 7.2 cm
- shape armhole nicely
- measure the complete armhole (front piece, back piece and yoke) M = approx. 57 cm (you will need this later for the sleeves)

Front edge
- on waistline *(WL*-line) from front-basic-line: mark to the left approx. 2/8 difference *DIFF* = 2 cm and draw center-front-line *CF*

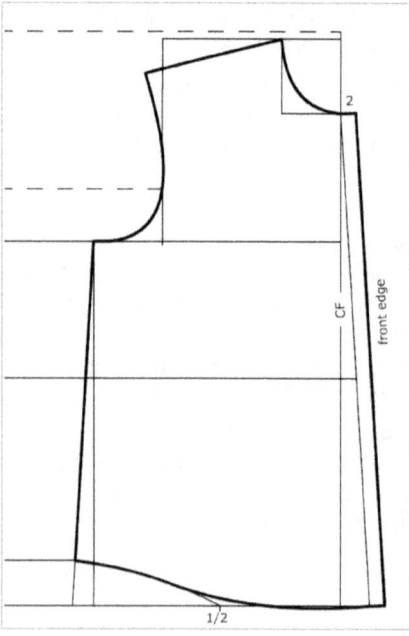

Front edge
- from *CF*: mark to the right 2 cm and square up and down

Hem
- halve hem-basic-line and shape hem nicely

Cutting
- cut front 2 x, cut back 1 x in fold, cut yoke 2 x in fold

Instructions
- all measures are in cm, all seams are without seam allowances
- with strong backs, the back fold can be enlarged
- if the waist in the pattern is too narrow: expand it at the side seams

Taken measurements
                                            1/2   1/4   1/8   1/16

Height	(HEI)	180 | 90 | 45 | 22.5 | 11.25
Chest	(CHE)	124 | 62 | 31 | 15.5
Waist	(WAI)	132 | 66
Hips	(HIP)	132 | 66
Neck	(NE)	45
Sleeve lenght	(SL)	62
Wrist	(WR)	24

Calculated measurements

Depth of scye	(DOS)	= 1/16 HEI + 1/8 CHE + 2 = 28.75 cm
Waist length	(WL)	= 1/4 HEI + 2 = 47 cm
Length	(LG)	= 1/2 HEI - 12 = 78 cm
Neckline	(NL)	= 1/6 NE + 1 = 8.5 cm
Width of scye	(WOS)	= 1/8 CHE + 4 = 19.5 cm
Difference	(DIFF)	= WAI - CHE = 8 cm
Width of cuffs	(WOC)	= WR + 5 = 29 cm

For clients that deviate from the 'norm' (broad shoulders, strong back, etc.), the taken measurements should be used instead of the calculated ones.

Armhole
The circumference of scye COS = approx. 57 cm is measured after finishing the shirt pattern.

Control
Compare the width of chest, width of waist and width of hips in the pattern with the taken measurements.
The fullness at the 1/2 chest and the 1/2 waist should be about 5 cm each and is already considered in the calculation. For broad shoulders, mark 1/2 of the full shoulder width from CVP to the outer shoulder point.

Grainline
CF and CB serve as grainline references.
The back yoke is cut across to the back part.

Seam allowances

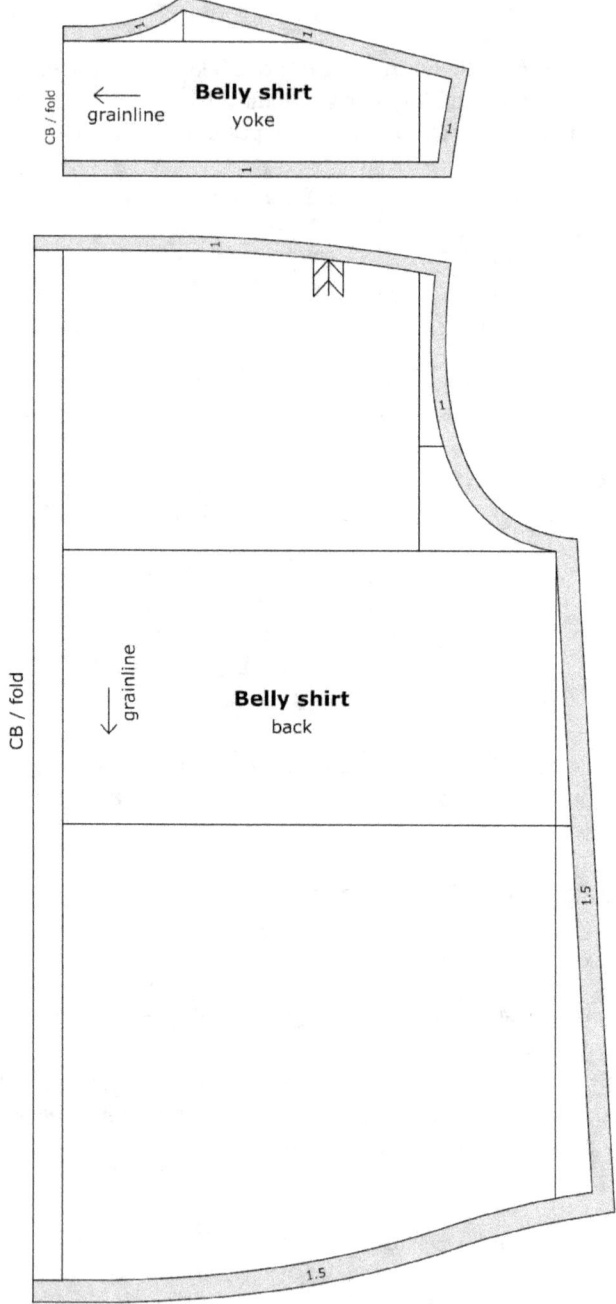

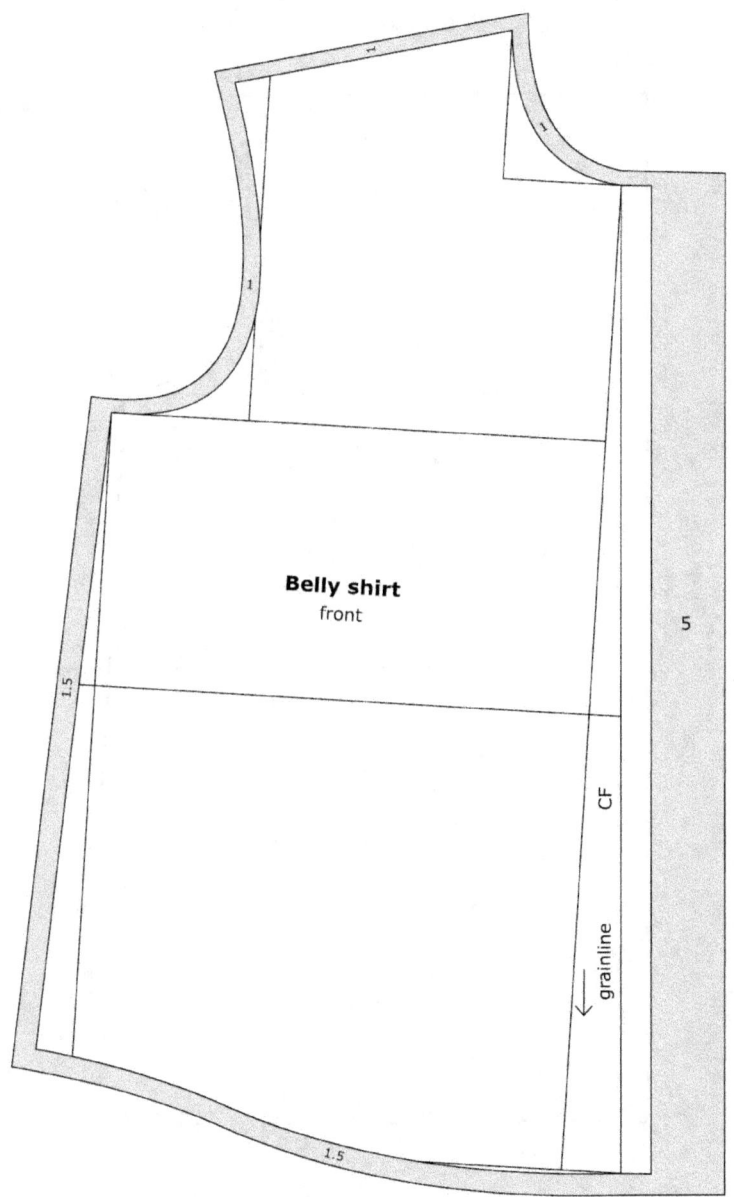

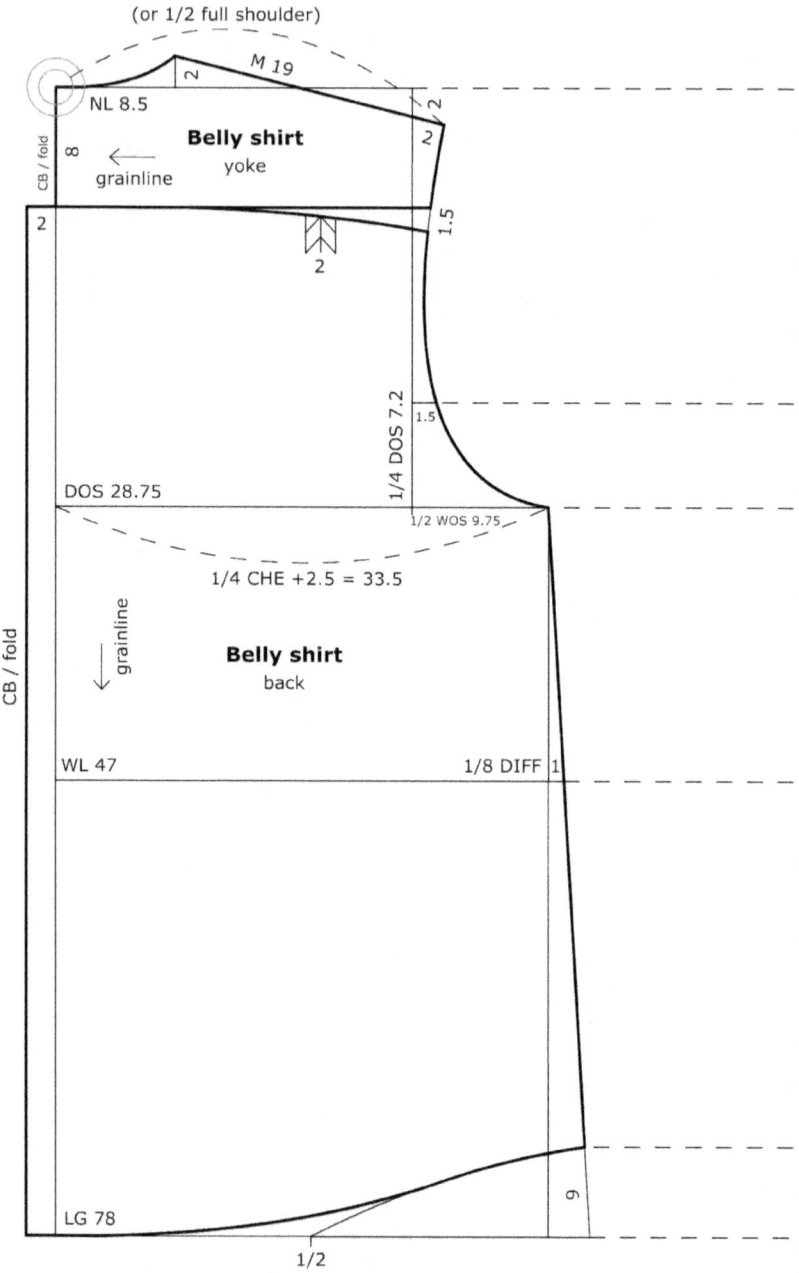

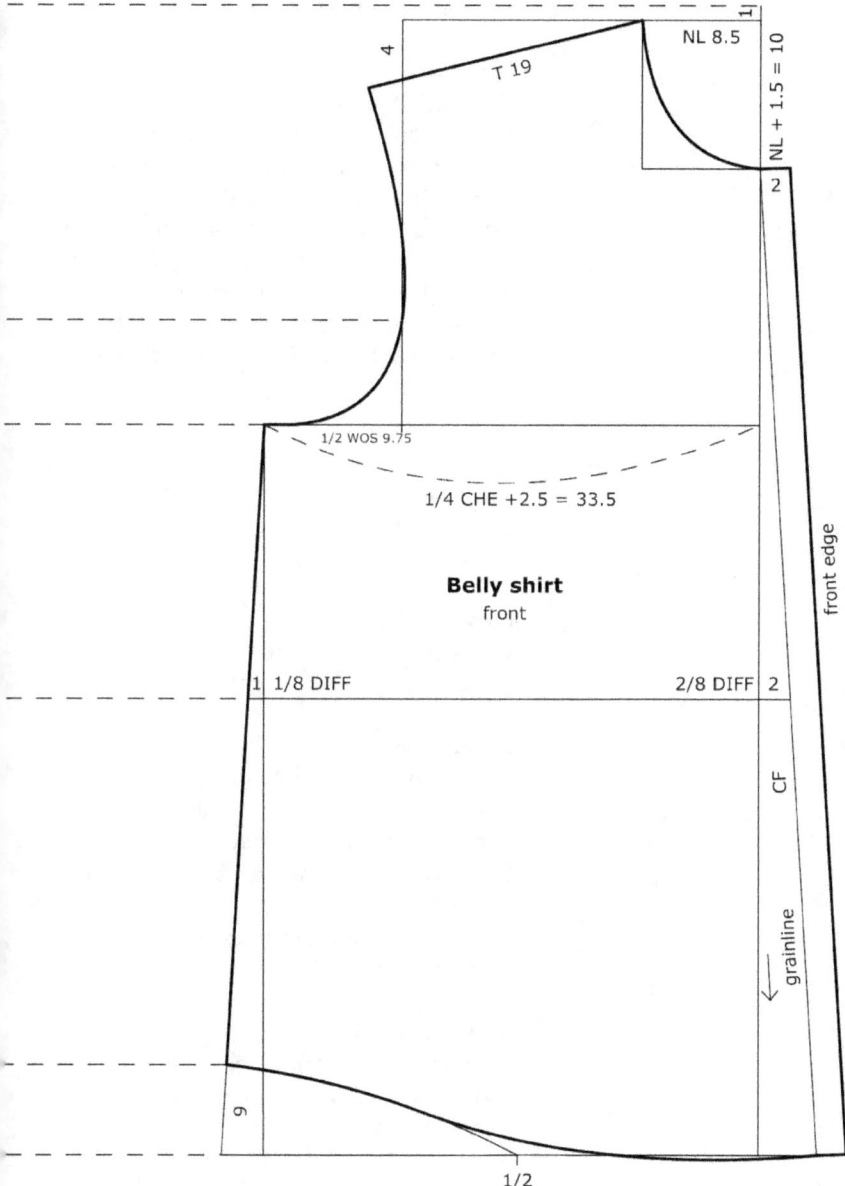

Manual for the sleeve for the belly shirt

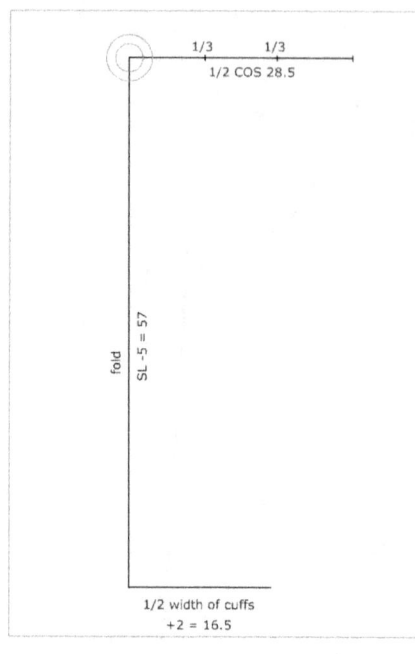

Measurements
The measurements and further information can be found on page 55.

Start
- draw a 90° angle
- on horizontal line: mark to the right 1/2 circumference of scye COS = 28.5 cm
- divide this distance into three
- on vertical line: mark down sleeve-length SL - 5 = 57 cm and square right
- on this line: mark to the right 1/2 width of the cuffs + 2 cm (for pleats) = 16.5 cm
- the vertical line is the fold and serves as the grainline

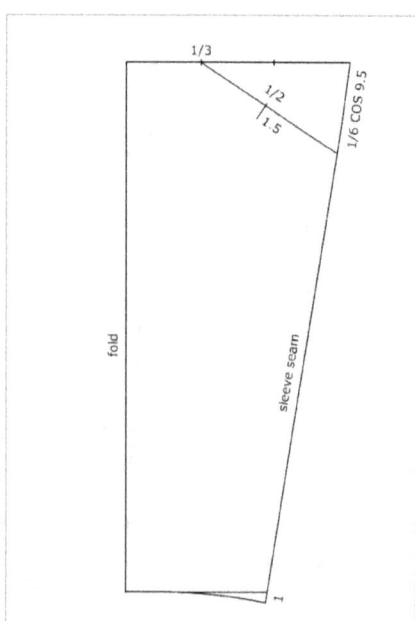

Sleeve seam
- connect the right outer points of the upper and lower horizontal lines

Sleeve head
- from upper horizontal line at sleeve-seam: mark down 1/6 COS = 9.5 cm
- connect this point with the first point on the upper horizontal line and halve this distance
- from 1/2-point square downward and mark 1.5 cm

Seam at wrist
- from lower horizontal line at sleeve seam: mark down 1 cm
- shape cuff seam nicely

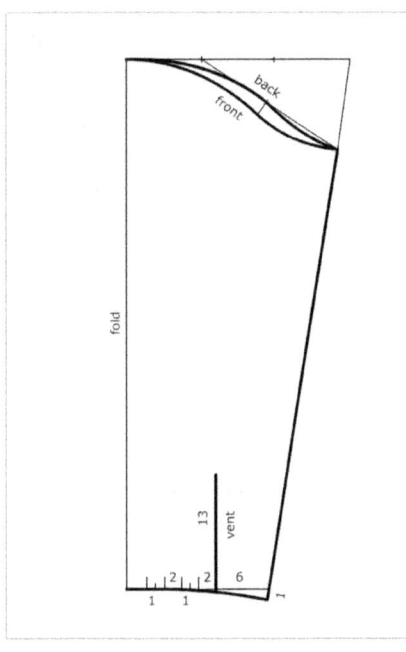

Sleeve head
- shape back sleeve-head nicely
- shape front sleeve-head as shown

Sleeve vent
- at cuff seam from sleeve seam: mark to the left 6 cm, square up and mark the length of the vent by approx. 13 cm

Folds
- from vent: for 1. pleat mark to the left 2 cm and mark depth of pleat (2 x 1 cm)
- from this point: for 2. pleat again mark to the left 2 cm and mark depth of pleat (2 x 1 cm)
- see also large pattern on page 63

Cutting
- cut 2 x in fold

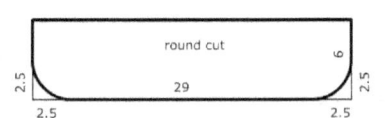

Round cut cuffs
- draw rectangle with a height of 6 cm and a width of 29 cm
- at the lower corners, mark 2.5 cm each and draw these corners round

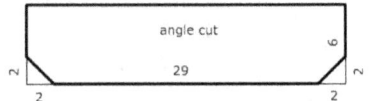

Angle cut cuffs
- draw rectangle with a height of 6 cm and a width of 29 cm
- at the lower corners, mark 2 cm each and draw the diagonals

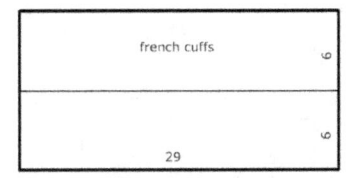

French cut cuffs
- draw rectangle with a height of 12 cm and a width of 29 cm
- divide the vertical line in half and square right

Cutting
- decide for one variation and cut 4 x

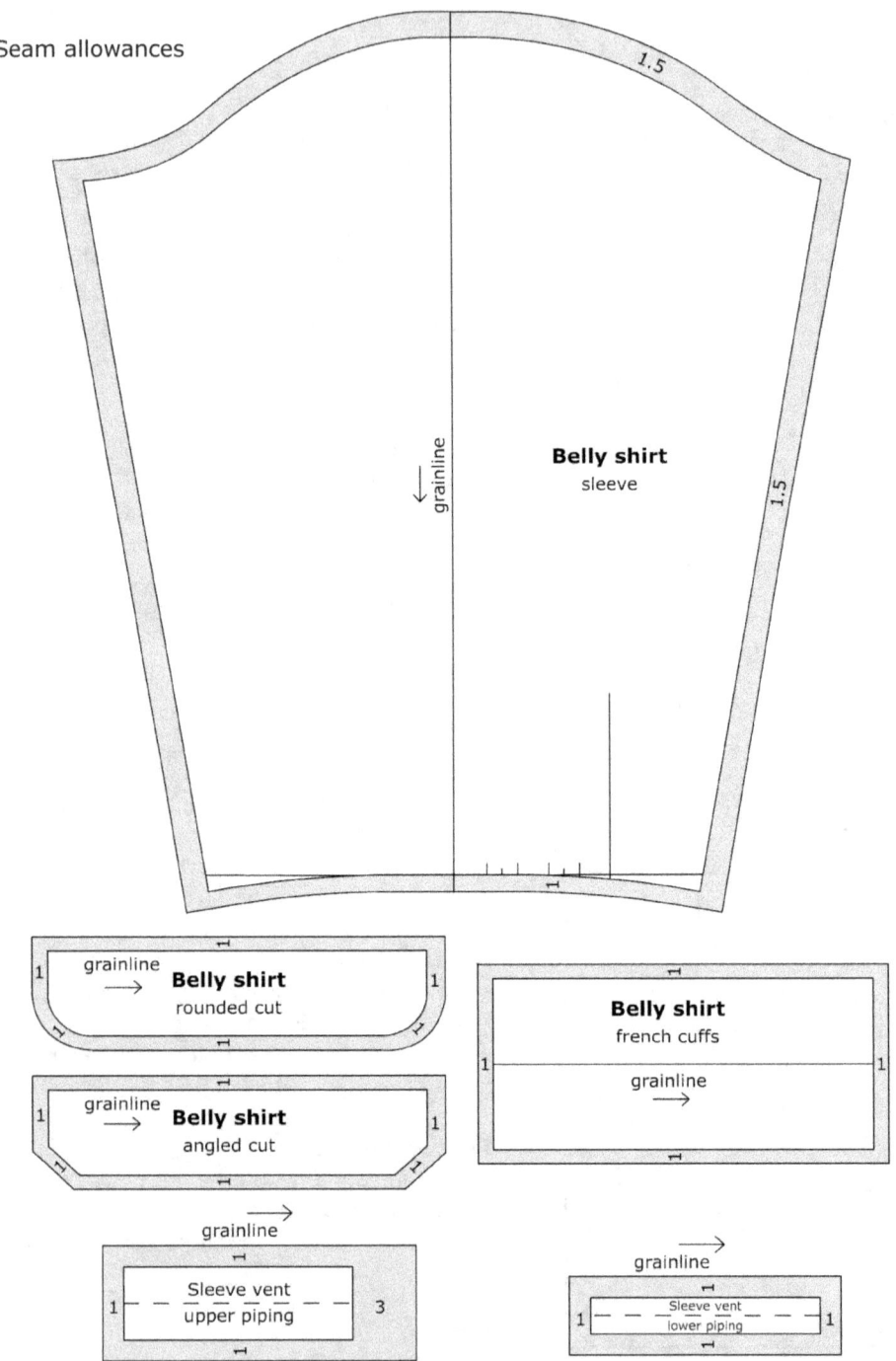

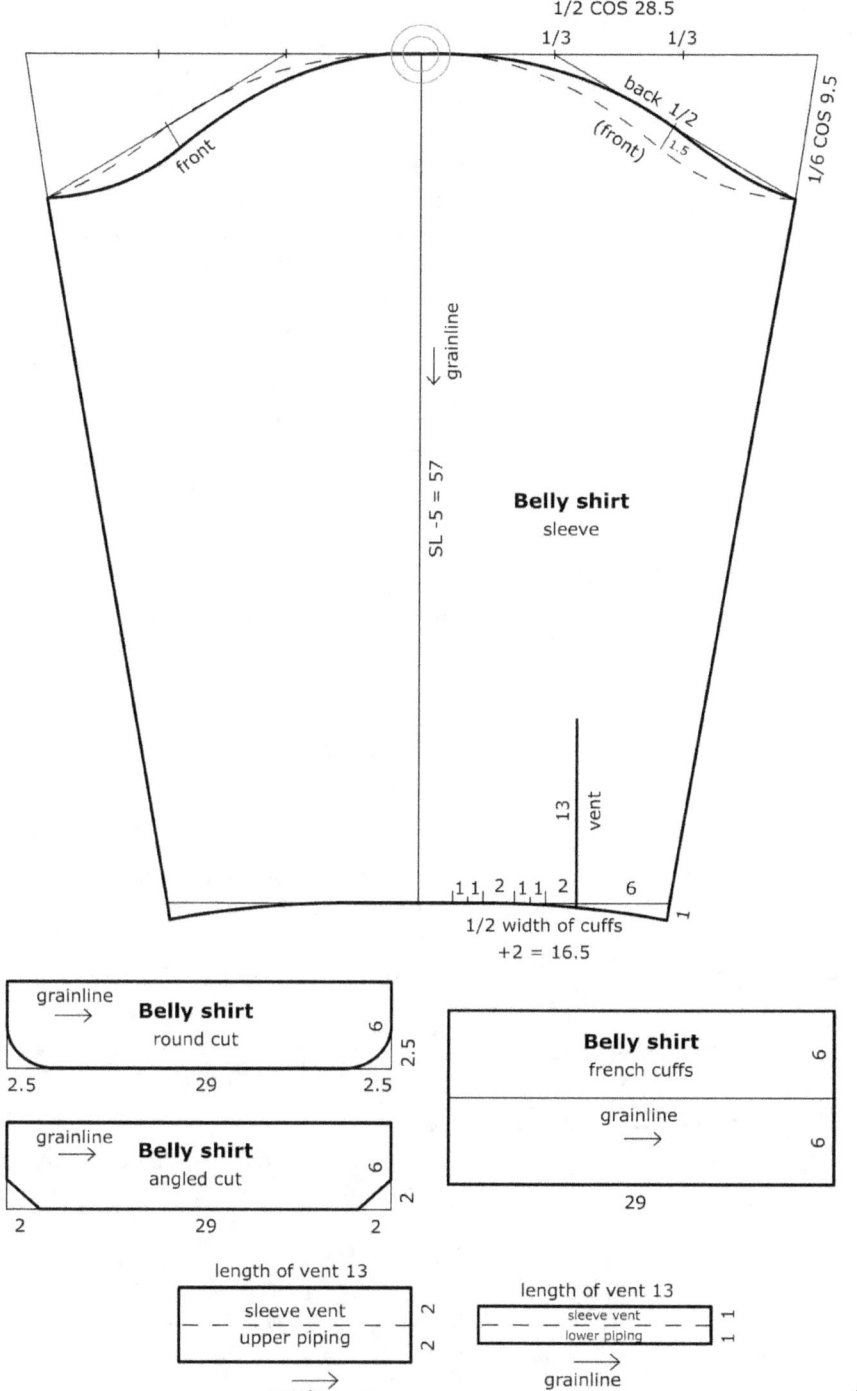

Manual for the classic collar

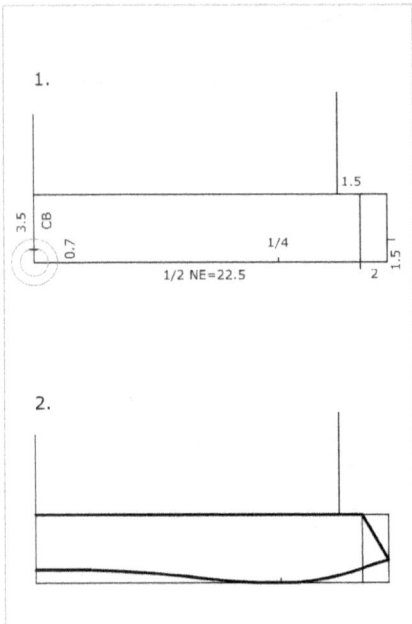

The measurements and further information can be found on page 55.

1. Start
- draw a 90° angle
- on vertical line at *CB*: mark up 0.7 cm
- from here, mark up 3.5 cm and square right
- on horizontal line: mark to the right 1/2 neck *NE* = 21 cm and divide this distance into four
- mark to the right 2 cm, square up and mark 1.5 cm
- on upper line: mark to the left 1.5 cm and square up

2.
- finish the collar stand as shown
- upfront: draw in diagonal line

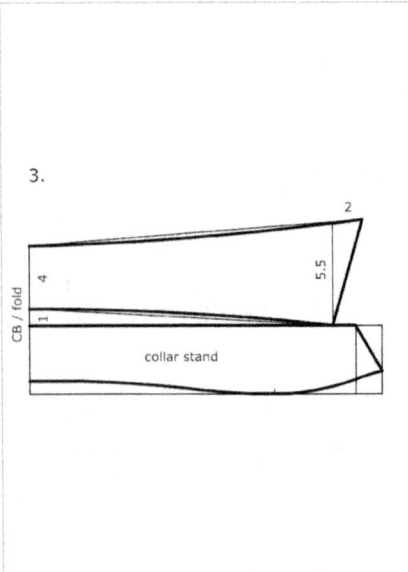

3. Collar tip
- on vertical line at *CB*: mark up 1 cm
- from here, mark up 4 cm
- upfront on vertical line: mark up 5.5 cm
- connect this point with upper point at center-back *CB* and extend this line forward by 2 cm
- finish the collar as shown

Cutting
- cut collar stand and turn down 2 x in fold

Note
You can find more collar shapes in our book: Modern Men's Tailoring (see p. 161).

Extra note
This pattern instruction also works for the bodybuilder's shirt; just change the neck measurements.

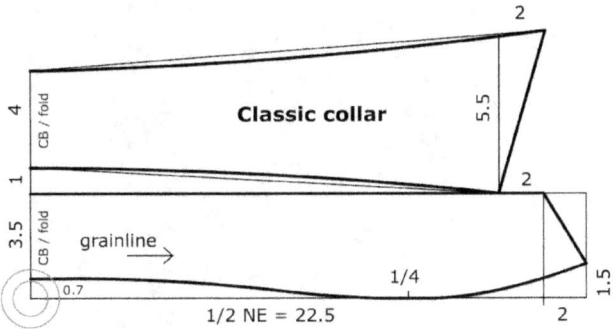

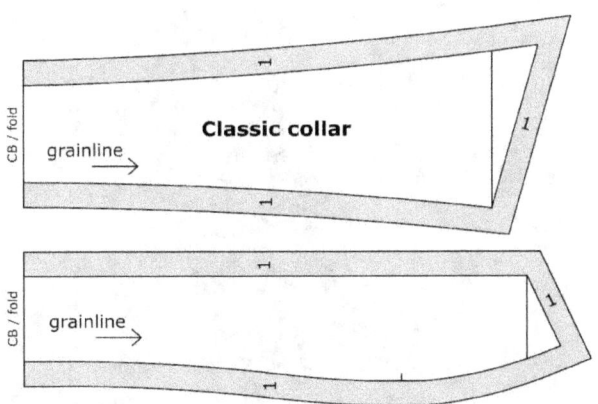

Note

This pattern also suits for the bodybuilder-shirt, just change the neck measure.

Manual for the belly jacket

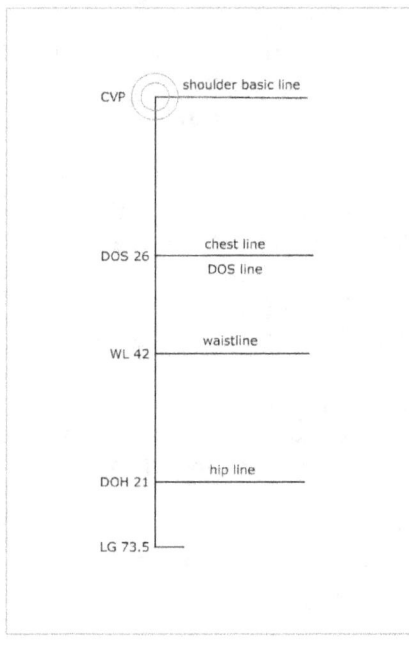

Start (for measurements, see page 75)
- draw a 90° angle
- vertical line is the center-back-basic-line
- horizontal line is the shoulder-basic-line
- on center-back-basic-line from the 7th cervical-vertebra-point *CVP:* mark down depth of scye *DOS* = 1/16 height *HEI* + 1/8 chest *CHE* - 1= 26 cm and square right (chest-line)
- from *CVP:* mark down waist-length *WL* = 1/4 *HEI* = 42 cm and square right (waistline)
- on center-back-basic-line from *WL:* mark down depth of hips *DOH* = 1/8 *HEI* = 21 cm and square right (hip-line)
- on center-back-basic-line from *CVP:* mark down length *LG* = approx. 1/8 *HEI* x 3.5 = 73.5 cm and square right

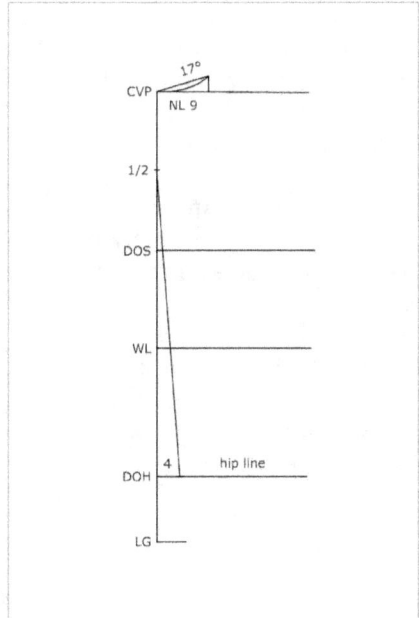

Length
- compare the length with your favourite jacket

Back seam
- on center-back-basic-line: halve the distance between *CVP* and *DOS*
- on *HIP*-line from *CB*-basic-line: mark to the right 4 cm and connect this point with previous point

Neck/Shoulder
- on shoulder-basic-line from *CVP:* mark to the right neckline *NL* = 1/6 *NE* + 1.5 = 9 cm and square up
- from *CVP:* create a 17° angle to the right up
- shape back neckline nicely

The belly jacket

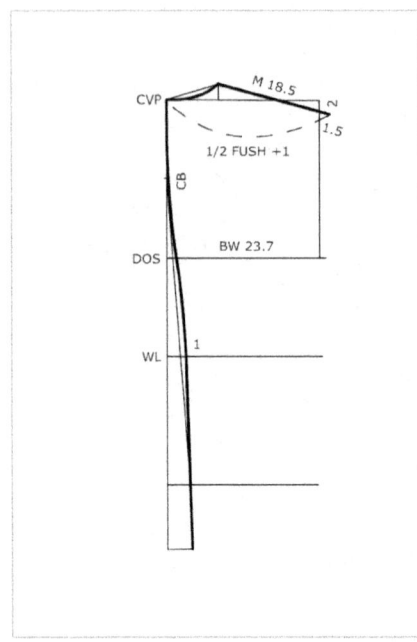

Center back seam
- on waistline from center-back-basic-line: mark to the right 1 cm
- shape back-seam CB nicely

Shoulder
- on chest-line from *CB*: mark to the right back-width $BW = 1/10\ CHE + 10.5 = 23.7$ cm and square up
- on *BW*-line from shoulder-basic-line: mark down 2 cm and connect with upper point at the neckline
- on shoulder from *BW*-line: extend shoulder-seam to the right by 1.5 cm and measure $M = 18.5$ cm (you will need this for the front shoulder)
- for broad shoulders, use the measure 1/2 *FUSH* + 1 from the CVP point to the outer shoulder point

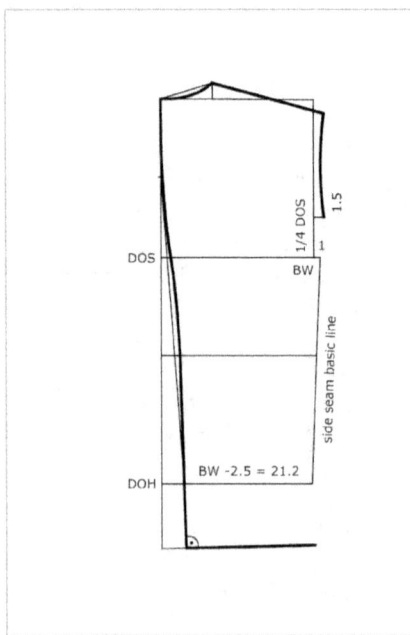

Scye / Armhole
- on *BW*-line from chest-line: mark up 1/4 *DOS* 6.5 cm, square right and mark 1.5 cm
- shape back-armhole nicely

Preparation for side seam
- on chest-line from *BW*-line: mark to the right 1 cm (to hide the side seam under the sleeve)
- on *HIP*-line from *CB*: mark to the right $BW - 2.5 = 21.2$ cm
- connect this point with previous point; this defines the side-seam-basic-line
- at *LG* from *CB*: square right

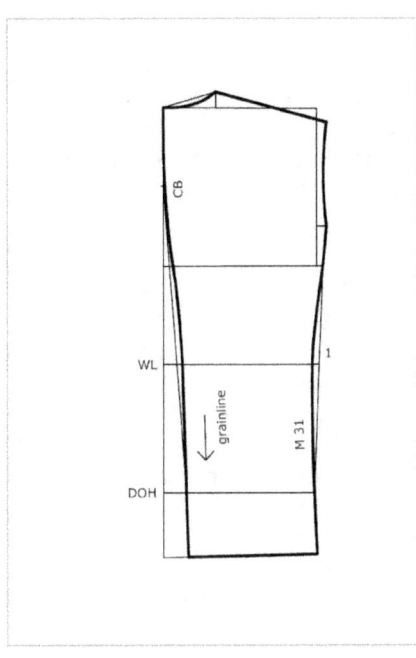

Side seam
- on waistline from side-seam-basic-line: mark to the left approx. 1 cm
- shape side seam nicely
- on side seam from waistline: measure down to *LG*, *M* = approx. 31 cm (you will need this for the side part)

Grainline
- draw in a 90° angle to the length

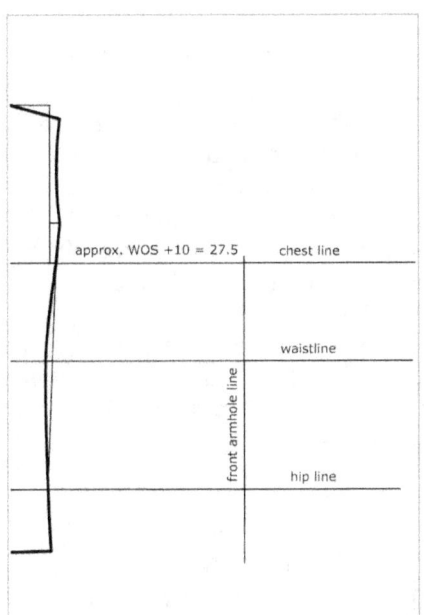

Extend lines for front and side part
- extend chest-line (also known as *DOS*-line), waistline and hip-line to the right
- on chest-line: mark to the right *WOS* + approx. 10 = 27.5 cm and square down (the 10 cm are chosen at random to get enough space between the back and the front part); this is the front-armhole-line

Note
The chest-line is called *BW*-line at the back and *CW*-line at the front.
The waistline is also called *WL*-line.

The belly jacket

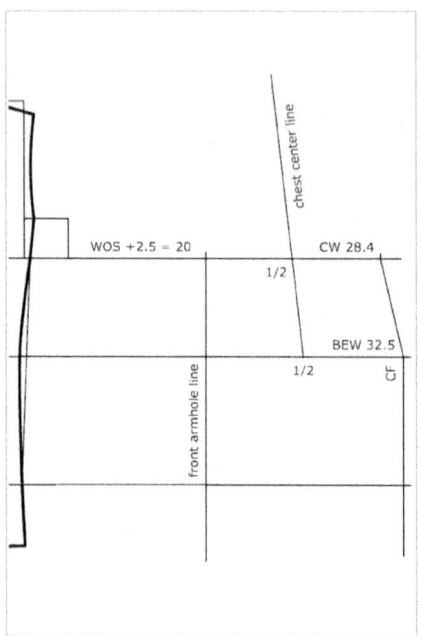

Width of scye
- on chest-line from front-armhole-line: mark to the left width of scye
  $WOS = 1/8\ CHE + 1 = 17.5$ cm $+ 2.5$
  (**for the inclination of the side part**, see page 75) $= 20$ cm

Chest width
- on chest-line from front-armhole-line: mark to the right chest-width
  $CW = 2/10\ CHE + 2 = 28.4$ cm
- on waistline from front-armhole-line: mark to the right belly-width BEW
  $= 1/4\ WAI - 1 = 32.5$ cm
- connect both points for the CF
- halve distance at CW
- halve distance at BEW
- connect both points as shown; this line defines the chest-center-line

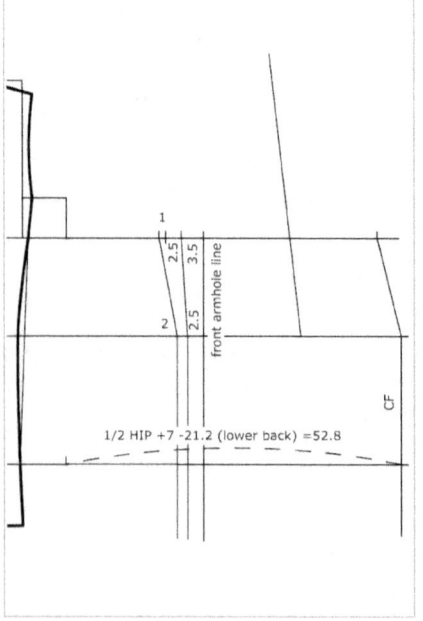

Side part
- on chest-line from front-armhole-line: mark to the left 3.5 cm
- from this point, mark to the left: 2.5 cm **for the inclination of the side part** (see explanation on page 75)
- from previous point: mark to the left 1 cm (the amount from the shifted side seam at the back, see also pic. 2 on page 68)
- on waistline from front-armhole-line: mark to the left 2.5 cm and square down
- from this point: mark to the left 2 cm and square down

Side seam
- on hip-line from CF: mark to the left 1/2 HIP - 21.2 cm (width of lower back) + 7 (fullness and seam allowances) = 52.8 cm

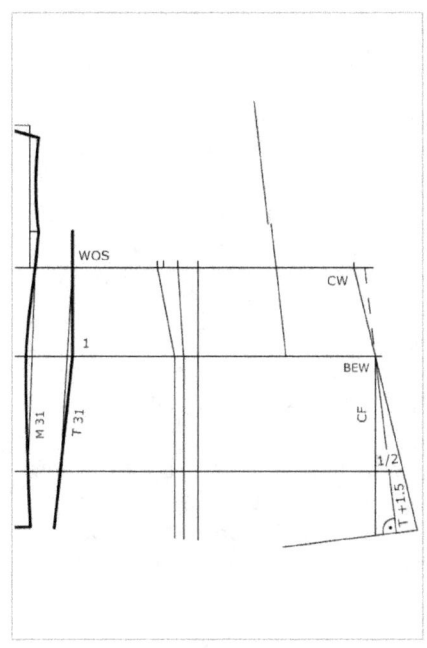

Side seam
- connect previous point on hip-line with *WOS*-point on chest-line
- on waistline: mark to the right approx. 1 cm and draw side seam
- at back side seam from elevated waistline: measure distance to length *M* = approx. 31 cm and transfer to front side seam *T* = 31 cm

Front edge
- upfront, between *CW* and *BEW*: extend line downward
- on hip line, between previous line and *CF*: halve distance and draw a diagonal line
- on this line from the waistline: transfer *T* the measured distance from the lower side seam + 1.5 = 32.5 cm downward and square left

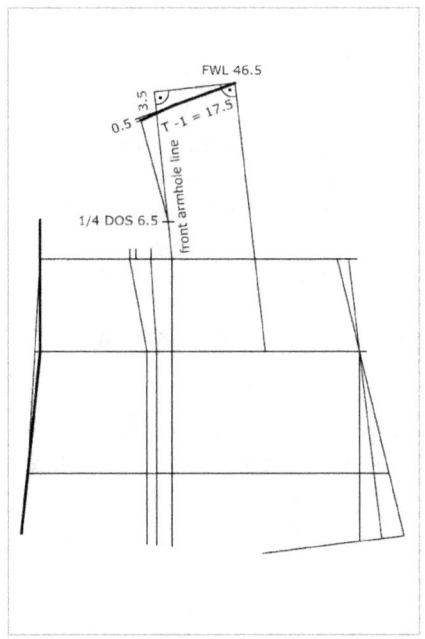

Front waist length
- on chest-center-line from waistline: mark up front-waist-length *FWL* = nape to front waist *NTFW* 54.5 - 9.5 (back neckline) + 1.5 (seam allowances at front and back shoulder) = 46.5 cm and square left
- from shoulder-basic-line: square down to crossing point of chest-line and front-armhole-line
- on this line from chest-line: mark up 1/4 *DOS* = 6.5 cm

Shoulder
- at front-armhole-line from the top: mark down 3.5 cm
- draw shoulder seam and transfer length of back-shoulder-seam - 1 cm = 17.5 cm
- lower the outer shoulder part by 0.5 cm, see pattern on page 79

The belly jacket

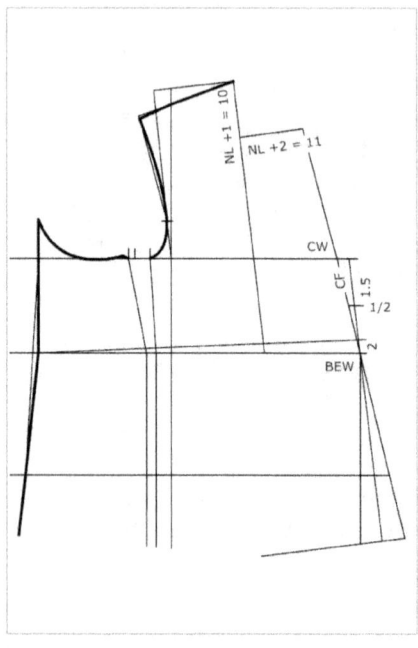

Armhole
- shape front and side part armhole nicely

Neckline
- on chest-center-line from front shoulder: mark down neckline
NL $(1/6$ $NE + 1.5) + 1 = 10$ cm, square right and mark $NL + 2 = 11$ cm
- connect this point with CF on chest-line

Front edge
- on CF between CW-line and BEW-line: halve the distance, square right and mark 1.5 cm
- on CF from waistline: mark up 2 cm and connect this point with side seam on waistline; this line becomes the new waistline

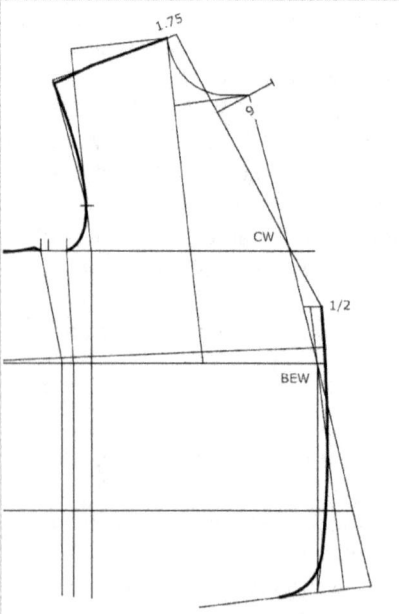

Neckline
- shape front neckline nicely

Lapel fall
- extend shoulder-line to the right and mark 1.75 cm
- connect this point with 1/2-point at front edge
- on lapel-fall: square right up to tip of CF/neckline
- on this line: mark 9 cm for lapel-width

Lower front edge
- from 1/2-point at front edge: draw down lower front edge slightly curved; see large pattern on page 79
- shape curve at lower front edge as shown

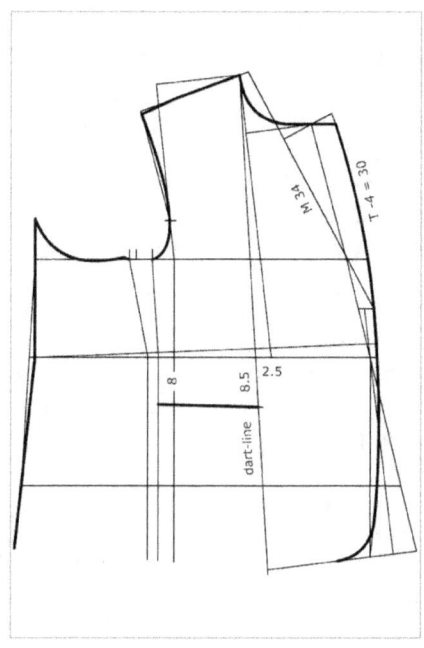

Lapel
- shape edge of lapel slightly curved
- measure lapel-fall M = approx. 34 cm and transfer T this measure - 4 = 30 cm to the lapel-edge
- from lapel tip at CF: draw line to top of lapel-fall

Pocket opening
- on waistline from chest-center-line: mark to the left 2.5 cm
- from tip of front shoulder: draw line downward through 2.5-cm-point
- on dart-line from waistline: mark down approx. 8.5 cm
- on side seam from waistline: mark down approx. 8 cm
- connect both previous points

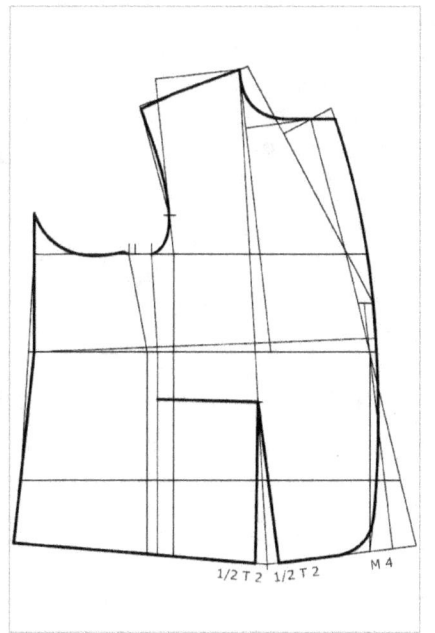

Hem
- connect lowest point of side seam with lowest point of dart-line

Belly dart
- measure distance at lower front edge $M = 4\ cm$
- at hem, form dart-line: transfer to each side left and right 1/2 of the previous measurement $T = 2$ cm
- connect both points with pocket opening at dart line
- this part will be cut out and put together; it will rotate the lower front part, which leads to a better fit

The belly jacket

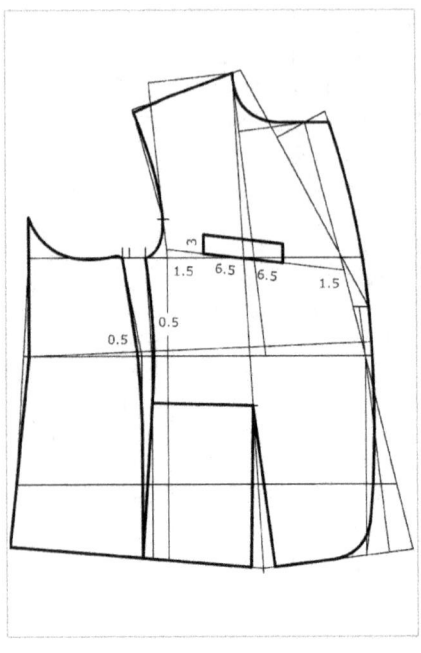

Chest pocket
- on front-armhole-line from chest-line: mark up 1.5 cm
- on chest-line from *CF*: mark down 1.5 cm
- connect both previous points
- on this line from dart-line: mark left and right approx. 6.5 cm
- mark height of welt pocket with approx. 3 cm

Side-part-seam
- at front side-part-seam from pocket opening: draw a curved line to the hem of the side part (see large pattern on page 79)

Narrow waist
- at side-part-seams, above the waistline: mark approx. 0.5 cm to each side

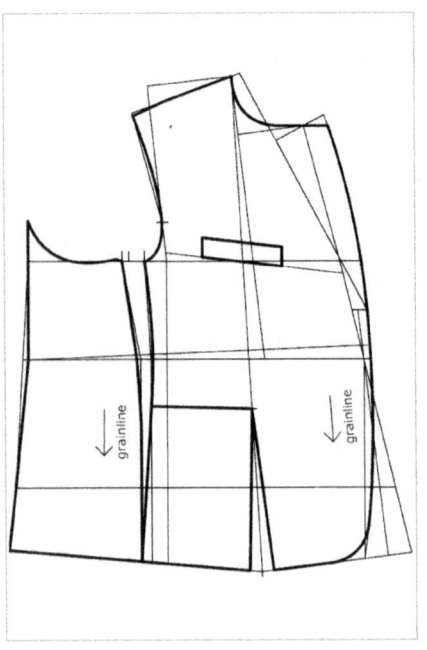

Grainline
- at the front part: the center of the dart defines the grainline
- at the side-part: the lower side-part-seam defines the grainline

Cutting
- cut front-, side- and back-part 2 x each

Instructions
- all measures are in cm. The fullness at the 1/2 chest, 1/2 waist and 1/2 hips should be 5.5 cm and is already considered in the calculation
- 0.75 cm seam allowances are included (sewing machine foot width) at the shoulder seam, the entire armhole and the side-part-seam, all other seams are without seam allowances (see pages 76/77)
- at the back-shoulder, the fullness of 1 cm is kept short during the pressing process for a better fit
- for clients that deviate from the 'norm' (broad shoulders, strong back, etc.), the taken measurements should always be used instead of the calculated ones

Inclination of side-part (Page 70)
The amount of the inclination at the upper side part results from the customer's body shape: regular 1.5 cm, strong 2 cm, short or with belly 2.5 cm

Taken measurements

		1/2	1/4	1/8	1/16
Height	(HEI)	168	84	42	21	10.5
Chest	(CHE)	132	66	33		16.5
Waist	(WAI)	134	67	33.5		
Hip	(HIP)	134	67	33.5		
Neck	(NE)	45			
Nape to front waist	(NTFW)	54.5			

Calculated measurements

Depth of syce	(DOS)	= 1/16 HEI + 1/8 CHE - 1 = 26 cm
Waist length	(WL)	= 1/4 HEI = 42 cm
Depth of hips	(DOH)	= 1/8 HEI = 21 cm
Length	(LG)	= 1/8 HEI x 3.5 = 73.5 cm
Neckline	(NL)	= 1/6 NE + 1.5 = 9 cm
Back width	(BW)	= 1/10 CHE + 10.5 = 23.7 cm
Width of scye	(WOS)	= 1/8 CHE + 1 = 17.5 cm
Chest width	(CW)	= 2/10 CHE + 2 = 28.4 cm
Belly width	(BEW)	= 1/4 WAI - 1 = 32.5 cm
Front waist length	(FWL)	= $NTFW$ - 9.5 (back neckline) + 1.5 (seam allowance at front and back shoulder) = 46.5 cm

Double-breasted jacket
Instructions for the double-breasted jacket can be found in our book 'Modern Men's Tailoring' (s. p. 161).

Seam allowances

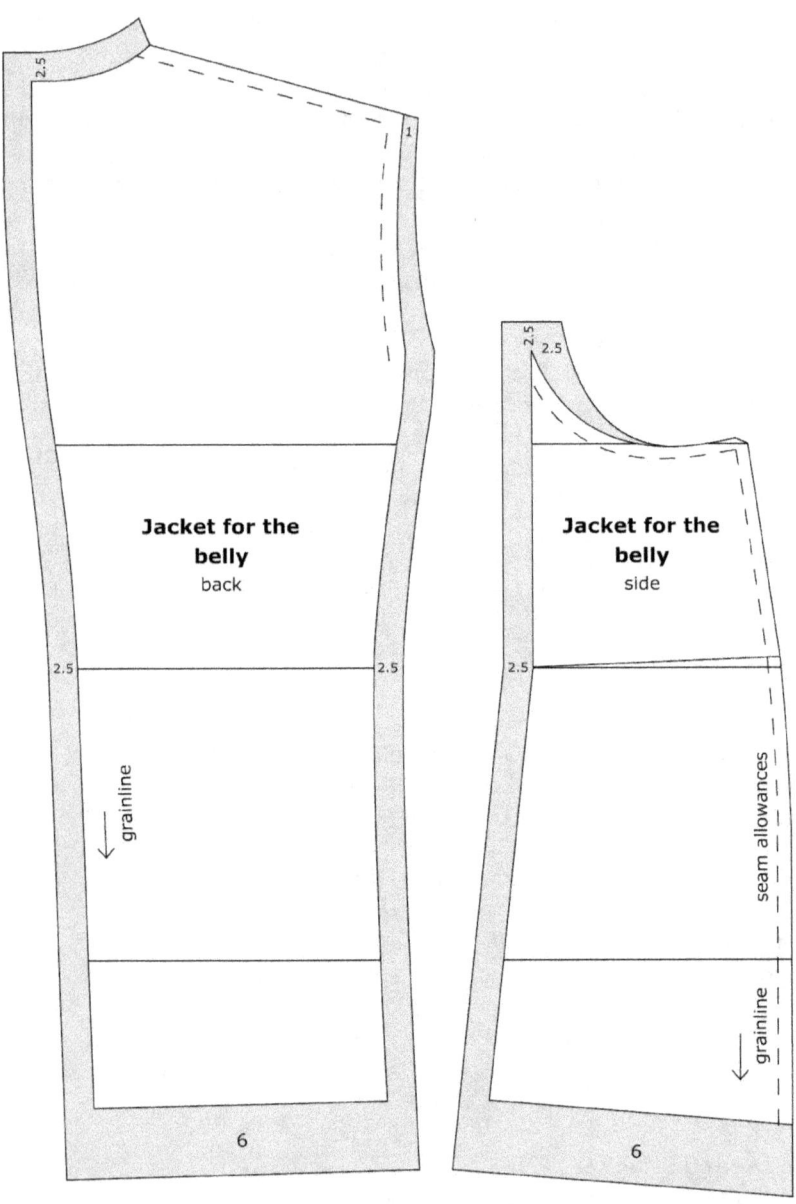

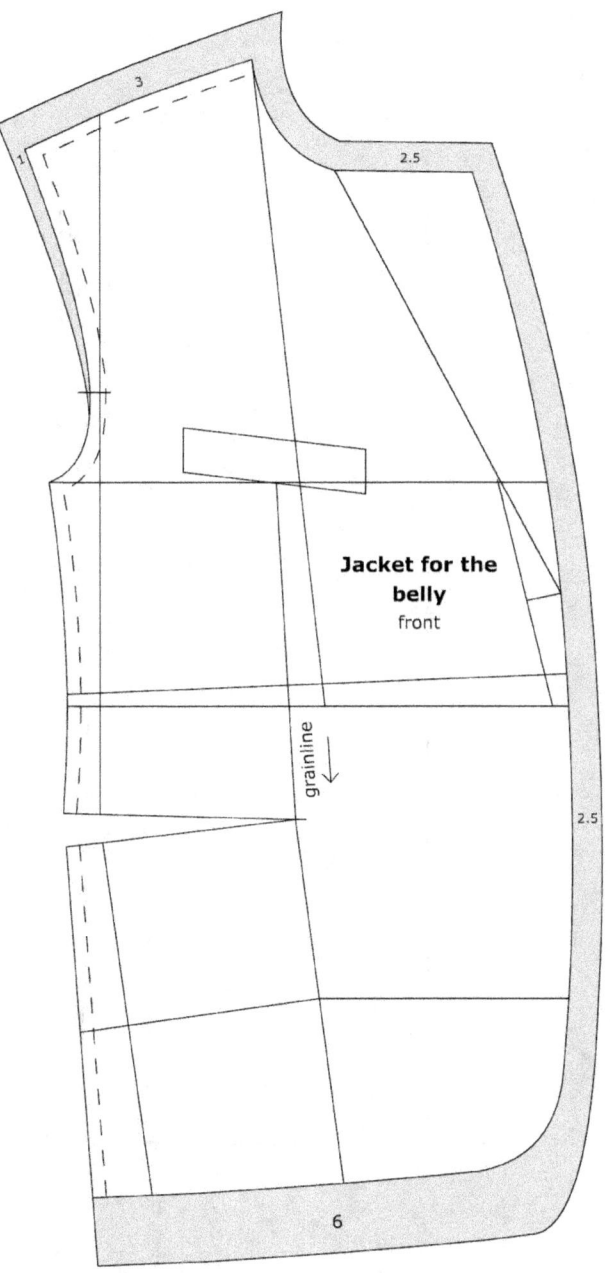

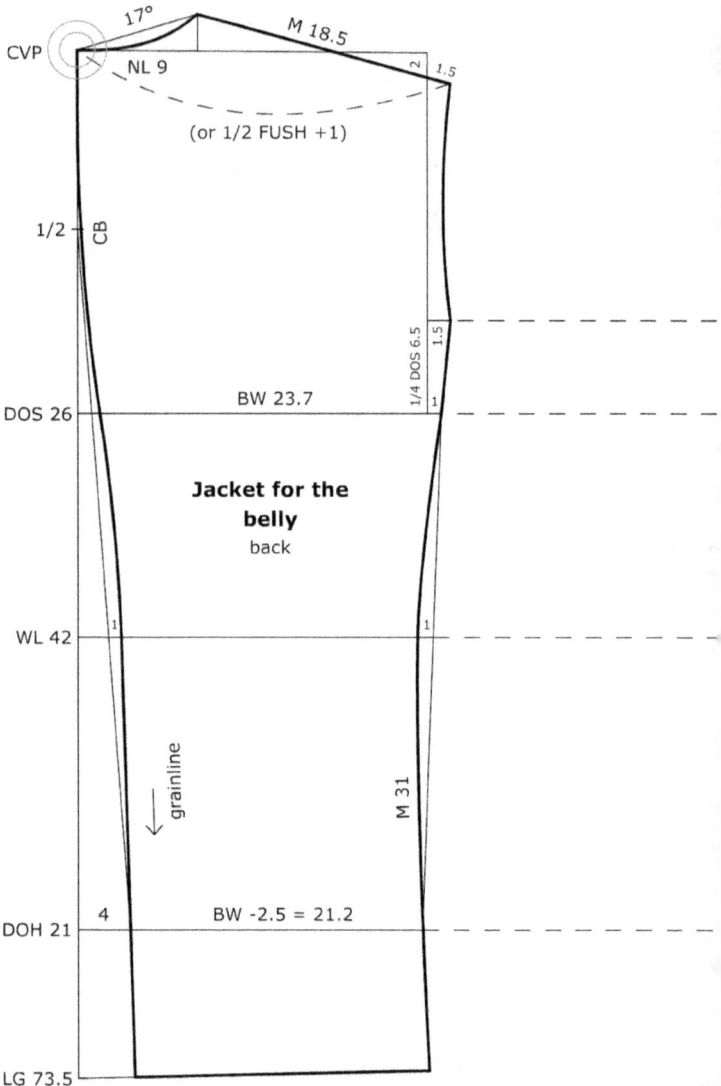

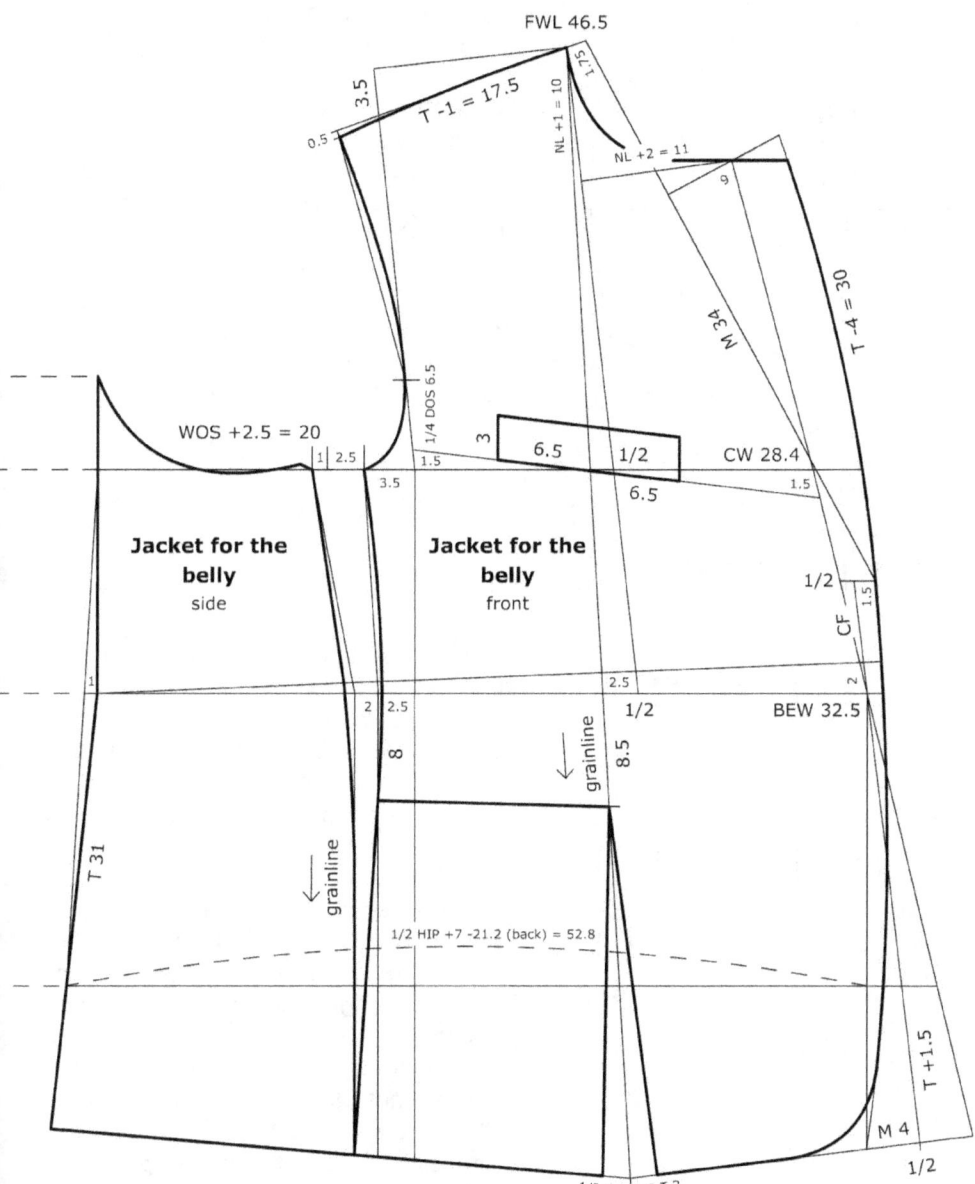

Manual for the belly jacket sleeve

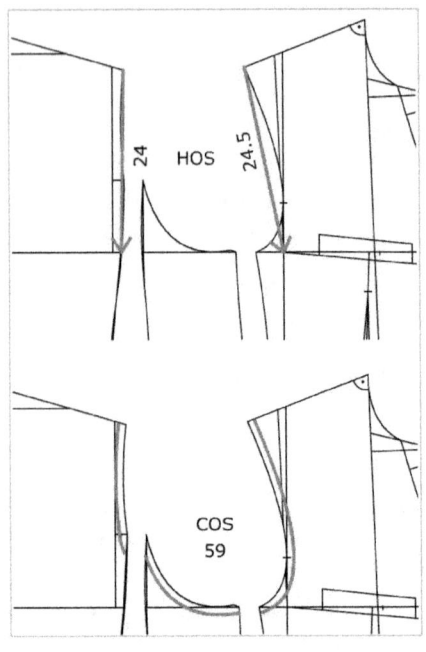

Height of scye
- measure front and back height-of-scye *HOS* and add up = 48.5 cm

Circumference of Scye
- measure circumference-of-scye *COS* minus seam allowances 3 cm = 59 cm (front and back-shoulder as well as front and back side-part-seam = 4 seams = 4 x 0.75 = 3 cm)

Note
For more information about the seam allowances, see pages 76 and 77.

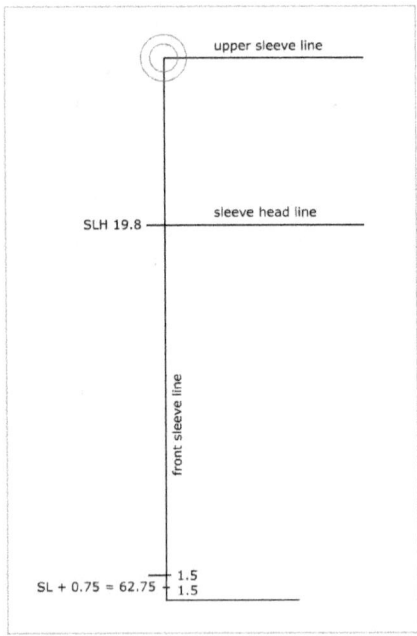

For measurements, see page 83.
Start
- draw a 90° angle
- vertical line defines the front-sleeve-line
- horizontal line defines the upper-sleeve-line

Basic frame
- at front-sleeve-line from upper-sleeve-line: mark down sleeve-head *SLH* = 1/2 *HOS* - (1/20 *HOS* + 2) = 19.8 cm and square right and left; this defines the sleeve-head-line
- from upper-sleeve-line: mark down sleeve-length *SL* + 0.75 cm (seam allowance at sleeve head) = 62.75 cm
- from sleeve-length *SL*: mark up 1.5 cm and square left
- from *SL*: mark down 1.5 cm and square right

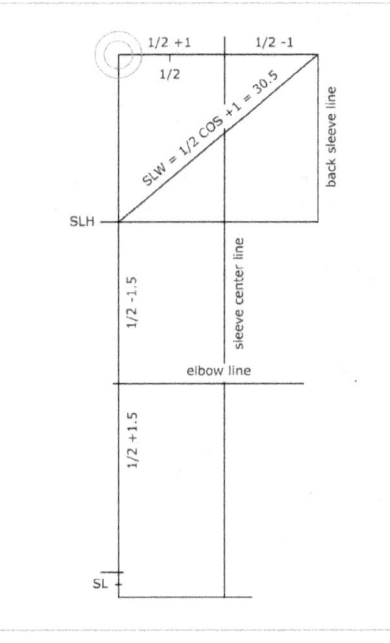

Sleeve width
- at front-sleeve-line from *SLH*:
  draw right upward, diagonal line touching the upper-sleeve-line, by the sleeve-width $SLW = 1/2\ COS + 1 = 30.5$ cm
- from previous point at upper-sleeve-line: square down; this defines the back-sleeve-line
- on upper-sleeve-line from start-point: mark $1/2 + 1$ and square down; this defines the sleeve-center-line
- halve the front part of the upper-sleeve-line

Elbow-line
- at front-sleeve-line: halve the distance between the point 1.5 cm above the *SL* and *SLH*, mark up 1.5 cm and square right; this defines the elbow-line

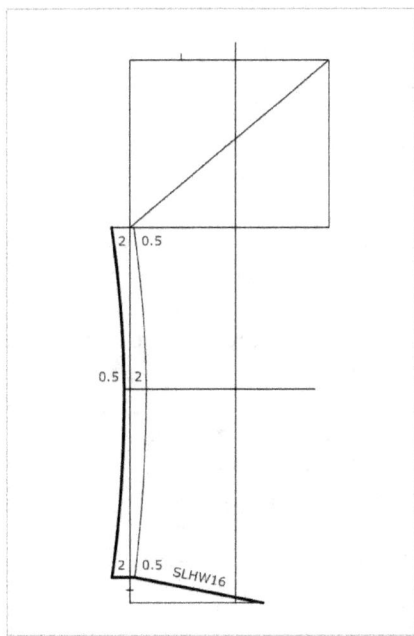

Front sleeve seam
- at the point, 1.5 cm above the *SL*, from front-sleeve-line: mark to the left 2 cm and 0.5 cm to the right
- on elbow-line from front-sleeve-line: mark to the left 0.5 cm and 2 cm to the right
- on sleeve-head-line from front-sleeve-line: mark to the left 2 cm and 0.5 cm to the right
- connect all points with a slightly curved line as shown

Sleeve hem width
- at the point 1.5 cm above the *SL*, from front-sleeve-line: mark right downward sleeve-hem-width *SLHW* 16 cm, touching the lower line as shown

The belly jacket sleeve

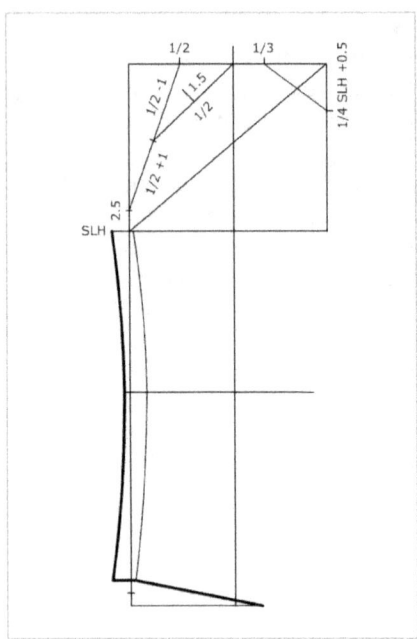

Sleeve head
- at front-sleeve-line from *SLH*: mark up 2.5 cm
- from this point, draw upward a diagonal line to left 1/2-point on upper-sleeve-line
- on previous line: mark up 1/2 + 1 and connect this point with sleeve-center-line on upper-sleeve-line
- halve previous line, square up left and mark 1.5 cm
- divide the back part of the upper-sleeve-line into three
- on back-sleeve-line from upper-sleeve-line: mark down 1/4 *SLH* + 0.5 = 5.5 cm
- connect this point with 1/3-point on upper-sleeve-line

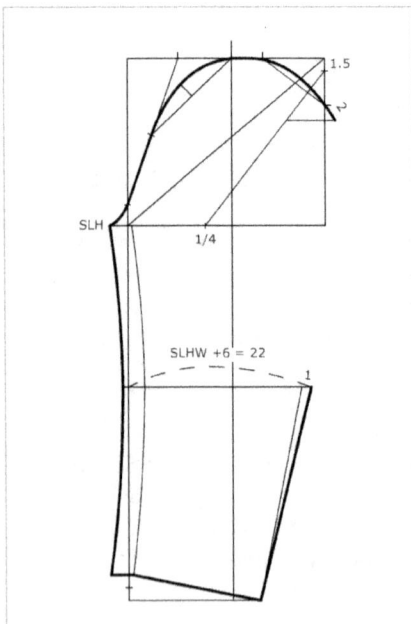

Top sleeve
- shape sleeve head as shown
- extend back part of sleeve-head-seam-line downward by 2 cm
- from previous point: square left as shown

Undersleeve
- on elbow-line from front-sleeve-line: mark to the right sleeve-hem-width *SLHW* + 6 = 22 cm
- from this point mark to the left 1 cm
- draw lines to point on sleeve hem as shown
- on back-sleeve-line from upper-sleeve-line: mark down 1.5 cm
- on *SLH*-line from sleeve-center-line: divide the distance into four
- connect this point with 1.5-cm-point at back-sleeve-line

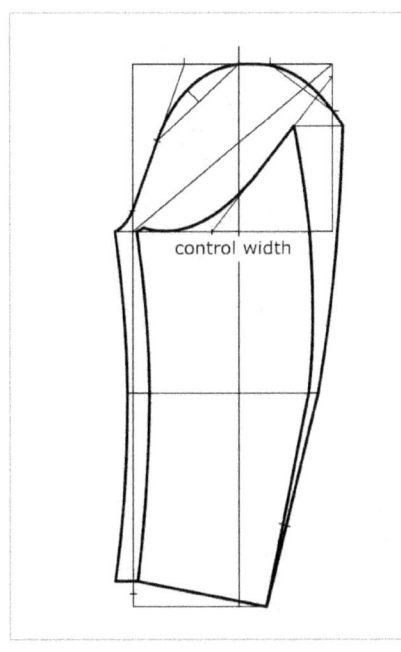

control width

Finish Sleeve
- draw back-seam with a curved line
- finish undersleeve as shown on page 85
- copy undersleeve as a separate pattern piece
- the fullness in the sleeve-head-seam is approx. 3.5 cm

Sleeve notches
In the pattern consciously no notch was defined on the sleeve-head because the arm pitch is different for each person.

Create notch
The sleeve is held at the top of the sleeve-head, placed to the shoulder and turned into the correct position. Then the position of the shoulder-seam is transferred to the sleeve-head.

Cutting
- cut top sleeve 2 x, cut undersleeve 2 x

Instructions
- back sleeve-seam and sleeve-hem are without seam-allowance
- all other seams include 0.75 cm seam allowance (sewing machine foot width), see also next page
- the sleeve-center-line serves as a grainline reference
- check if there will be enough space for the biceps on the *SLH* lines
- the sleeve already has a fullness of approx. 3.5 cm; for more or less fullness, vary the sleeve width *SLW*

Measurements   1/2
Sleeve length	(SL)	62	
Circumference of scye	(COS)	59	| 29.5
Heigth of scye	(HOS)	48.5	| 24.25
Sleeve head	(SLH)	1/2 HOS - (1/20 HOS + 2) = 19.8 cm	
Sleeve width	(SLW)	1/2 COS + 1 = 30.5 cm	
Sleeve hem width	(SLHW)	approx. 16 cm	

Seam allowances

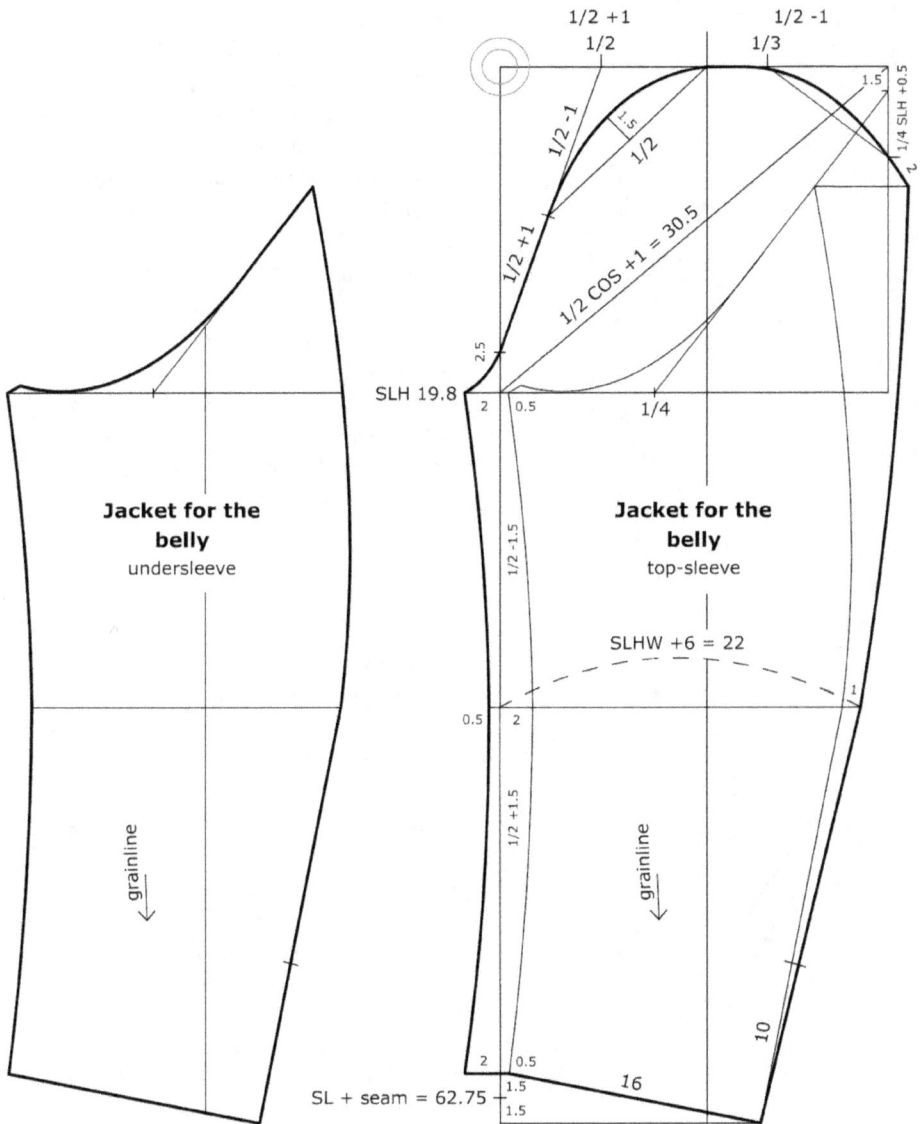

Manual for the belly jacket collar

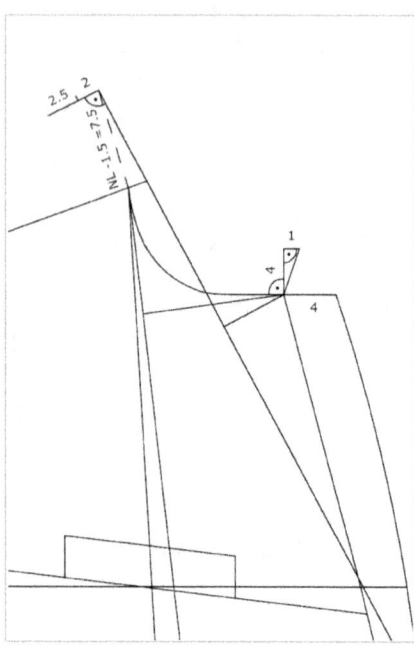

Start
- extend the line of the lapel-fall
- from tip of shoulder/neckline: mark up neckline NL (1/6 NE + 1.5 = 9 cm)
  - 1.5 (seam allowances at front and back shoulder, see also pages 76 and 77)
  = 7.5 cm touching the extended lapel-fall
- from this point: square to the left using the extended lapel-fall-line
- on this line: first mark to the left 2 cm and then mark 2.5 cm as shown
- from lapel-tip: mark to the left 4 cm and square up
- on this line, mark up 4 cm, square right and mark 1 cm
- connect both previous points as shown

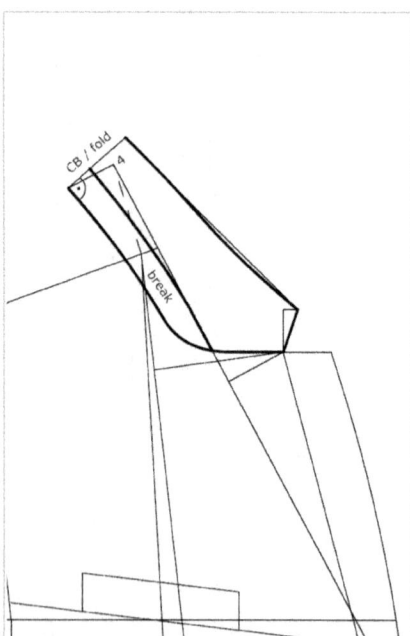

Finish collar
- draw curved line for neckline-seam
- at center back CB/fold from neckline-seam: square right
- draw curved line for collar-break-line
- at CB from collar-break-line: mark to the right 4 cm
- connect previous point with point at collar-tip
- shape collar nicely as shown

Note
The processing of the under- and top collar can be found in our book 'Guide to Men's Tailoring Volume 2' (see p. 162).

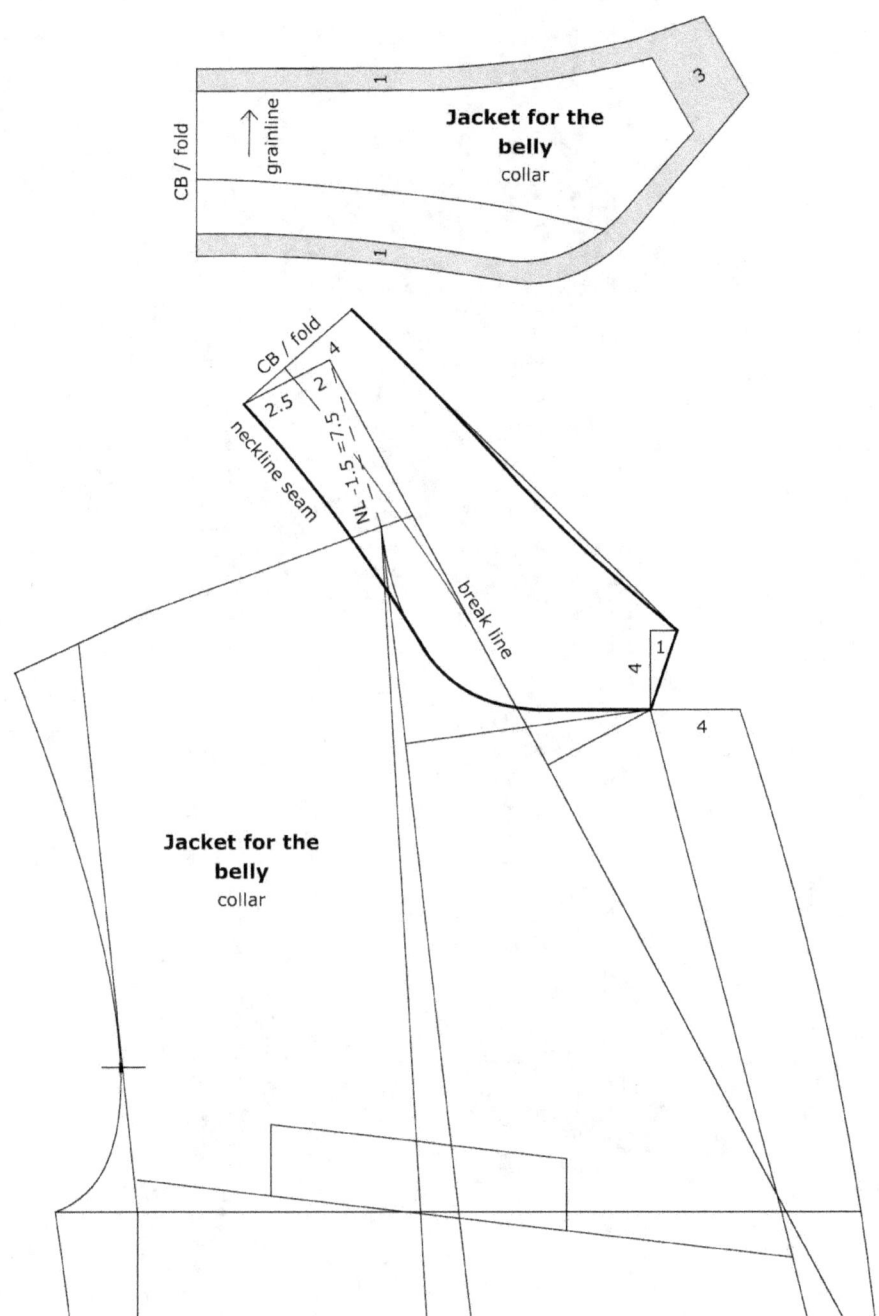

Manual for the pants for muscular thighs

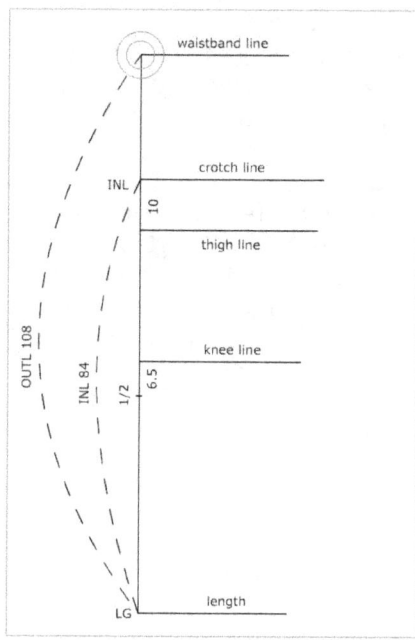

The measurements and further information can be found on page 95.

Start basic structure of front pattern
- draw a 90° angle
- the horizontal line is the waistband-line
- from starting point: mark down outside-leg *OUTL* 108 cm and square right, this line is the length *LG*
- from *LG*: mark up inside-leg *INL* 84 cm and square right; this line is the crotch-line
- from *LG*: mark up 1/2 *INL* + 6.5 cm and square right; this line is the knee-line
- from *INL*: mark down approx. 10 cm and square right for the thigh-line

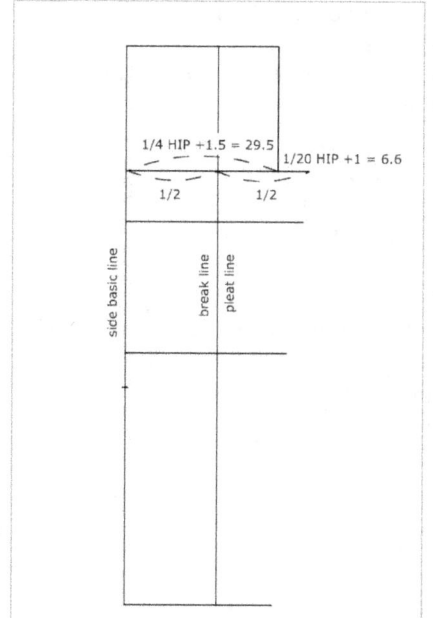

Basic structure
- on crotch-line from side-basic-line: mark to the right 1/4 hip-width *HIP* 28 + 1.5 (1/4 depth of pleat at the break line) = 29.5 cm and square up
- from this point: mark to the right 1/20 *HIP* + 1 = 6.6 cm
- on crotch-line: halve the hole section and square up and down; this line is the break-line or pleat-line
  (see also page 97)

Note
For clients with strong muscular thighs, you should always plan for at least one pleat.

The pants for muscular thighs

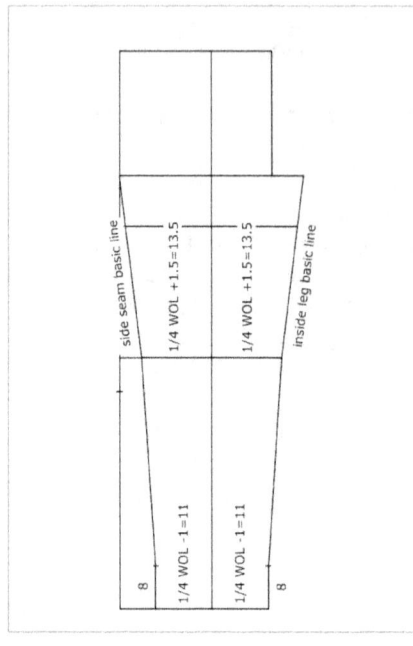

Width of length WOL
- on *LG*-line from break-line: mark to each side, 1/4 width of leg *WOL* - 1 = 11 cm, square up and mark 8 cm

Knee-width
- on knee-line from break-line: mark to each side 1/4 *WOL* + 1.5 = 13.5 cm
- connect the points at the knee-line with the points at the length
- connect the points at the knee-line with the points at the crotch-line

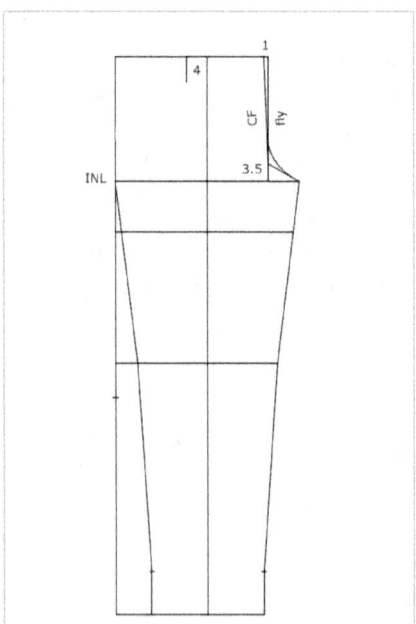

The fly - center front *CF*
- on fly-line from crotch-line: mark up 3.5 cm and connect with right point on crotch-line
- on waistband-line from fly-line: mark to the left approx. 1 cm and connect with previous point at center-front *CF*
- shape lower fly seam

The pleat
- on waistband-line from break-line: mark to the left 4 cm (2 x 2 cm for the pleat) and square down

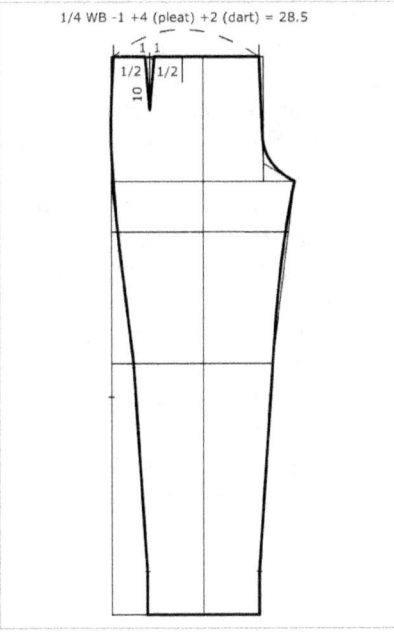

Waistband-line
- on waistband-line from 1-cm-marking at CF: mark to the left 1/4 WB - 1 (will be added at the waistband of the back pattern) + 4 (for the pleat) + 2 (for the dart) = 28.5 cm

Front dart
- on waistband-line between side seam and pleat: halve the distance, square down and mark approx. 10 cm
- on waistband-line from dart-line: mark to each side approx. 1 cm

Finish the front-pattern
- shape side seam and inseam nicely
- compare the taken measurements of the front pants length *FPL* with your pattern

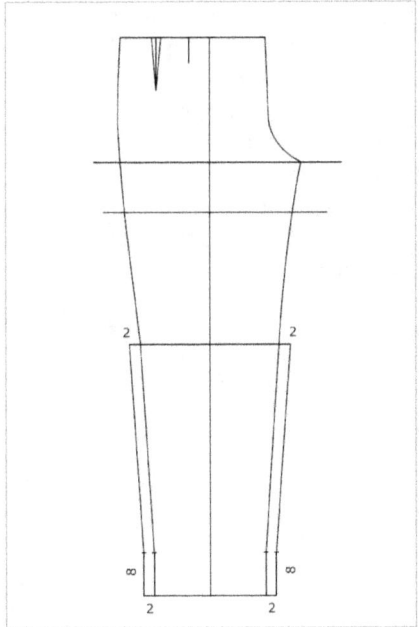

Back pattern
Cut out the front pattern and use it as a basis. Then, place it on a new piece of pattern paper.

- extend all lines (waistband-line, thigh-line, knee-line, length and break-line)
- on *LG*-line from the front pattern: mark 2 cm to each side, square up and mark 8 cm
- on knee-line from the front pattern: mark 2 cm to each side
- connect the points at the knee-line with the lower points

The pants for muscular thighs

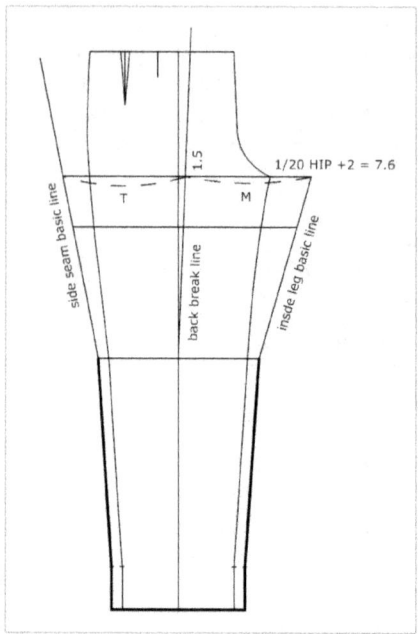

Width of back pants
- on crotch-line from front-break-line: mark to the right approx. 1.5 cm
- at the crossing of the front-break-line and knee-line: draw up a line through the previous point
- this line is the re-placed back-break-line
- on the crotch-line from the tip of the front trousers: mark to the right 1/20 HIP + 2 = 7.6 cm
- on crotch-line: measure *M* the entire distance from the tip of the back trousers to the new back-break-line and transfer *T* to the left
- finish inseam-basic-line and side-seam-basic-line as shown

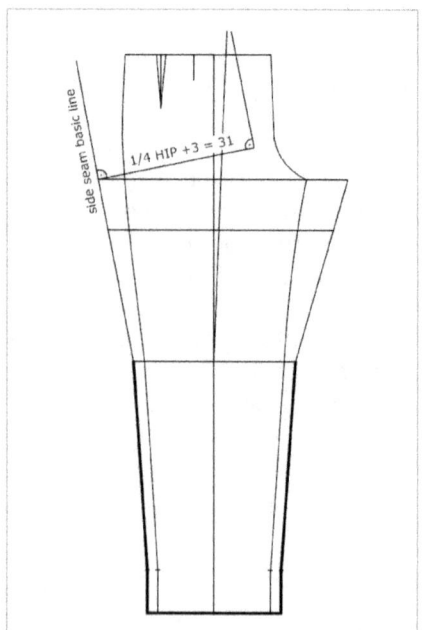

The inclination of the butt seam
- at the crossing of crotch-line and side-seam-basic-line of the back pants: square upward to the right
- on that line from side-seam-basic-line: mark to the right 1/4 *HIP* + 3 fullness = 31 cm and square up
- pierce this point with the tip of the pencil to transfer it to the lower paper

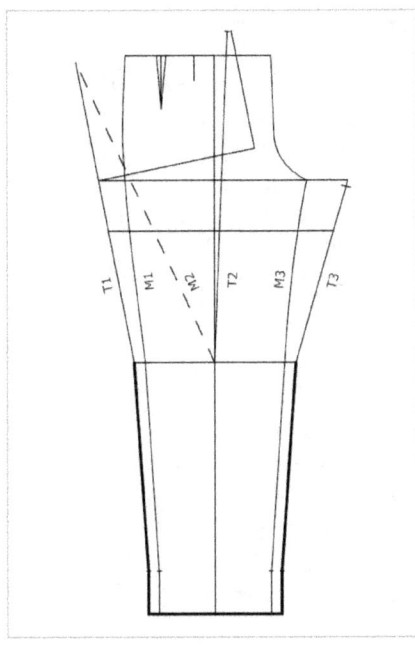

Back pants length *BPL*

- measure the length of the side-seam-basic-line at the front pants from the knee point up *M1* = 59.5 cm and transfer it to the side-seam-basic-line of the back pants *T1*

- from the crossing front-break-line / knee-line: measure up to the side-seam-basic-line of the back pants *M2* = 64 cm and transfer it to the back-break-line *T2*
- measure here from the top to the length *LG* and compare this measure with the taken measurement *BPL* (see page 16)

- measure the length of the inseam-basic-line of the front pants from the knee-point up *M3* = 35.5 cm and transfer it to the back pants *T3*

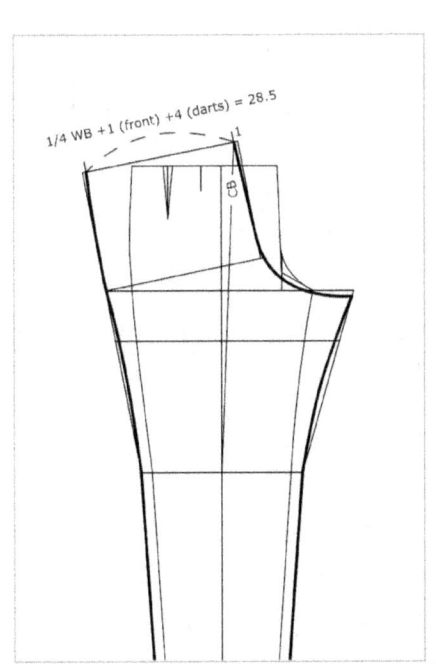

Waistband back pants

- connect the top points for the waistband of the back pants
- from right point on waistband-line: mark to the left approx. 1 cm
- from the center back *CB*: mark to the left 1/4 waistband *WB* + 1 cm (reduced at the front pattern) + 4 cm (for the darts) = 28.5 cm
- this measure should not go beyond the side seam, otherwise decrease the darts
- if only one dart is required due to a smaller difference between the waistband and the hip, then the fullness at the back-waistband is also calculated with just one dart
- remove the front pants pattern and retrace all lines below
- shape inseam and side seam

The pants for muscular thighs

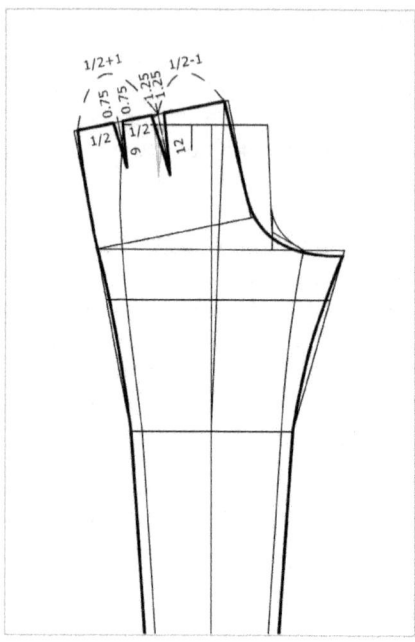

Darts at the back pants

Dart 1
- at waistband from *CB*: mark to the left 1/2 - 1 cm of the entire length of the back-waistband (including fullness for darts) and square down
- the dart length is approx. 12 cm
- the 1/2 dart is about 1.25 cm on both sides (it depends on the difference between hips and waistband)

Dart 2
(the quantity of darts depends on the difference between hips and waistband)
- halve the distance between side seam and 1st dart and square down
- the dart length is approx. 9 cm
- the 1/2 dart is about 0.75 cm
- the width for both darts is approx. 4 cm in total

Shaping the seat-seam
- put the inseam of the front pants to the inseam of the back pants and shape the seat-seam

Note
Make sure that the curve of the seat-seam is not too flat (a) and definitely not too deep (b).
Otherwise, the back pants will be to tight at the butt.

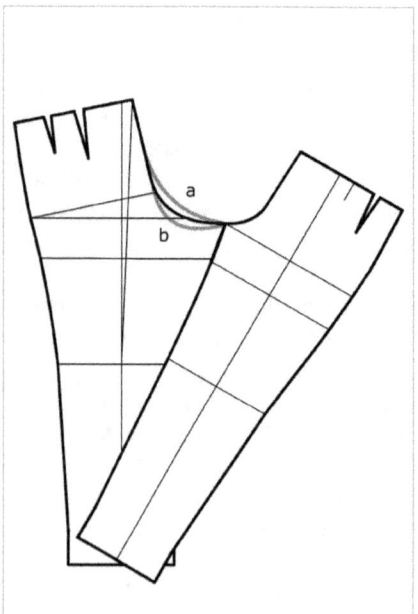

Cutting
- cut front pants 2 x
- cut back pants 2 x

Instructions
- all measures are in cm
- all seams are without seam allowances
- the lower parts of the front and back pants' break-line serve as the grainline

Fullness
At the waistband, the measure should fit exactly. The fullness at the 1/2 hips should be about 3 cm + 1/4 of the pleat-measure. This fullness is already considered in the calculation.

Measurements for the pants

			1/2	1/4
Waistband	(*WB*)	94	47	23.5
Hips	(*HIP*	112	56	28
Outside leg	(*OUTL*)	108		
Inside leg	(*INL*)	84		
Thigh	(*TH*)	68	34	
Width of length	(*WOL*)	48	24	12

Note
If the width at the thigh is too tight, increase the front (s. p. 89, picture 2) and rear crotch diameters (s. p. 92, picture 1) equally, or follow the steps on page 98.

Seam allowances

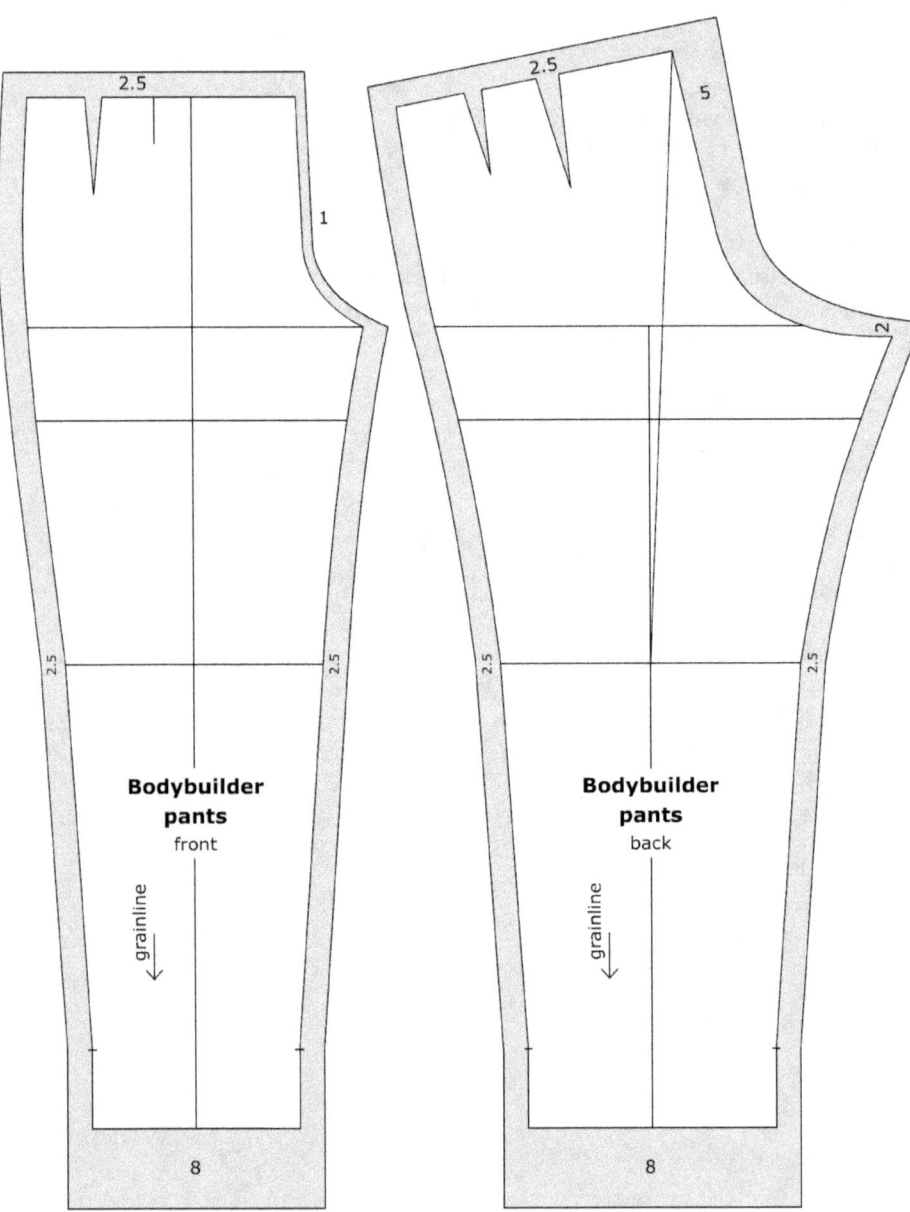

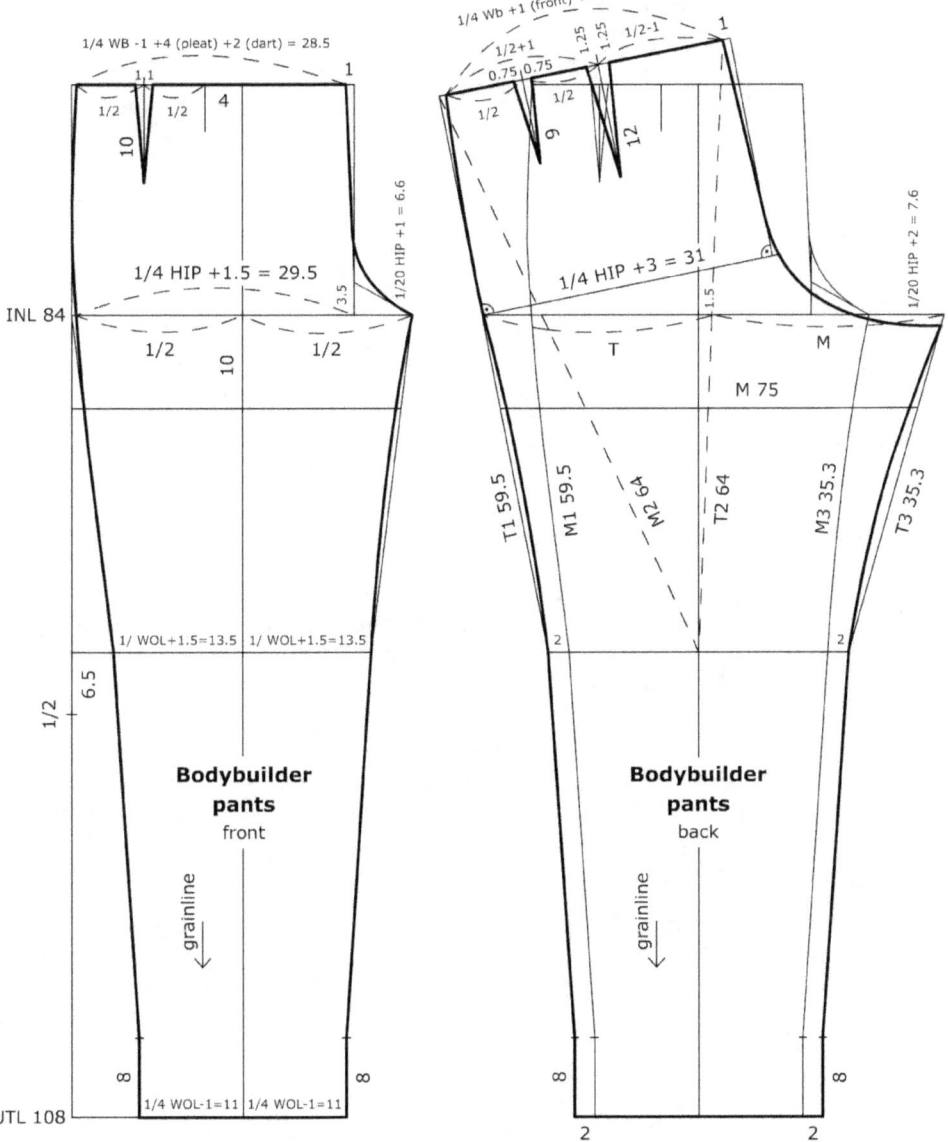

Altering a regular pattern

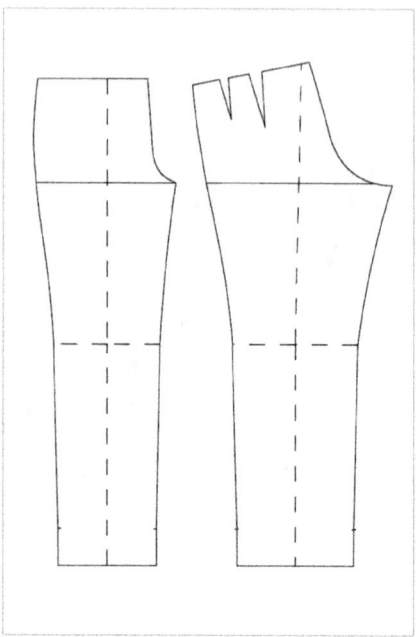

Front pattern

Cut the front pattern apart at the centerline and the knee line (dashed lines).

back pattern

Cut the back pattern apart at the centerline and the knee line (dashed lines).

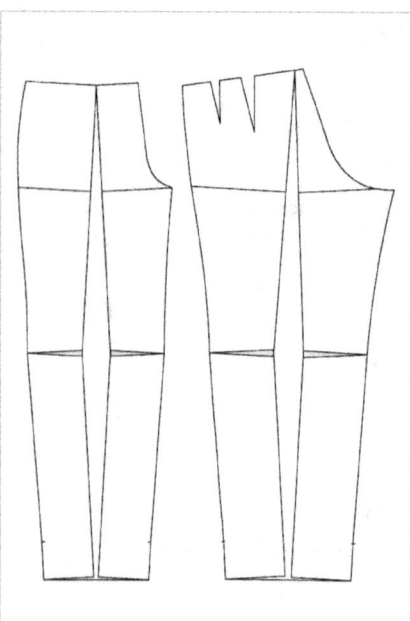

Rotate to open the pattern

Rotate to open the pattern of the front and back pants so that you have enough room at the thighs.

Note

The shape of the side seam and inseam, as well as the length, now has to be balanced out a bit.

Manual for the bodybuilder vest

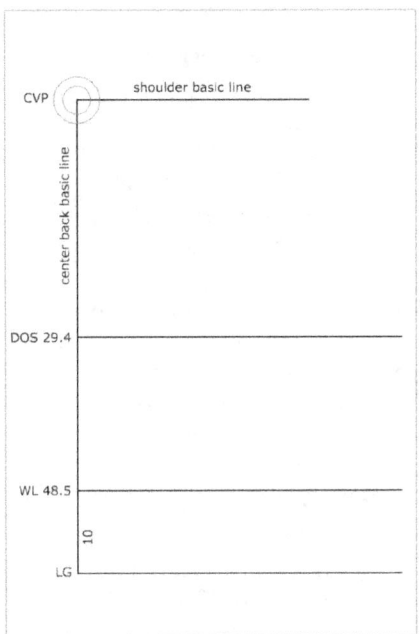

The measurements and further information can be found on page 107.

Start
- draw a 90° angle
- vertical line is the center-back-basic-line
- horizontal line is the shoulder-basic-line
- on center-back-basic-line from 7th cervical-vertebra-point *CVP*: mark down depth-of-scye *DOS* = 1/16 *HEI* + 1/8 *CHE* = 29.4 cm and square right
- on center-back-basic-line from *CVP*: mark down waist-length *WL* = 1/4 *HEI* = 48.5 cm and square right
- on center-back-basic-line from *WL*: mark down approx. 10 cm and square right
- When drawing the length, make sure that the waistcoat covers the pants' waistband

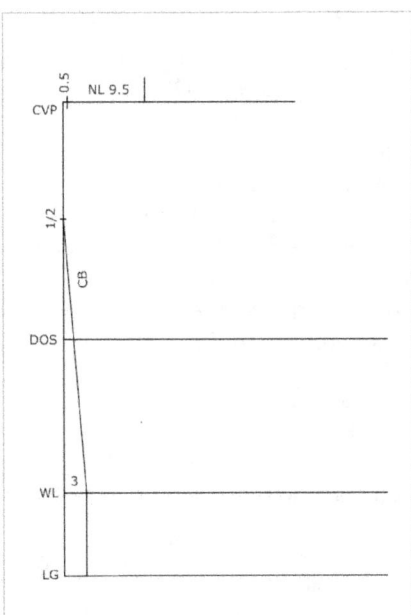

Center-back-seam
- on center-back-basic-line: halve the line between *CVP* and *DOS*
- on *WL*-line from center-back-basic-line: mark to the right approx. 3 cm and square down
- connect this point with previous 1/2-point; this line will become the center-back *CB*

Neckline, shoulder
- on shoulder-basic-line from *CVP*: mark to the right approx. 0.5 cm
- on shoulder-basic-line from 0.5-cm-point: mark to the right neckline *NL* = 1/6 *NE* + 1 = 9.5 cm and square up

101

The bodybuilder vest

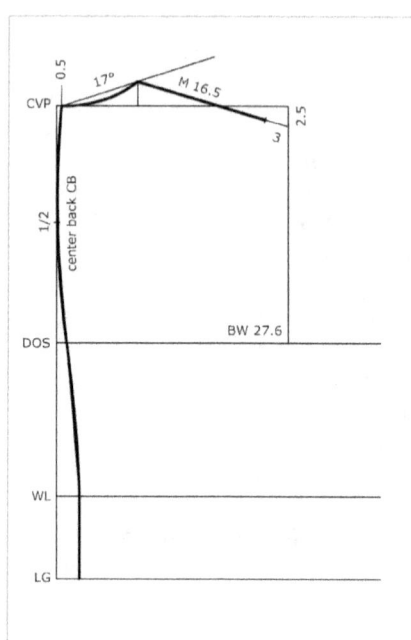

Center-back-seam
- shape seam at center-back *CB*

Shoulder
- on chest-line (*DOS*-line) from seam at *CB*: mark to the right back-width *BW* = 2/10 *CHE* = 27.6 cm and square up
- from 0.5-cm-point: create a 17° angle to the right up
- on *BW*-line from shoulder-basic-line: mark down 2.5 cm and connect this point with previous point at neckline
- mark shoulder seam from *BW*-line 3 cm narrower and measure this line *M* = approx. 16.5 cm
- shape back-neckline

Note
The shoulder can be drawn broader or narrower, just as you wish for your design.

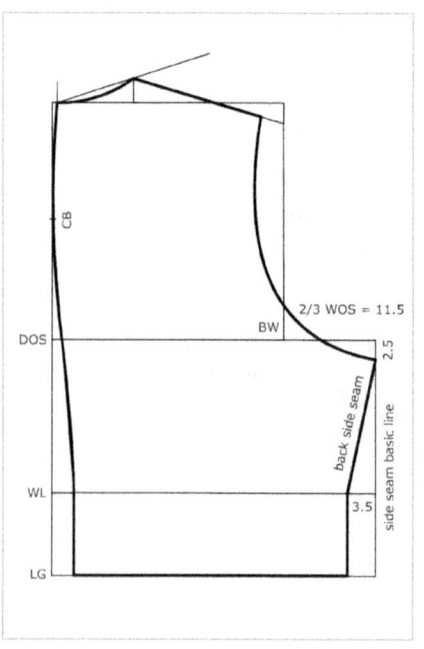

Side seam
- on chest-line from *BW*-line: mark to the right 2/3 width-of-scye *WOS* = 1/8 *CHE* (17.25) ÷ 3 × 2 = 11.5 cm and square down
- at side seam from chest-line: mark down 2.5 cm; this armhole enlargement is to give the wearer more room for moving his arms
- at waistline from side-seam-basic-line: mark to the left approx. 3.5 cm and square down
- finish back side seam

Armhole
- shape back armhole nicely

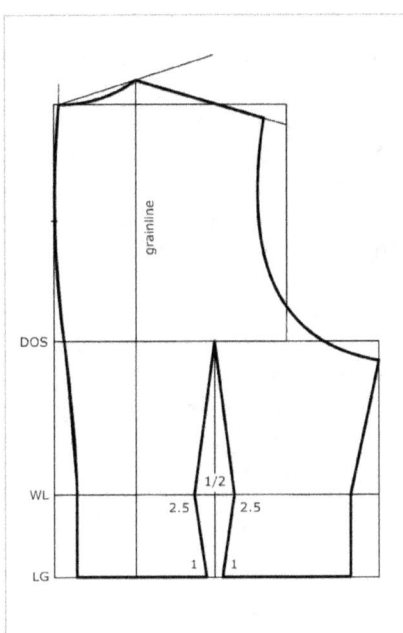

Dart
- on waistline between *CB* and side seam: halve distance at *WL*-line and square up to the *DOS*-line
- at hem-line (*LG*-line) from dart-line: mark to each side approx. 1 cm
- on waistline: mark depth of the dart with approx. 2.5 cm to each side
- the depth of the dart depends on the shaping at the back waist, it can also be less or more
- finish dart as shown

Grainline
- draw a line parallel to the center-back-basic-line

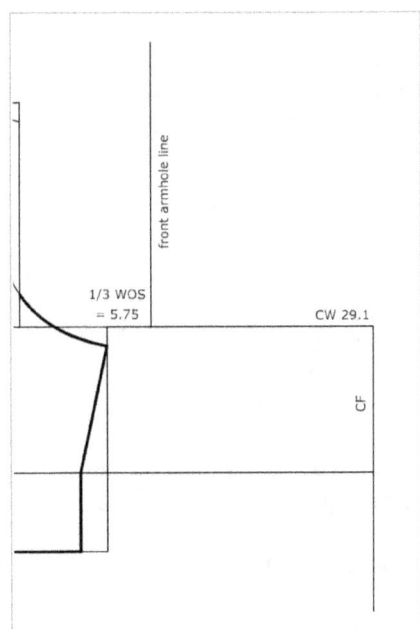

Basic front frame
- extend chest-line and waistline to the right
- at chest-line from side-seam-basic-line: mark to the right $1/3\ WOS = 1/8\ CHE \div 3 = 5.75$ cm and square up; this is the front-armhole-line
- from here on chest-line: mark to the right chest-width $CW = 2/10\ CHE + 1.5 = 29.1$ cm and square down; this line is the center-front *CF*

Note
The chest-line is called *DOS*-line or *BW*-line at the back and *CW*-line at the front.
The *WL*-line is also called waistline.

The bodybuilder vest

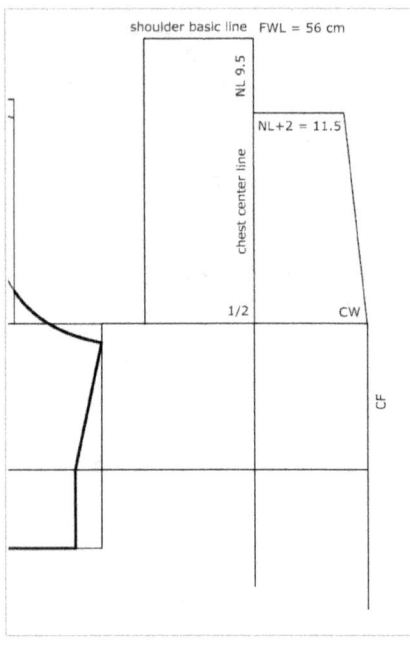

Shoulder
- halve chest-width CW and square up and down
- on chest-center-line from WL-line: mark up front-waist-length FWL = nape-to-front-waist NTFW - 10 (back neckline) = 56 cm and square left; this creates the shoulder-basic-line

Neckline
- on chest-center-line from shoulder-basic-line: mark down front neckline $NL = 1/6\ NE + 1 = 9.5$ cm square right and mark $NL + 2 = 11.5$ cm
- connect this point with CF on chest-line

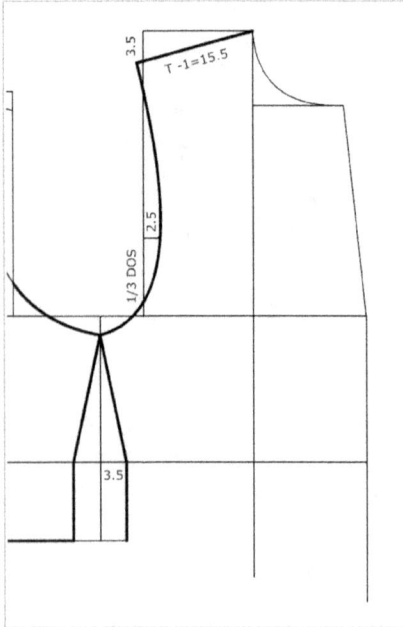

Shoulder
- at front-armhole-line from shoulder-basic-line: mark down 3.5 cm
- connect this point with point at neckline and transfer T the measure from back-shoulder - 1 cm = 15.5 cm

Armhole
- at front-armhole-line from CHE-line: mark up $1/3\ DOS = 9.8$ cm, square right and mark approx. 2.5 cm
- shape front armhole nicely

Side seam
- at WL-line from side-seam-basic-line: mark to the right approx. 3.5 cm and square down
- extend the hem at the back-side-seam to the right

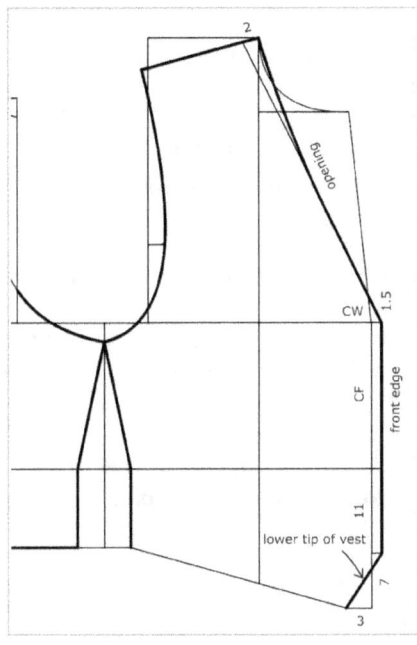

Opening
- at shoulder tip: mark to the left 2 cm
- at *CF* from *CW*-line: mark to the right 1.5 cm and square down
- connect 2-cm-point at the shoulder with front edge at *CW*-line
- shape opening by hollowing it slightly

Tip of vest
- at *CF* from waistline: mark down 11 cm and square right
- from this point: mark down 7 cm, square left and mark 3 cm
- connect this point with lower front-side-seam
- finish the lower tip of the vest at the lower front edge

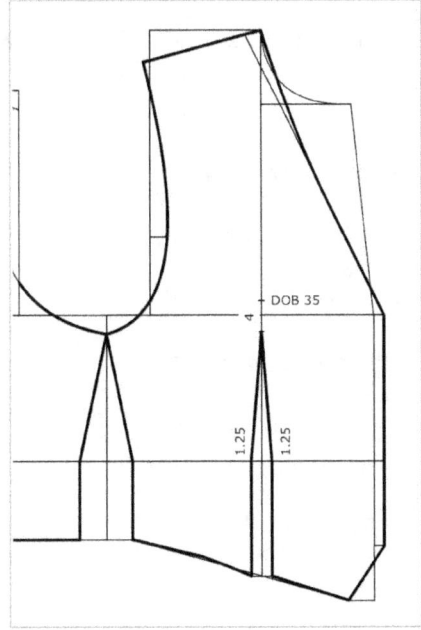

Front dart
- on chest-center-line from shoulder: mark down depth-of-breast *DOB* = nape-to-breast *NTB* - 10 (back neckline) = 35 cm
- on chest-center-line from *DOB*: mark down 4 cm
- at waistline from chest-center-line: mark depth-of-dart with approx. 1.25 cm to each side and square down each
- finish dart as shown
- balance hem at the dart as shown

The bodybuilder vest

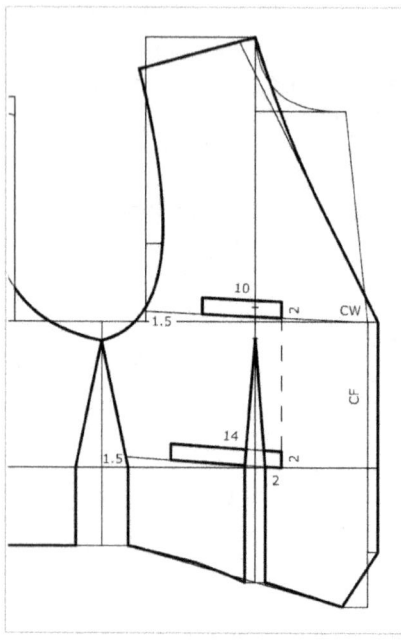

Chest pocket
- at front-armhole-line from chest-line: mark up 1.5 cm
- connect previous point with CF at CW
- mark heigth of welt with approx. 2 cm
- mark pocket-opening with approx. 10 cm

Waist pocket
- at side seam from waistline: mark up 1.5 cm
- on waistline from dart-line (chest-center-line): mark to the right 2 cm and square up
- connect both previous points
- mark heigth of welt with approx. 2 cm
- mark pocket-opening with approx. 14 cm

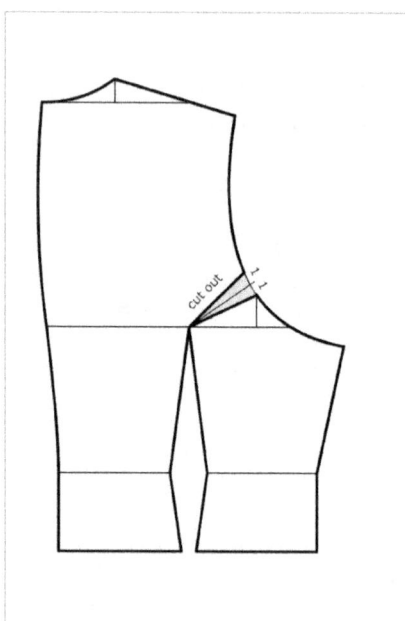

Narrow armhole
When the pattern is finished, the back pattern is cut out, and the back armhole will be narrowed (reshaped).

- from armhole: draw a 90° angle toward the dart
- mark about 1 cm on each side
- cut out this amount and join together
- this opens the back-dart and the back gets a better fit at the armhole and around the scapula, see p. 108

Cutting
- cut front 2 x
- cut back 2 x (plus 2 x for the lining)

Instructions
- all measures are in cm
- all seams are without seam allowances

Taken measurements

		1/2	1/4	1/8	1/16
Height	(HEI)	194	97	48.5	24.25	12.12
Chest	(CHE)	138	69	34.5	17.25
Waist	(WAI)	106	53
Neck	(NE)	51
Nape to front waist	(NTFW)	66
Nape to breast	(NTB)	45

Calculated measurements

Depth of scye	(DOS)	$= 1/16\ HEI + 1/8\ CHE = 29.4$ cm
Waist length	(WL)	$= 1/4\ HEI = 48.5$ cm
Neckline	(NL)	$= 1/6\ NE + 1 = 9.5$ cm
Back width	(BW)	$= 2/10\ CHE = 27.6$ cm
Width of scye	(WOS)	$= 1/8\ CHE = 17.25$ cm
Chest width	(CW)	$= 2/10\ CHE + 1.5 = 29.1$ cm
Difference	(DIFF)	$= CHE - WAI = 32$ cm
Front waist length	(FWL)	$=$ NTFW - 10 (back neckline) $= 56$ cm
Depth of breast	(DOB)	$= NTB - 10$ (back neckline) $= 35$ cm

For clients that deviate from the 'norm' (broad shoulders, strong back, etc.), the taken measurements should be used instead of the calculated ones.

Control
Compare chest and waist with the taken measurements. The fullness at the 1/2 chest and the 1/2 waist should be about 4.5 cm for each and is already considered in the calculation.

Grainline
In the front part, the center front *CF* serves as a grainline reference; in the back part, the line marked parallel to the center-back-basic-line is doing this job.

Seam allowances

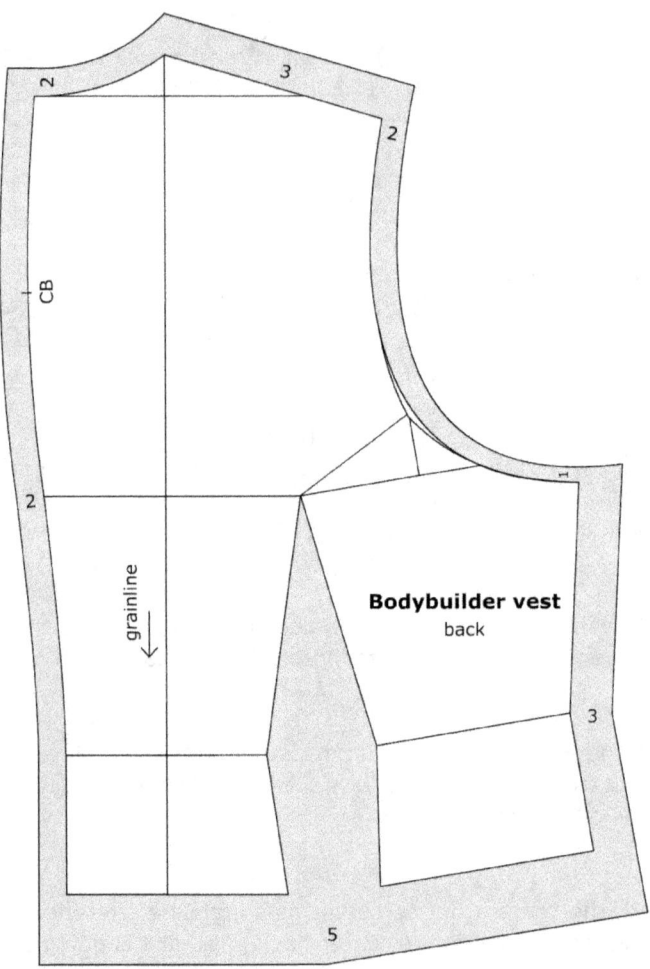

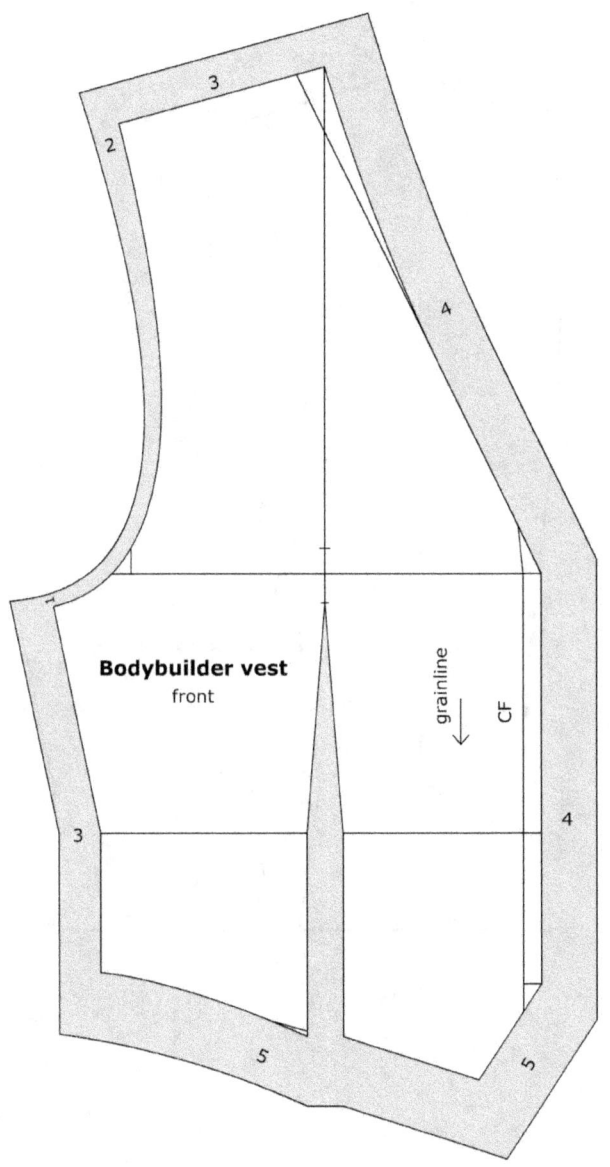

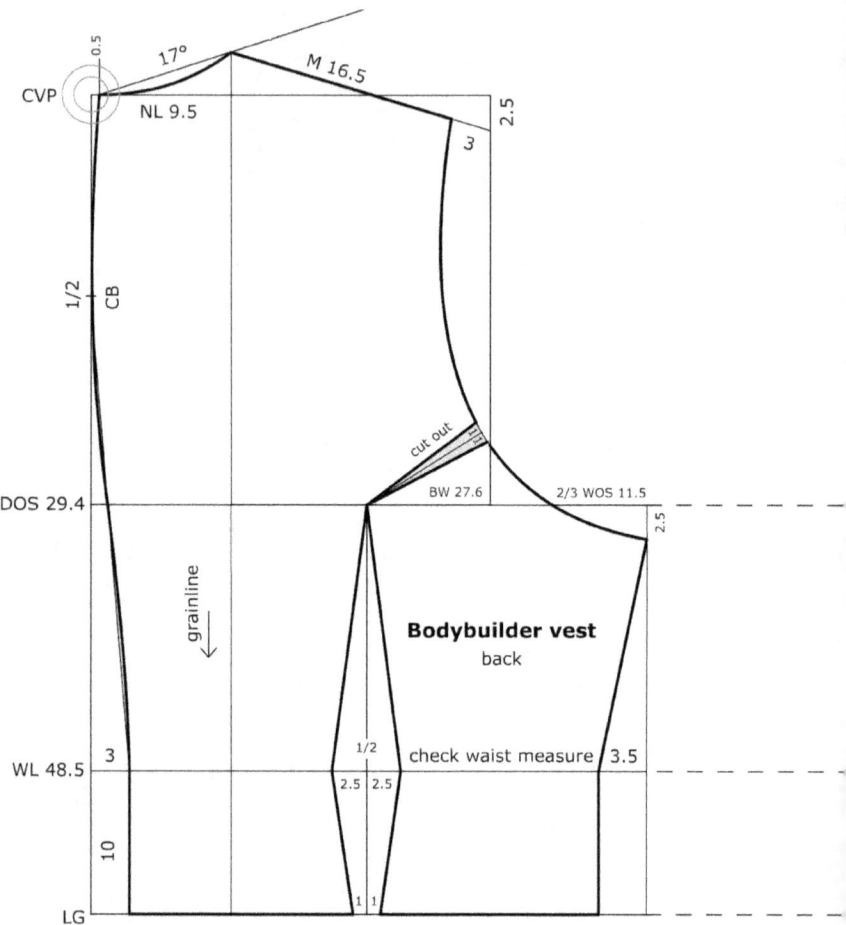

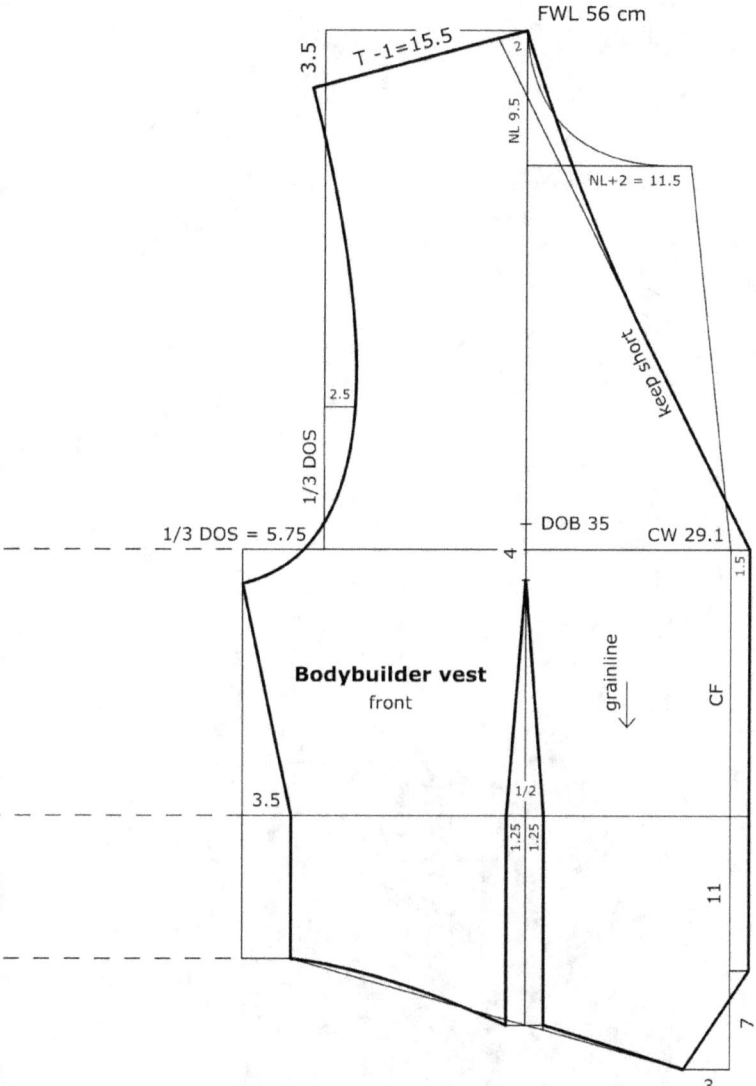

Manual for the bodybuilder shirt

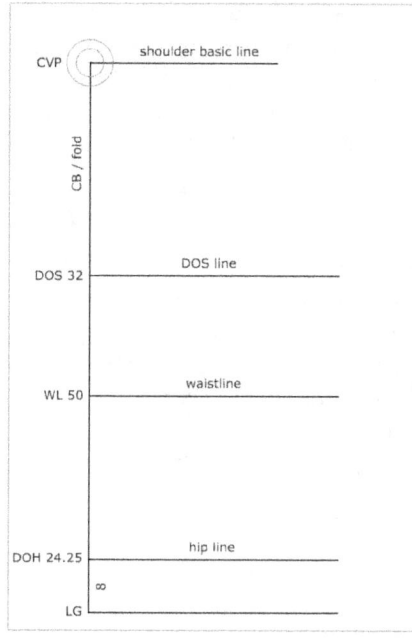

For measurements, see page 117.

Start
- draw a 90° angle
- on *CB*-line from the 7th cervical-vertebra-point *CVP*: mark down depth-of-scye *DOS* = 1/16 *HEI* + 1/8 *CHE* + 2.5 = 32 cm and square right (*DOS*-line/chest-line)
- on *CB*-line from *CVP*: mark down waist-length *WL* = 1/4 *HEI* + 1.5 = 50 cm and square right (waistline)
- on *CB*-line from *WL*: mark down depth-of-hips *DOH* = 1/8 *HEI* = 24.25 cm and square right (hip line)
- from *DOH*: mark down 8 cm and square right (hem-line)
- compare the length with your favourite shirt

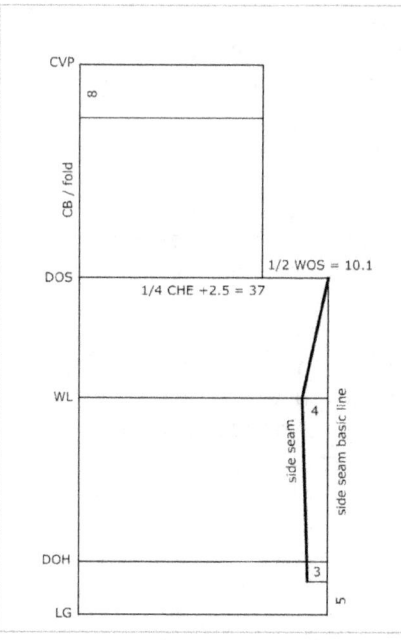

Chest width
- on *DOS*-line from *CB*: mark to the right 1/4 *CHE* + 2.5 = 37 cm and square down

Back width
- on *DOS*-line from side-seam-basic-line: mark to the left 1/2 width-of-scye *WOS* = (1/8 *CHE* + 3) ÷ 2 = 10.1 cm and square up

Side seam
- on *WL*-line from side-seam-basic-line: mark to the left approx. 4 cm
- from hem-basic-line mark up 5 cm, square left and mark approx. 3 cm
- finish side seam as shown

Yoke
- on *CB*-line from *CVP*: mark down 8 cm and square right

The bodybuilder shirt

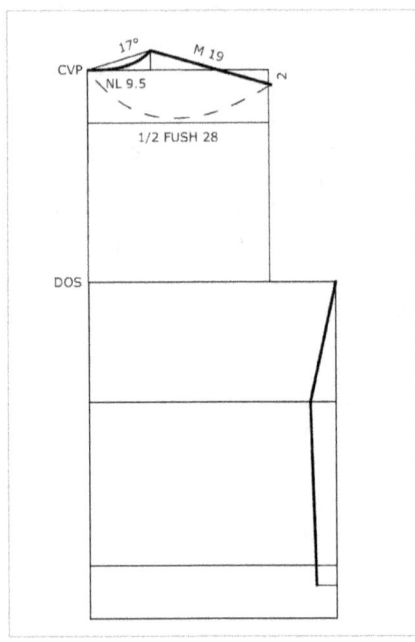

Back neckline
- on shoulder-basic-line from *CVP*: mark to the right neckline *NL* = 1/6 *NE* + 1 = 9.5 cm and square up
- from *CVP*: create a 17° angle to the right up
- shape neckline nicely

Shoulder
- on back-width-line from shoulder-basic-line: mark down 2 cm
- from upper point at neck draw shoulder-seam through previous point
- on shoulder-seam from *CVP*: mark to the right 1/2 full shoulder *FUSH* 28 cm
- measure width of shoulder seam *M* = approx. 19 cm

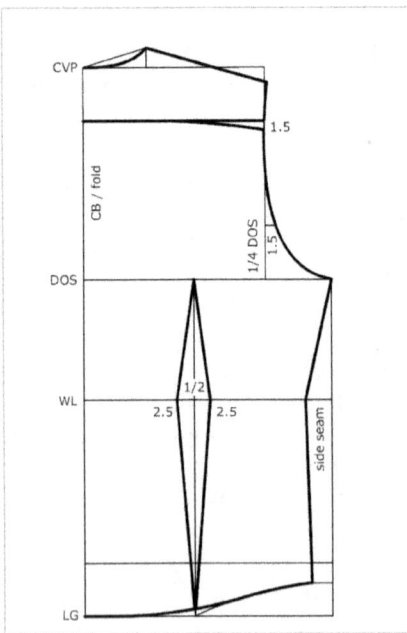

Back armhole
- on back-width-line: mark up 1/4 *DOS* = 8 cm, square right and mark 1.5 cm
- shape armhole nicely

Yoke
- at back-armhole from yoke-line: mark down 1.5 cm and shape seam nicely

Dart
- halve the distance on waistline and square up and down
- for the depth-of-dart: mark to each side approx. 2.5 cm

Hem
- shape hem nicely

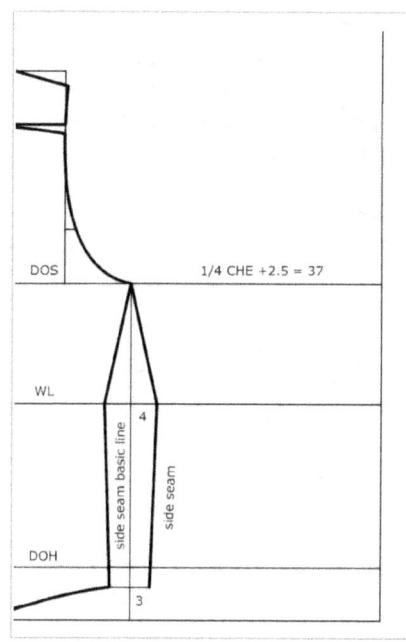

Basic frame front piece
- extend shoulder-basic-line, chest-line, waistline, hip-line and hem-basic-line to the right

Chest
- on chest-line from side-seam-basic-line: mark to the right 1/4 *CHE* + 2.5 = 37 cm and square up and down; this is the center-front *CF*

Side seam
- on waistline at side-seam-basic-line: mark to the right approx. 4 cm
- on side-seam-basic-line from hem-line: mark to the right approx. 3 cm
- finish front-side-seam as shown

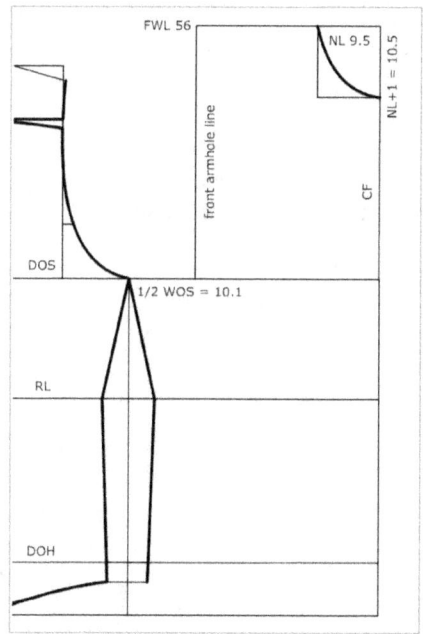

Chest width / front armhole width
- on chest-line from side-seam-basic-line: mark to the right 1/2 width-of-scye *WOS* = (1/8 *CHE* + 3) ÷ 2 = 10.1 cm and square up
- on front-armhole-line from chest-line: mark up *FWL* = *NTFW* - 10 (back neckline) = 56 cm and square right

Front neck
- on shoulder-basic-line from center front *CF*: mark to the left neckline *NL* = 1/6 *NE* + 1 = 9.5 cm and square down
- on *CF*-line from the top: mark down *NL* + 1 = 10.5 cm and square left
- shape front neckline

The bodybuilder shirt

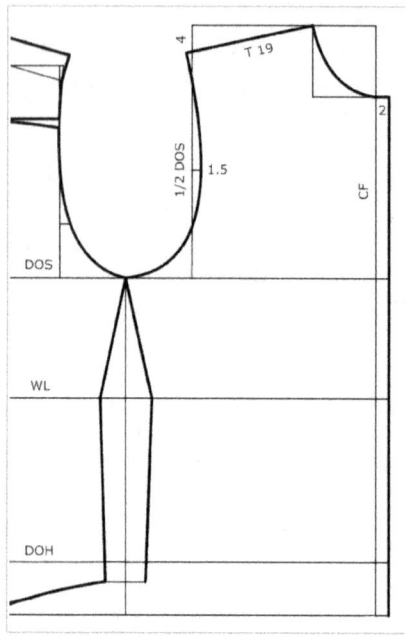

Front shoulder
- on front-armhole-line from shoulder-basic-line: mark down 4 cm, draw shoulder seam and transfer width-of-back shoulder $T = 19$ cm

Front armhole
- on front-armhole-line from chest-line: mark up 1/2 $DOS = 16$ cm, square right and mark approx. 1.5 cm
- shape armhole nicely
- measure the complete armhole circumference-of-scye COS (front piece, back piece and yoke) $M =$ approx. 72 cm

Front edge
- from CF: mark to the right 2 cm and square down

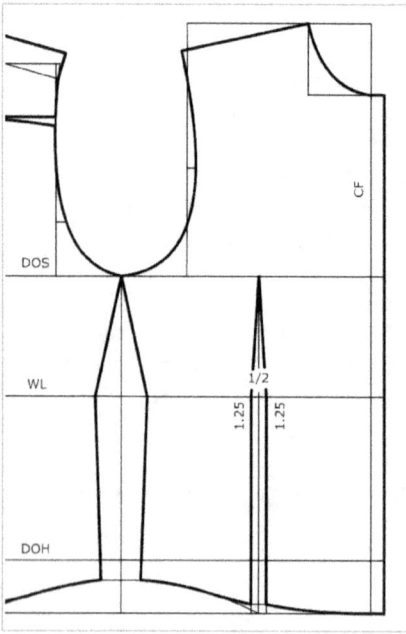

Chest dart
- on waistline: halve the distance between CF and side seam and square up and down

- on waistline from dart-line: mark to each side approx. 1.25 cm and finish dart

Hem
- shape hem nicely

Cutting
- cut front 2 x, cut back 1 x in fold, cut yoke 2 x in fold

Instructions
- all measures are in cm
- all seams are without seam allowances

Taken measurements

		1/2	1/4	1/8	1/16
Height	(HEI)	194	97	48.5	12.12
Chest	(CHE)	138	69	34.5	17.25
Waist	(WAI)	106	53		
Hips	(HIP)	116	58		
Neck	(NE)	51			
Nape to front waist	(NTFW)	66			
Full shoulder	(FUSH)	56			
Sleeve lenght	(SL)	69			
Wrist	(WR)	25			

Calculated measurements

Depth of scye	(DOS)	= 1/16 HEI + 1/8 CHE + 2.5 = 32 cm
Waist length	(WL)	= 1/4 HEI + 1.5 = 50 cm
Depth of hips	(DOH)	= 1/4 HEI = 24.25 cm
Neckline	(NL)	= 1/6 NE + 1 = 9.5 cm
Width of scye	(WOS)	= 1/8 CHE + 3 = 20.25 cm
Length	(LG)	= 1/2 HEI - 15 = approx. 82 cm
Difference	(DIFF)	= 1/2 CHE - 1/2 WAI = 16 cm
Front waist length	(FWL)	= NTFW - 10 (back neckline) = 56 cm
Width of cuff	(WOC)	= WR + 5 = 30 cm

For clients that deviate from the 'norm' (broad shoulders, strong back, etc.), the taken measurements should be used instead of the calculated ones.

Armhole
The circumference of scye COS = approx. 72 cm is measured after finishing the shirt pattern.

Control
The fullness at the 1/2 chest and the 1/2 waist should be about 5 cm each and is already considered in the calculation.

Grainline
CF and CB serve as grainline references.

Seam allowances

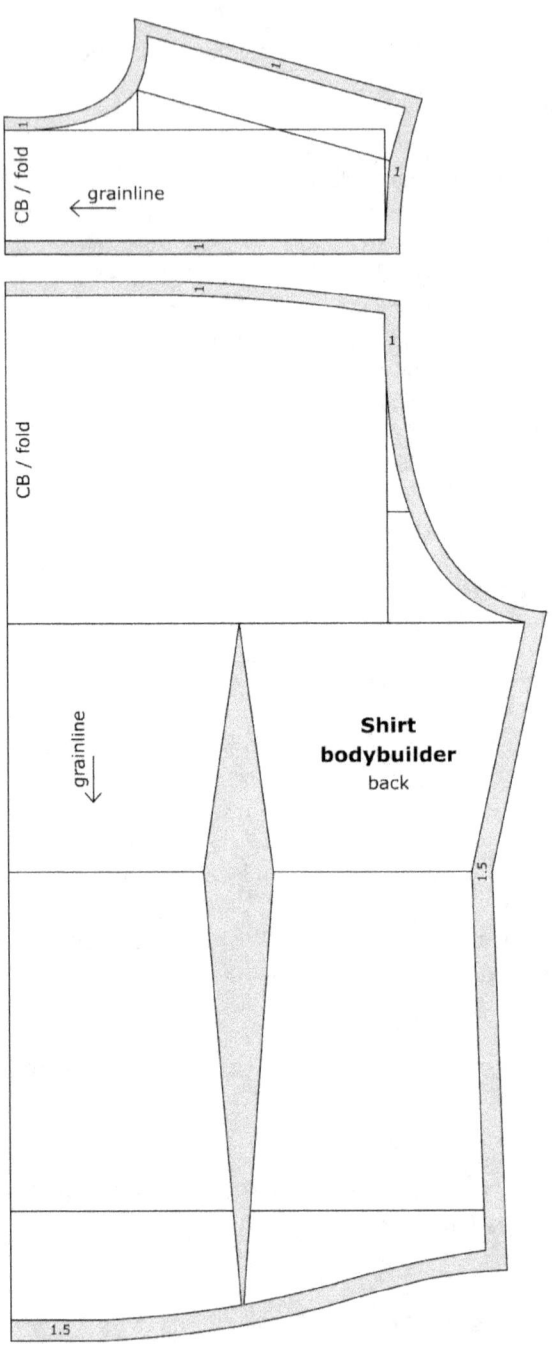

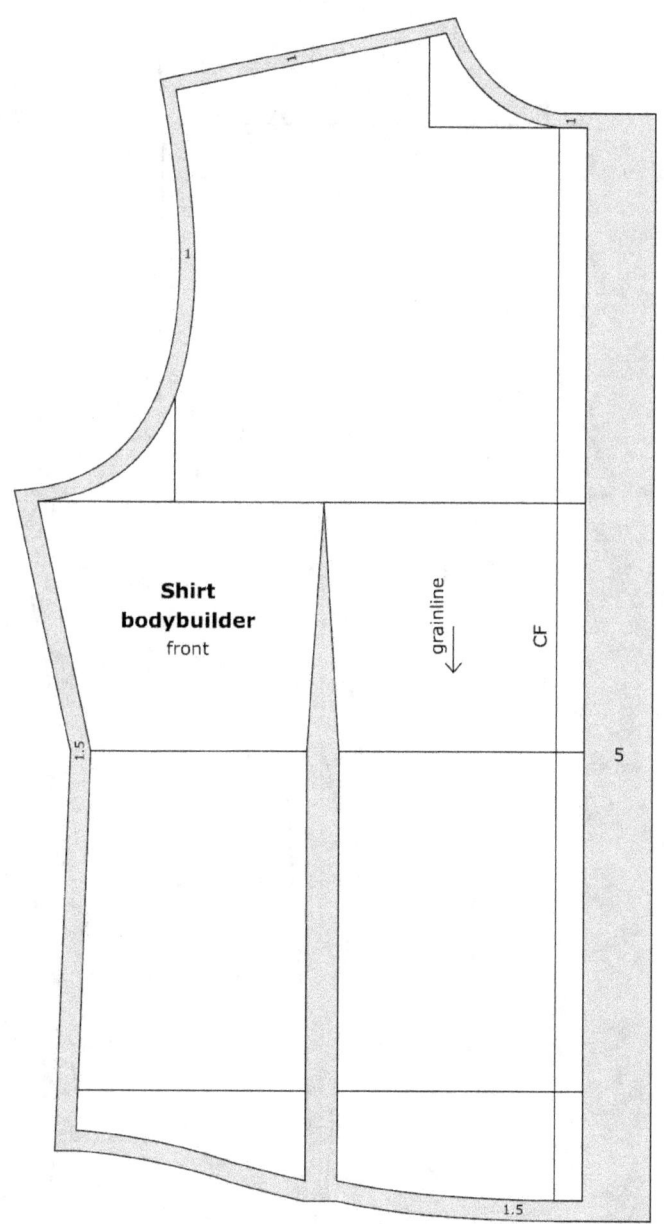

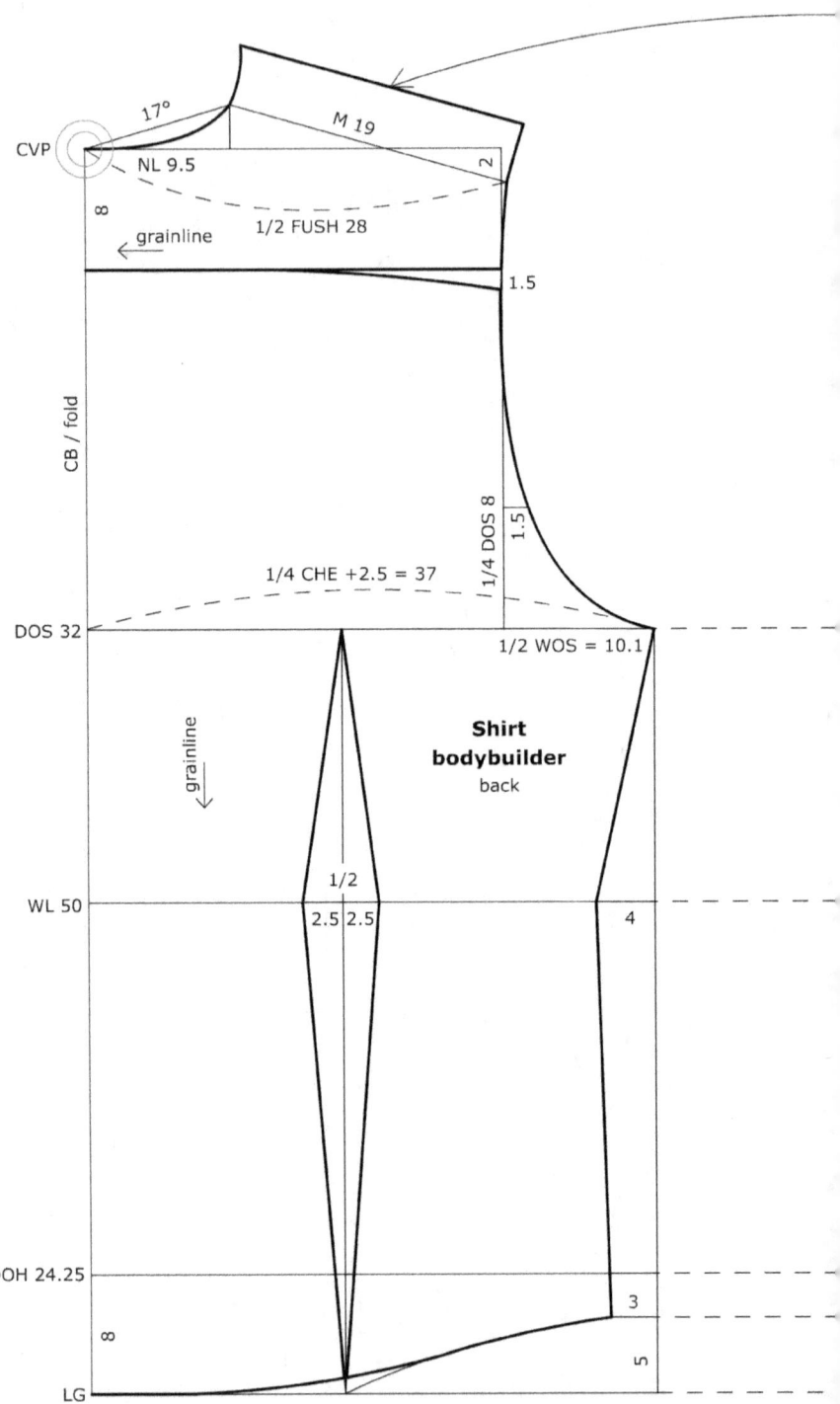

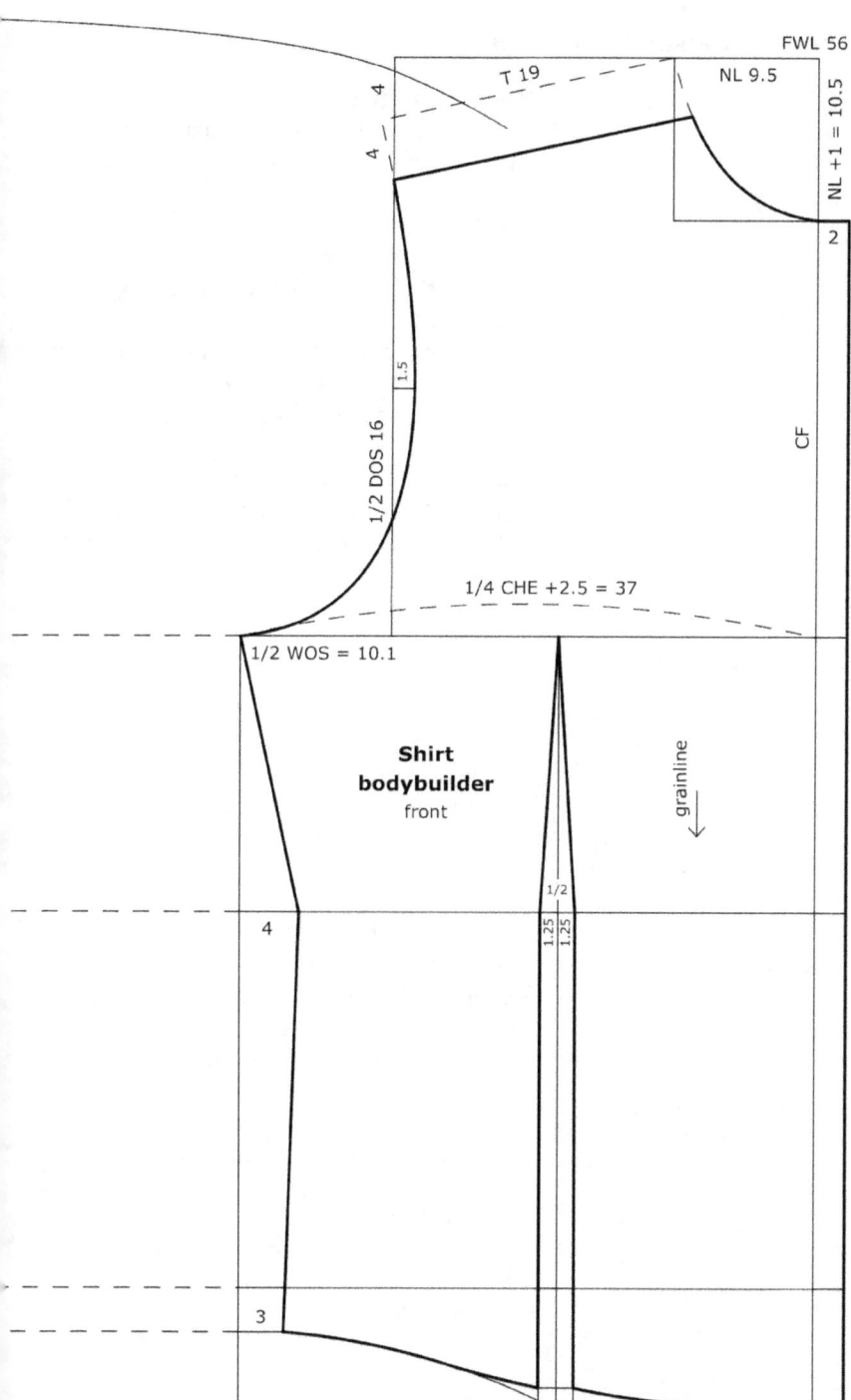

Manual for the bodybuilder's shirt sleeve

Measurements
The measurements and further information can be found on page 117.

Start
- draw a 90° angle
- the vertical line is the fold and serves as the grainline
- on upper horizontal line: mark to the right 1/2 circumference of scye COS = 36 cm
- divide this distance into three
- on vertical line: mark down sleeve-length SL - 5 = 64 cm and square right
- on this line: mark to the right 1/2 width of the cuffs + 3 cm (for pleats) = 18 cm

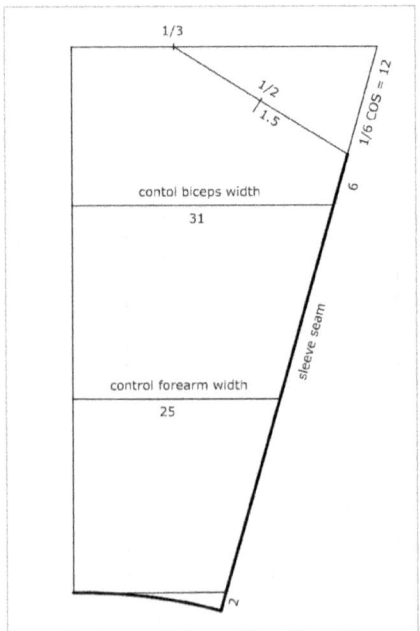

Sleeve seam
- connect the right outer points of the upper and lower horizontal lines

Sleeve head
- from upper horizontal line at sleeve-seam: mark down 1/6 COS = 12 cm
- connect this point with 1/3-point on the upper horizontal line and halve distance
- from 1/2-point: square downward and mark 1.5 cm
- on sleeve seam from sleeve-head-seam: mark down approx. 6 cm and square left

Seam at wrist
- from lower horizontal line at sleeve seam: mark down 2 cm
- shape cuff seam nicely

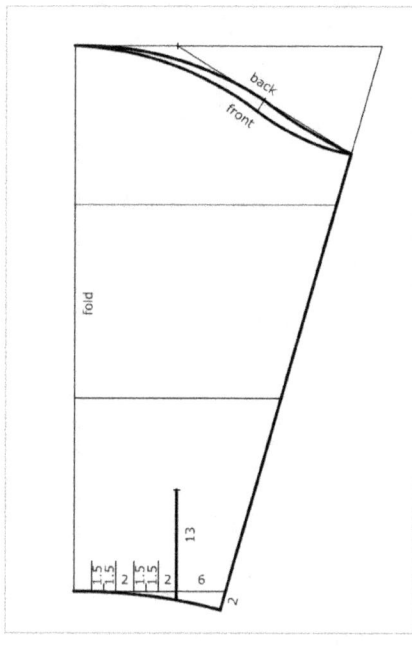

Sleeve head
- shape back sleeve-head nicely
- shape front sleeve-head as shown

Sleeve vent
- at cuff seam from sleeve seam:
  mark to the left 6 cm, square up and
  mark the length of the vent by approx.
  13 cm

Folds
- from vent: for 1. pleat mark to the left
  2 cm and mark depth of pleat (2 x 1.5 cm)
- from this point: for 2. pleat mark again
  to the left 2 cm and mark depth of pleat
  (2 x 1.5 cm)
- see also the bigger pattern on page 125

Cutting
- cut 2 x in fold

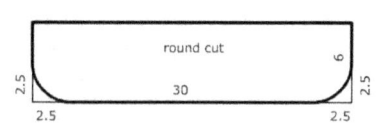

Round cut cuffs
- draw rectangle with a height of 6 cm
  and a width of 30 cm
- at the lower corners, mark 2.5 cm each
  and draw these corners round

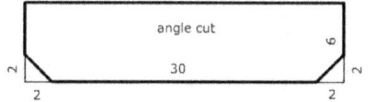

Angle cut cuffs
- draw rectangle with a height of 6 cm
  and a width of 30 cm
- at the lower corners, mark 2 cm each
  and draw the diagonals

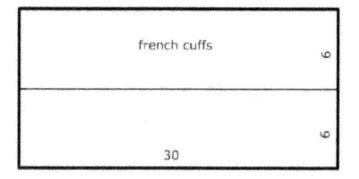

French cut cuffs
- draw rectangle with a height of 12 cm
  and a width of 30 cm
- divide the vertical line in half and square
  right

Cutting
- decide for one variation and cut 4 x

Seam allowances

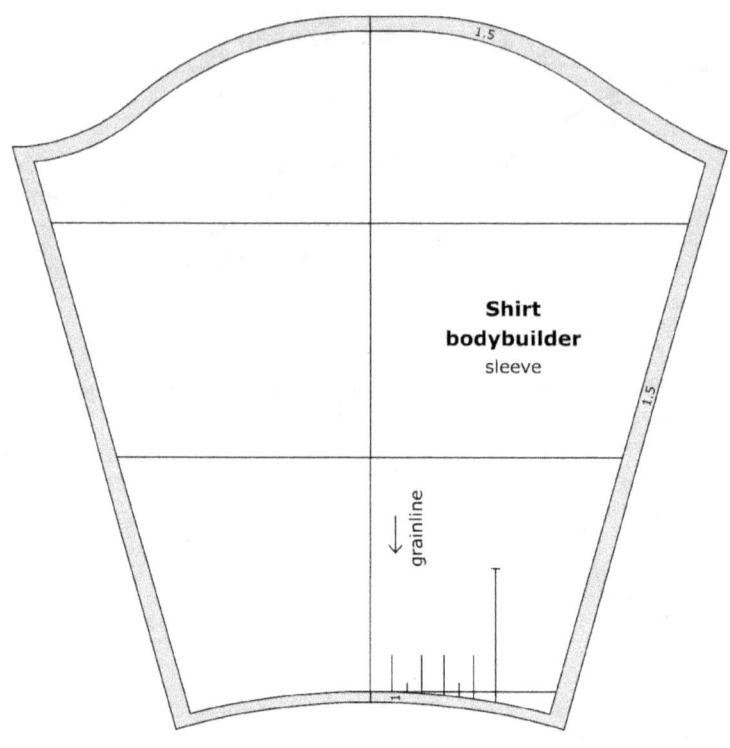

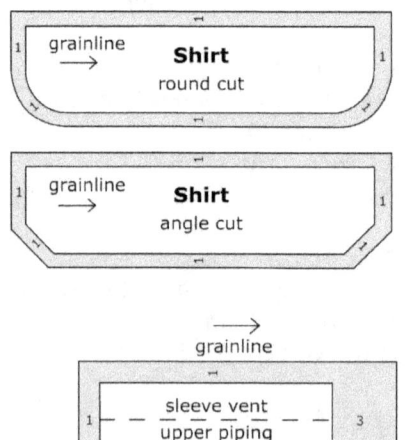

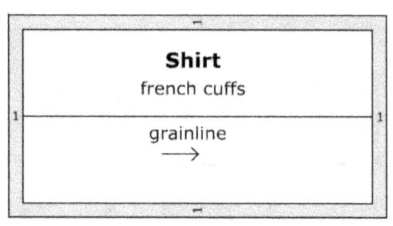

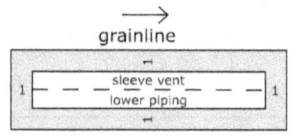

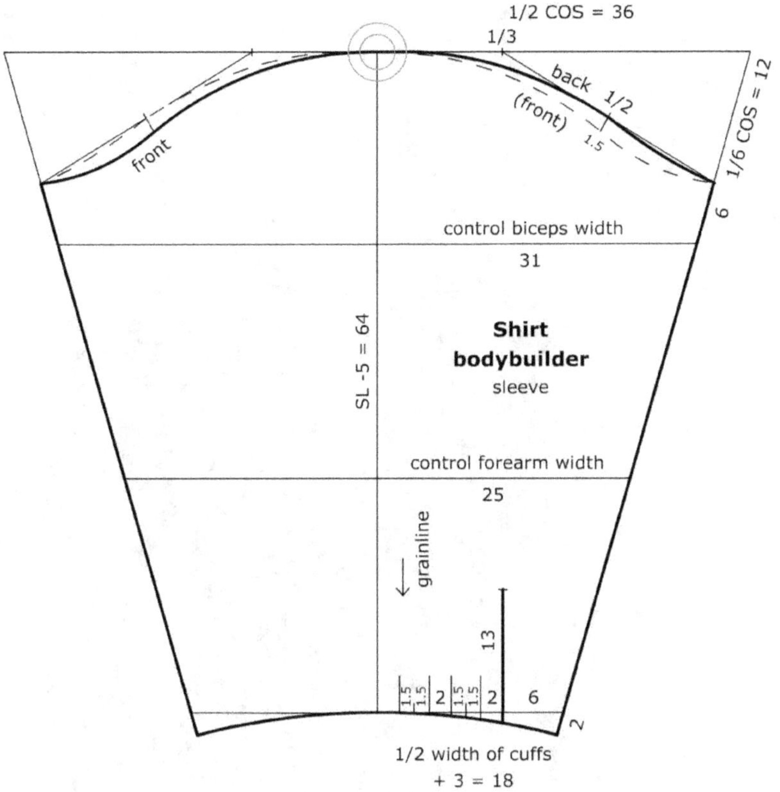

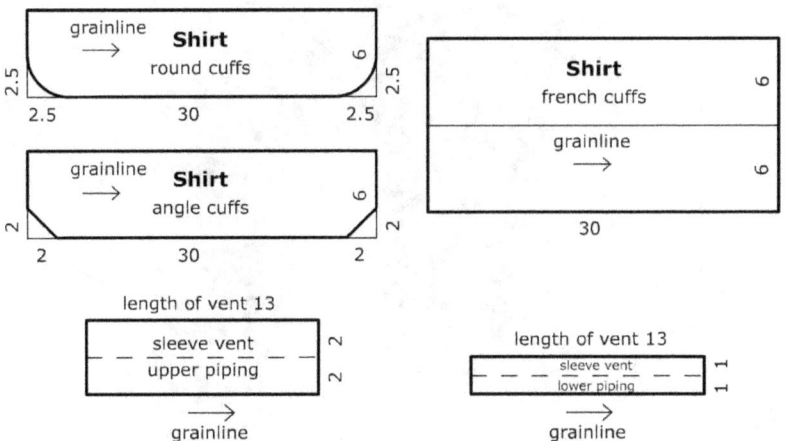

Manual for the bodybuilder jacket

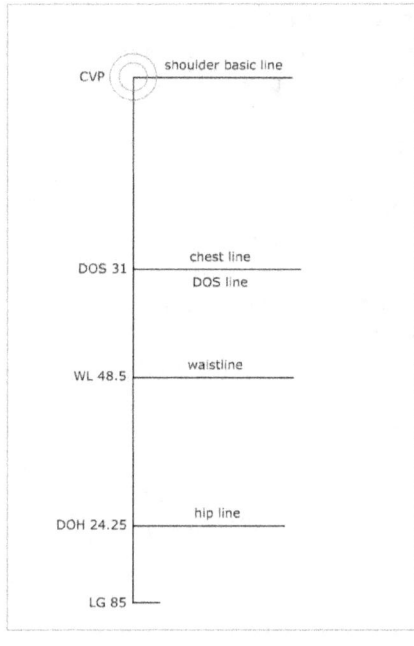

Start (for measurements, see page 135)
- draw a 90° angle
- vertical line is the center-back-basic-line
- horizontal line is the shoulder-basic-line
- on center-back-basic-line from the 7th cervical-vertebra-point *CVP:* mark down depth of scye *DOS* = 1/16 height *HEI* + 1/8 chest *CHE* + 2.5 = 31 cm and square right
- from *CVP*: mark down waist-length *WL* = 1/4 *HEI* = 48.5 cm and square right
- from *WL*: mark down depth of hips *DOH* = 1/8 *HEI* = 24.25 cm and square right
- from *CVP*: mark down length *LG* = approx. 1/8 *HEI* x 3.5 = 85 cm and square right
- compare the length with your favourite jacket

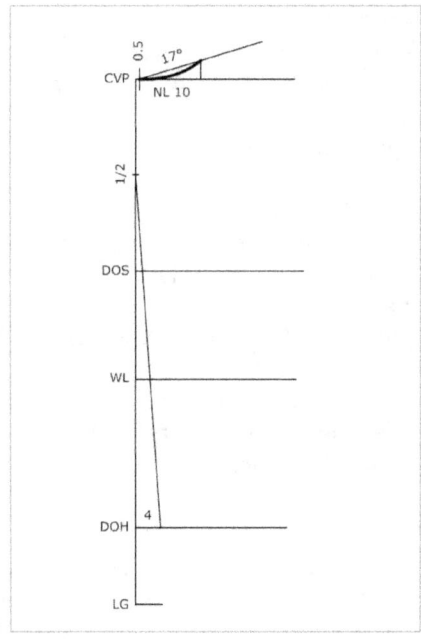

Back seam
- on center-back-basic-line: halve the distance between *CVP* and *DOS*
- on *HIP*-line from *CB*-basic-line: mark to the right 4 cm and connect this point with previous point

Neck/Shoulder
- on shoulder-basic-line from *CVP*: mark to the right 0.5 cm
- on shoulder-basic-line from 0.5-cm-point: mark to the right *NL* = 1/6 *NE* + 1.5 = 10 cm and square up
- from 0.5-cm-point: create a 17° angle to the right up
- shape back neckline nicely

The bodybuilder jacket

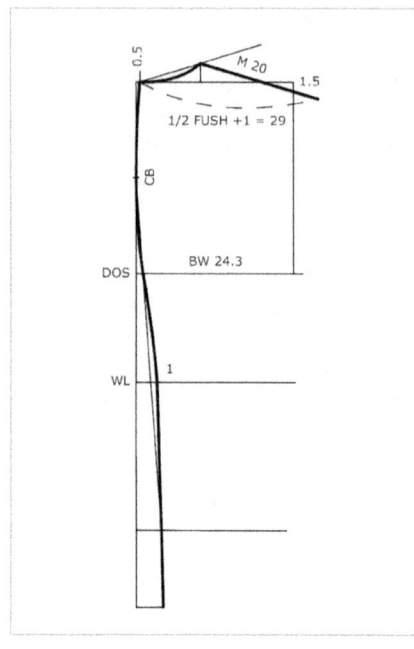

Center back seam
- on waistline: mark to the right 1 cm
- shape back-seam nicely

Shoulder
- on chest-line from *CB*: mark to the right back-width $BW = 1/10\ CHE + 10.5 = 24.3$ cm and square up
- on *BW*-line from shoulder-basic-line: mark down 1.5 cm and connect with upper point at the neckline
- on shoulder-basic-line from 0.5-cm-point: mark to the right onto shoulder 1/2 full shoulder $FUSH +1 = 29$ cm
- measure shoulder $M = 20$ cm (you will need this for the front shoulder)

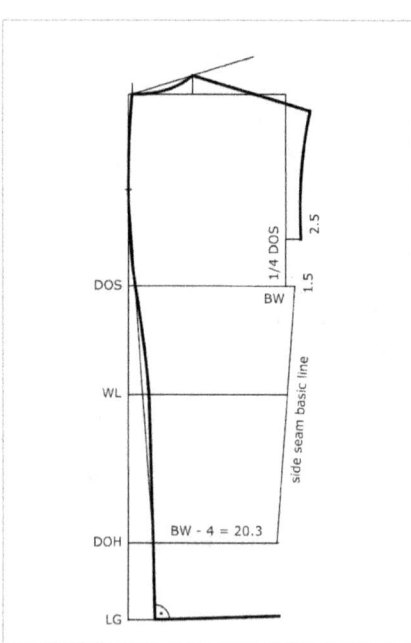

Scye / Armhole
- on *BW*-line from chest-line (*DOS*-line): mark up $1/4\ DOS = 7.75$ cm, square right and mark 2.5 cm
- shape back-armhole nicely

Preparation for side seam
- on chest-line from *BW*-line: mark to the right 1.5 cm (to hide the side seam under the sleeve)
- on *HIP*-line from *CB*: mark to the right BW - approx. $4 = 20.3$ cm
- connect this point with previous point; this defines the side-seam-basic-line
- on *LG* from *CB*: square right

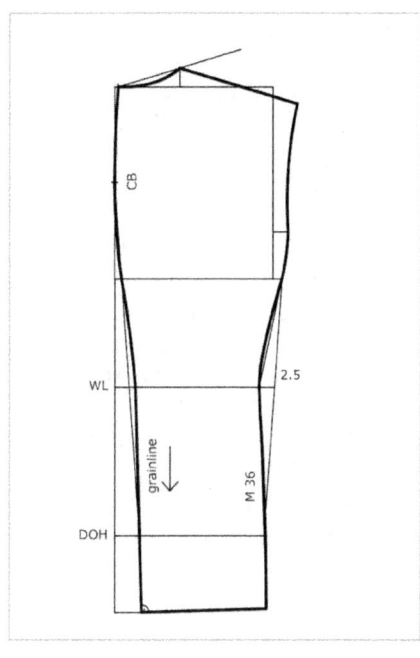

Side seam
- on waistline from side-seam-basic-line: mark to the left approx. 2.5 cm
- shape side seam nicely
- on side seam from waistline: measure down to *LG*, *M* = approx. 36 cm (you will need this for the side part)

Grainline
- draw in a right angle to the length

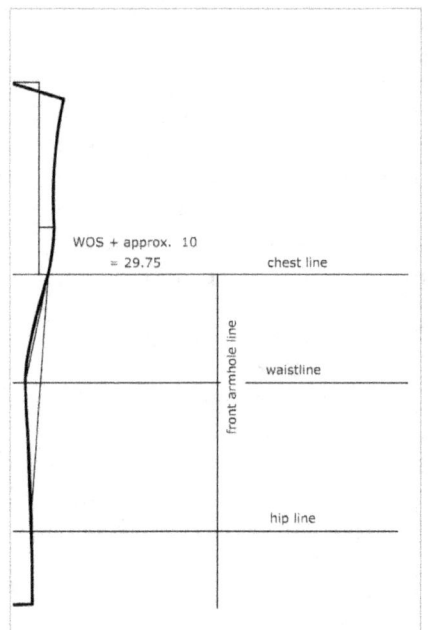

Extend lines for front and side part
- extend chest-line (also known as *DOS*-line), waistline and hip-line to the right
- on chest-line from back pattern: mark to the right *WOS* + approx. 10 = 29.75 cm and square down (the 10 cm are chosen at random to get enough space between the back and the front part); this is the front-armhole-line

Note
The chest-line is called *BW*-line at the back and *CW*-line at the front.

The bodybuilder jacket

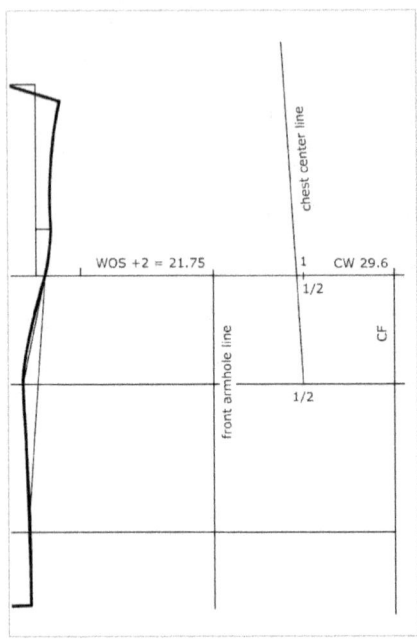

Width of scye
- on chest-line from front-armhole-line:
  mark to the left width of scye
  $WOS = 1/8\ CHE + 2.5 = 19.75$ cm + 2
  (for the inclination of the side part,
  see page 135) = 21.75 cm

Chest width
- on chest-line from front-armhole-line:
  mark to the right chest-width
  $CW = 2/10\ CHE + 2 = 29.6$ cm and
  square down; this is the center-front CF
- halve CW and mark to the left 1 cm
  (this helps for a better fit at the shoulder)
- halve distance at waistline
- connect both points as shown; this line
  defines the chest-center-line

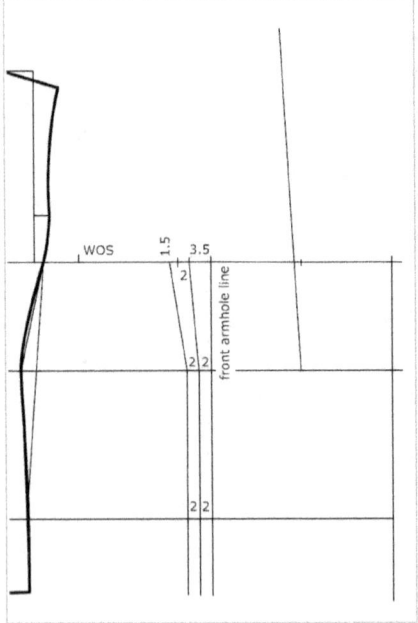

Side part
- on chest-line from front-armhole-line:
  mark to the left 3.5 cm
- from this point, mark to the left: 2 cm
  for the inclination of the side part
  (see explanation on page 135)
- from previous point: mark to the left
  1.5 cm (the amount from the shifted
  side seam at the back, see also pic. 2
  on page 128)
- on waistline from front-armhole-line:
  mark to the left 2 cm
- from this point: mark to the left 2 cm
- on hip-line from front-armhole-line:
  mark to the left 2 cm
- from this point mark to the left 2 cm
- connect all points at side-part-seam
  as shown

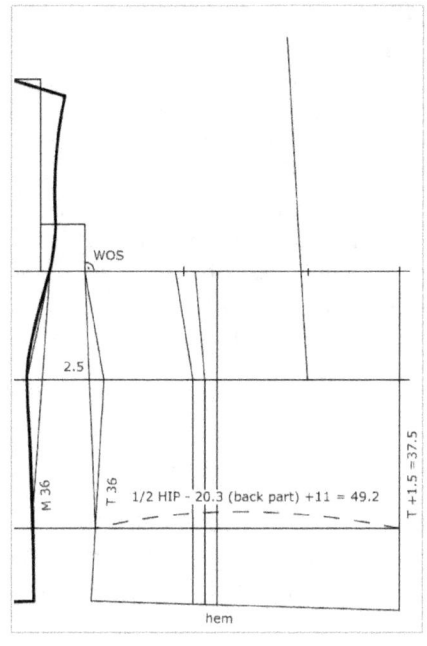

Side seam
- on hip-line from *CF*: mark to the left
  1/2 *HIP* - 20.3 cm (width of lower back)
  + 11 (fullness and seam-allowances)
  = 49.2 cm
- connect this point with *WOS*-point on chest-line
- on waistline: mark to the right
  approx. 2.5 cm (same amount as for the back part) and draw side seam
- on chest-line from side seam: square up to the line coming from the back part
- at back side seam from waistline: measure distance to length *M* = approx. 36 cm and transfer to front side seam *T* = 36 cm
- at *CF* from waistline: transfer *T* down this distance + 1.5 = 37.5 cm
- connect both points at length for the hem-line

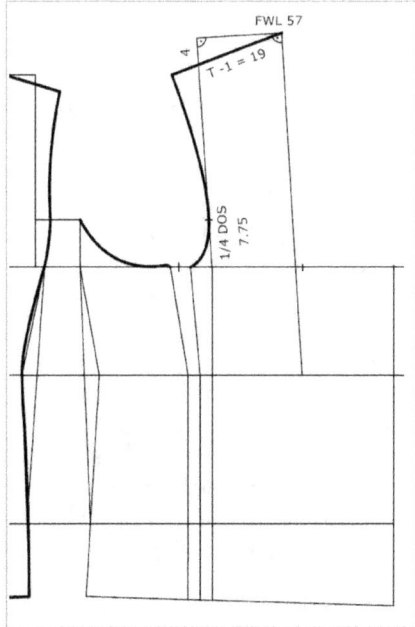

Front armhole
- on chest-center-line from waistline: mark up front-waist-length *FWL* = nape-to-front-waist *NTFW* - 10.5 (back neckline) + 1.5 cm (seam allowances at front and back shoulder) = 57 cm and square left (see also calculation on page 135)
- from shoulder-basic-line: square down to crossing point of chest-line and front-armhole-line
- on previous line from chest-line: mark up 1/4 *DOS* = 7.75 cm

Shoulder / armhole
- on front-armhole-line from the top: mark down approx. 4 cm
- draw shoulder seam and transfer length of back-shoulder - 1 cm = 19 cm
- shape front armhole nicely
- shape armhole of side part nicely

The bodybuilder jacket

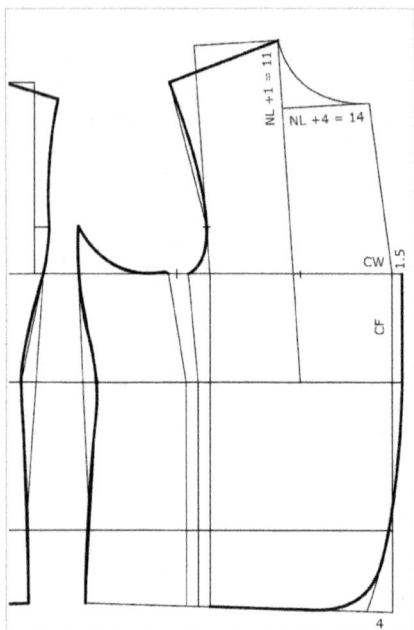

Side seam
- shape side seam nicely
- the side seam is without any seam allowance (see also page 137)

Neckline
- on chest-center-line from front shoulder: mark down neckline *NL* (1/6 *NE* + 1.5) + 1 = 11 cm, square right and mark *NL* + 2 + 2 (chest dart s. p. 139) = 14 cm
- connect this point with *CF* on chest-line
- shape front neckline nicely

Lower front edge
- on chest-line from *CF*: mark to the right 1.5 cm
- on hem-line from *CF*: mark to the left 4 cm and draw front edge slightly curved
- shape curve at lower front edge as shown

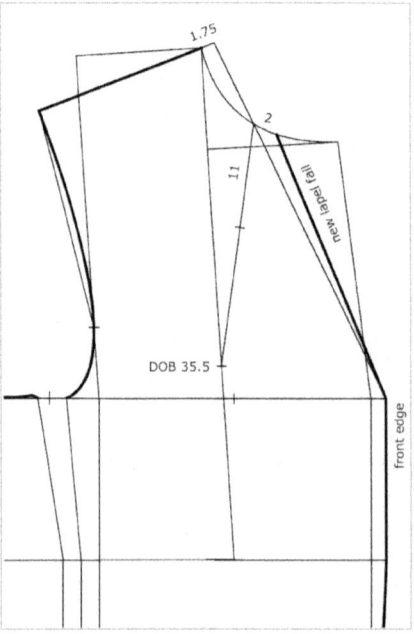

Lapel fall
- extend shoulder-line to the right and mark 1.75 cm
- connect shoulder-point with front edge on chest-line

New lapel fall
- at neckline from lapel-fall: mark to the right approx. 2 cm (measure of the chest dart) and define the new lapel fall

Chest-dart
- on chest-center-line front shoulder: mark down depth-of-breast *DOB* = nape-to-breast *NTB* - 10.5 (back neckline) + 1.5 (seam allowances at front and back shoulder) = 35.5 (s. p. 135)
- connect *DOB* with old lapel fall
- on chest-dart-line from neckline: mark down approx. 11 cm

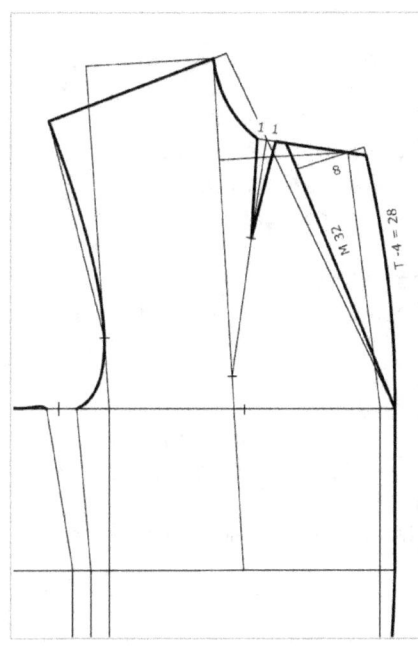

Chest-dart
- at neckline from chest-dart-line: mark to each side approx. 1 cm
- finish chest dart

Lapel
- on new lapel-fall: square right up to tip of *CF*/neckline
- on this line: mark 8 cm for lapel-width
- shape front edge of lapel slightly curved
- measure lapel-fall *M* = approx. 32 cm and transfer *T* this measure - 4 = 28 cm to the lapel-edge
- from lapel tip at *CF*: draw line to top of chest-dart

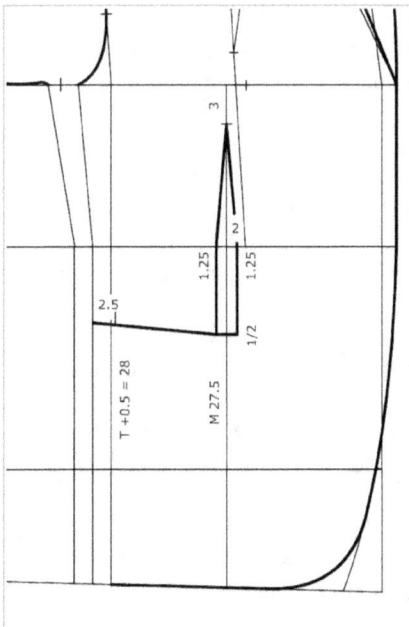

Waist-dart
- on waistline from chest-center-line: mark to the left 2 cm and square up and down
- halve this dart-line between chest-line and hem as shown
- on dart-line from chest-line: mark down approx. 3 cm
- from end of dart to hem: measure length of lower dart-line *M* = approx. 27.5 cm and transfer length *T* + 0.5 = 28 cm to side-part-seam
- mark depth of dart with 1.25 cm on each side and finish dart as shown
- draw pocket-opening as shown
- at pocket opening from side-part-seam: mark to the right 2.5 cm (same amount as for the full dart, s. p. 139)

The bodybuilder jacket

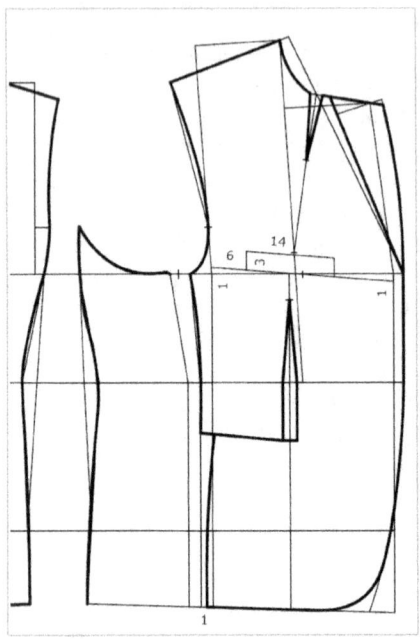

Chest pocket
- on front-armhole-line from chest-line: mark up 1 cm
- on CF from chest-line: mark down 1 cm and draw line to previous point
- on chest-pocket-line from front-armhole-line: mark to the right approx. 6 cm and square up
- mark pocket opening with approx. 14 cm
- mark height of welt pocket with approx. 3 cm

Side-part-seam
- on hem-line from front-armhole-line: mark to the left 1 cm (see also pattern on page 139)
- shape front side-part-seam as shown

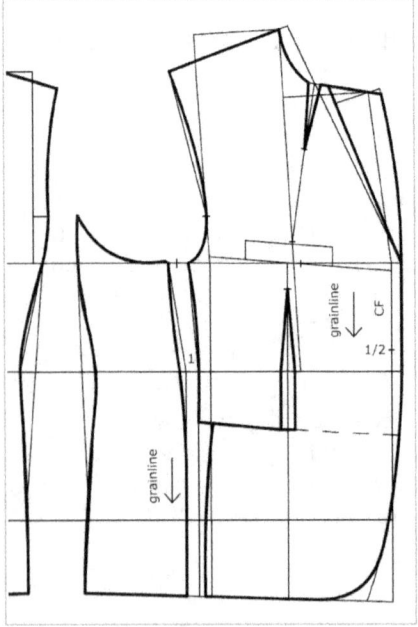

Narrow waist
- at side part on waist-line: mark approx. 1 cm at side-part-seam and shape nicely

Grainline
- at the front part: the center front CF defines the grainline
- at the side-part: the lower part of the front side-part-seam defines the grainline

Buttons
- extend the line of the pocket opening forward
- halve the distance between chest-line and previous line

Note
The top button should always stay at the strongest point of the chest.

Cutting
- cut front-, side- and back-part 2 x each

Instructions
- all measures are in cm. The fullness at the 1/2 chest, 1/2 waist and 1/2 hips should be 5.5 cm and is already considered in the calculation
- 0.75 cm seam allowances are included (sewing machine foot width) at the shoulder seam, the entire armhole and the side-part-seam, all other seams are without seam allowances
- at the back-shoulder, the fullness of 1 cm is kept short for a better fit
- in our other books, you can find more information about the shoulder seam and the shoulder pad; you will find a preview starting on page 161
- for clients that deviate from the 'norm' (broad shoulders, strong back, etc.), the taken measurements should always be used instead of the calculated ones

Inclination of side-part (page 130)
The amount of the inclination at the upper side part results from the customer's body shape: regular 1.5 cm, strong 2 cm, short or with belly 2.5 cm.

Taken measurements

		1/2	1/4	1/8	1/16
Height	(HEI)	194	97	48.5	24.25	12.12
Chest	(CHE)	138	69	34.5	17.25
Waist	(WAI)	106	53
Hip	(HIP)	116	58
Neck	(NE)	51
Full shoulder	($FUSH$)	56
Nape to front waist	($NTFW$)	66
Nape to breast	(NTB)	44.5

Calculated measurements

Depth of syce	(DOS)	$= 1/16\ HEI + 1/8\ CHE + 2.5 = 31$ cm
Waist length	(WL)	$= 1/4\ HEI = 48.5$ cm
Depth of hips	(DOH)	$= 1/8\ HEI = 24.25$ cm
Length	(LG)	$= 1/8\ HEI \times 3.5 = 84.87 \sim 85$ cm
Neckline	(NL)	$= 1/6\ NE + 1.5 = 10$ cm
Back width	(BW)	$= 1/10\ CHE + 10.5 = 24.3$ cm
Width of scye	(WOS)	$= 1/8\ CHE + 2.5 = 19.75$ cm
Chest width	(CW)	$= 2/10\ CHE + 2 = 29.6$ cm
Front waist length	(FWL)	$= NTWF - 10.5$ (back neckline) $+ 1.5$ cm (seam allowance at front and back shoulder) $= 57$ cm
Depth of breast	(DOB)	$= NTB - 10.5$ (back neckline) $+ 1.5$ cm (seam allowance at front and back shoulder) $= 35.5$ cm

Seam allowances

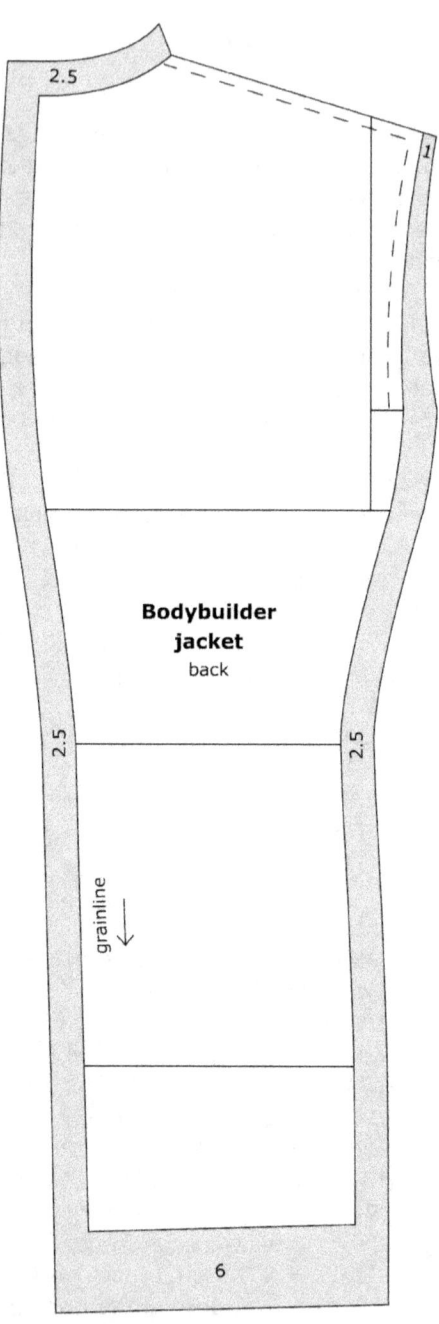

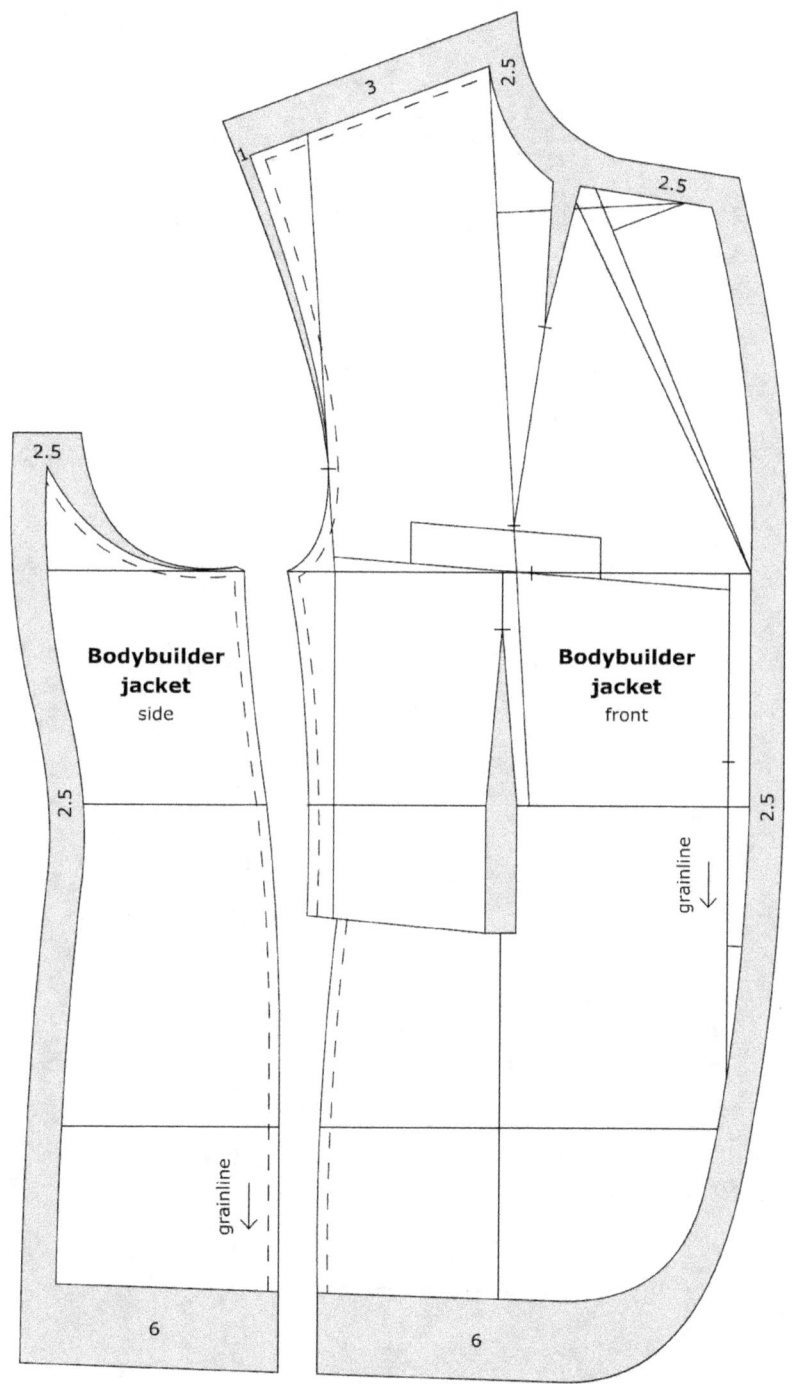

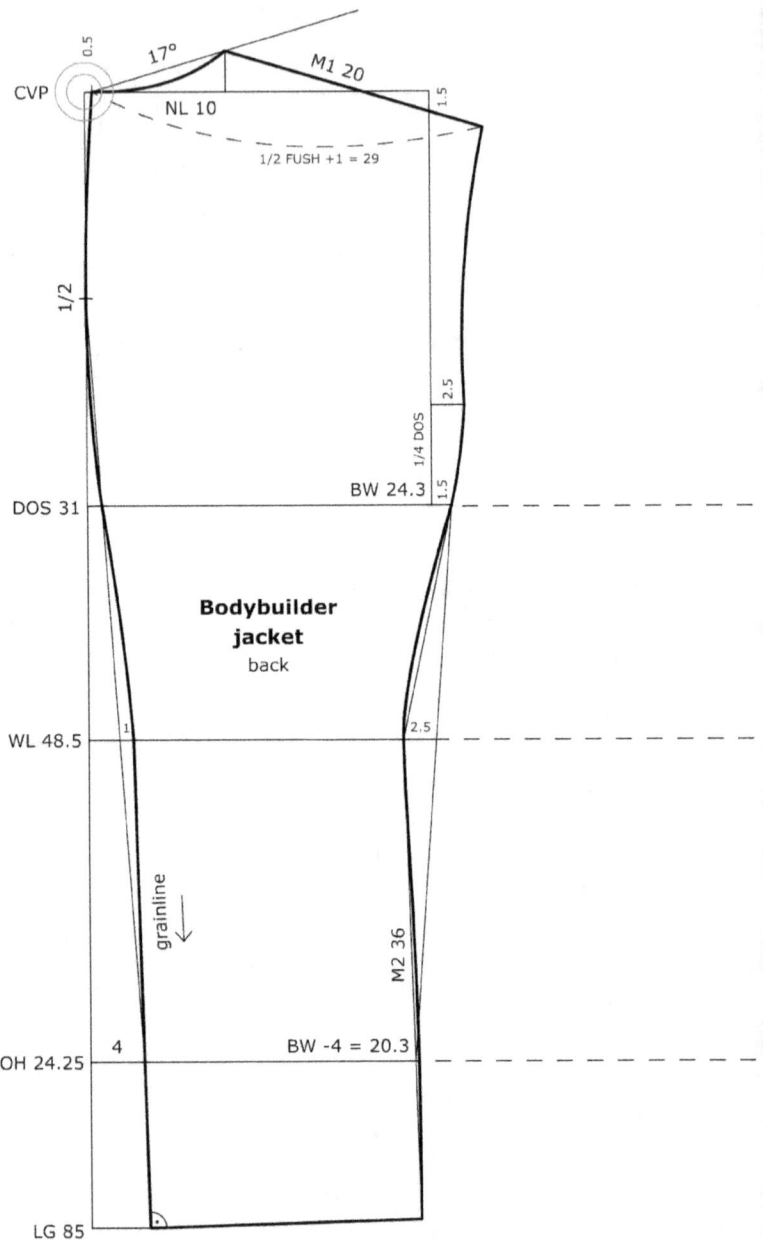

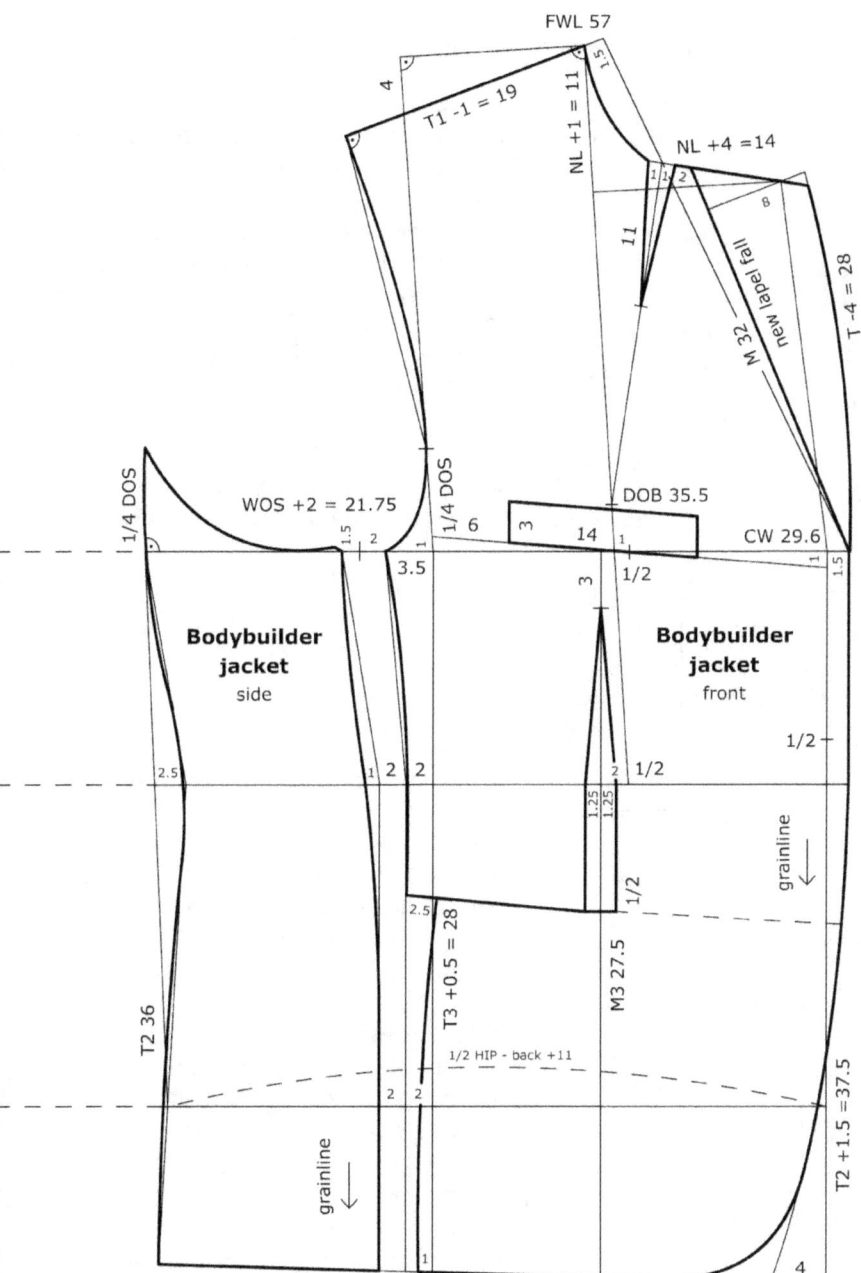

Manual for the bodybuilder jacket sleeve

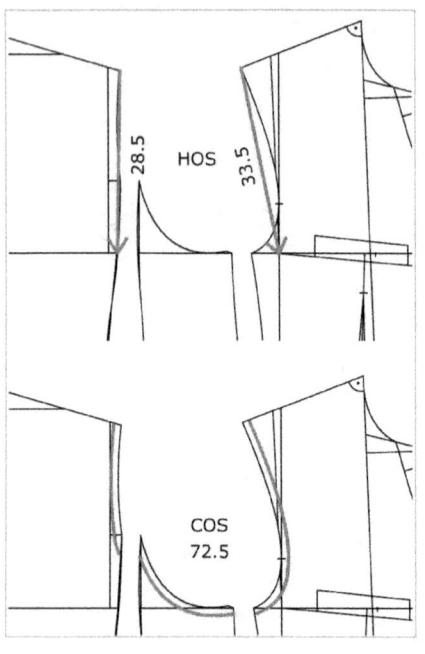

Height of scye
- measure front and back height-of-scye *HOS* and add up = 62 cm

Circumference of Scye
- measure circumference-of-scye *COS* minus seam allowances 3 cm = 72.5 cm (front and back-shoulder as well as front and back side-part-seam = 4 seams = 4 x 0.75 = 3 cm)

Note
For more information about the seam allowances, see pages 136 and 137.

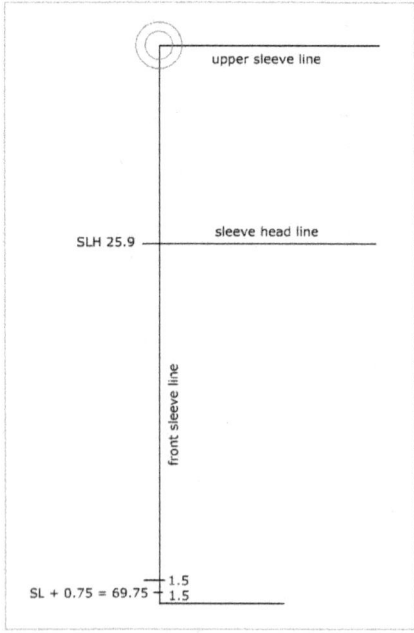

You will find the measurements on page 143.

Start
- draw a 90° angle
- vertical line defines the front-sleeve-line
- horizontal line defines the upper-sleeve-line

Basic frame
- at front-sleeve-line from upper-sleeve-line: mark down sleeve-head *SLH* = 1/2 *HOS* - (1/20 *HOS* + 2) = 25.9 cm and square right and left; this defines the sleeve-head-line
- from upper-sleeve-line: mark down sleeve-length *SL* + 0.75 cm (seam allowance at sleeve head) = 69.75 cm
- from sleeve-length *SL*: mark up and down 1.5 cm each and square left and right as shown

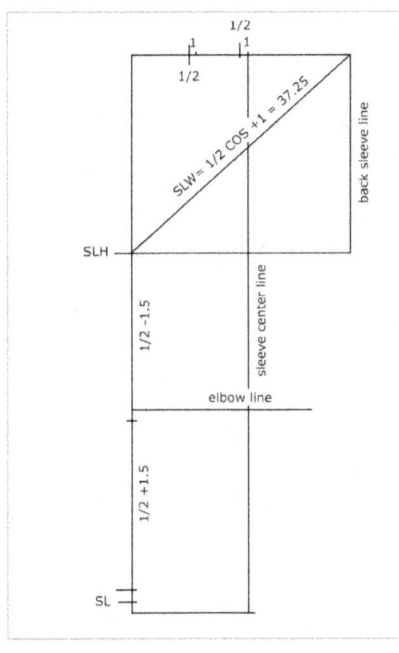

Sleeve width
- at front-sleeve-line from *SLH:*
  draw right upward a diagonal line touching the upper-sleeve-line, by the sleeve-width *SLW* = 1/2 *COS* + 1 = 37.25 cm
- from previous point at upper-sleeve-line: square down for the back-sleeve-line
- halve upper-sleeve-line, mark 1 cm to the right and square down; this defines the sleeve-center-line and also the grainline
- halve the front part of the upper-sleeve-line and mark 1 cm to the right

Elbow-line
- at front-sleeve-line: halve the distance between the point 1.5 cm above the *SL* and *SLH*, mark up 1.5 cm and square right; this defines the elbow-line

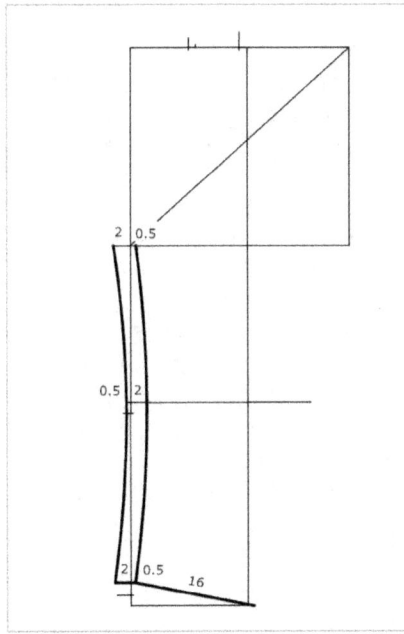

Front sleeve seam
- at the point, 1.5 cm above the *SL*, from front-sleeve-line: mark to the left 2 cm and 0.5 cm to the right
- on elbow-line from front-sleeve-line: mark to the left 0.5 cm and 2 cm to the right
- on sleeve-head-line from front-sleeve-line: mark to the left 2 cm and 0.5 cm to the right
- connect all points with a slightly curved line as shown

Sleeve hem width
- at the point 1.5 cm above the *SL*, from front-sleeve-line: mark right downward sleeve-hem-width *SLHW* 16 cm, touching the lower line as shown

The jacket sleeve for the bodybuilder

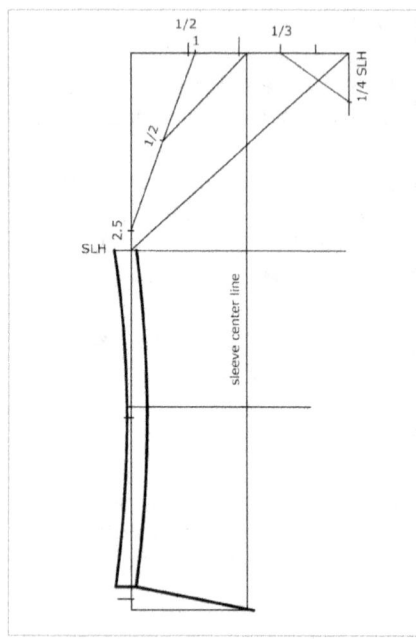

Sleeve head
- at front-sleeve-line from *SLH*: mark up 2.5 cm
- from this point, draw upward a diagonal line to first 1-cm-point on upper-sleeve-line
- halve this line and connect this point with sleeve-center-line on upper-sleeve-line
- divide the back part of the upper-sleeve-line into three
- on back-sleeve-line from upper-sleeve-line: mark down 1/4 *SLH* = 6.5 cm
- connect this point with 1/3-point on upper-sleeve-line
- see also bigger pattern drawing on page 145

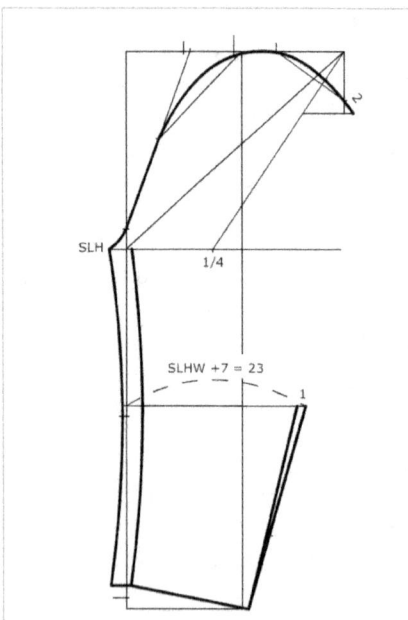

Top sleeve
- shape sleeve head as shown
- extend back part of sleeve-head-seam-line downward by 2 cm
- from previous point: square left as shown

Undersleeve
- on elbow-line from front-sleeve-line: mark to the right sleeve-hem-width *SLHW* + approx. 7 = 23 cm
- from this point mark to the left 1 cm
- draw lines to point on sleeve hem as shown
- on *SLH*-line from sleeve-center-line: divide the distance into four
- connect this point with right point at upper-sleeve-line

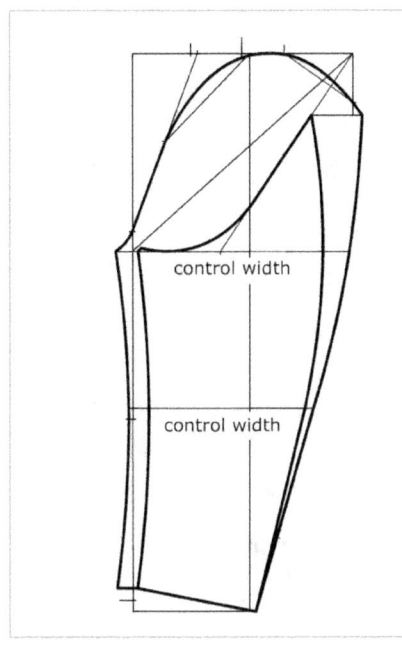

- finish back-seam with a curved line
- finish undersleeve as shown on page 145
- copy undersleeve as a separate pattern piece
- the fullness in the sleeve-head-seam is approx. 4.5 cm

Sleeve notches

In the pattern consciously no notch was defined on the sleeve-head because the arm pitch is different for each person.

Create notch

The sleeve is held at the top of the sleeve-head, placed to the shoulder and turned into the correct position. Then the position of the shoulder-seam is transferred to the sleeve-head.

Cutting
- cut top sleeve 2 x, cut undersleeve 2 x

Instructions
- back sleeve-seam and sleeve-hem are without seam-allowance
- all other seams include 0.75 cm seam allowance (sewing machine foot width); see also next page
- the sleeve-center-line serves as a grainline reference
- check if there is enough space for the biceps on the *SLH* lines, and on the elbow-line if there is space for the forearm
- the sleeve already has a fullness of approx. 4.5 cm; for more or less fullness, vary the sleeve-width *SLW*

Measurements

Sleeve length	(*SL*)	69
Circumference of scye	(*COS*)	72.5 | 36.25
Heigth of scye	(*HOS*)	62 | 31
Sleeve head	(*SLH*)	1/2 *HOS* - (1/20 *HOS* + 2) = 25.9 cm
Sleeve width	(*SLW*)	1/2 *COS* + 1 = 37.25 cm
Sleeve hem width	(*SLHW*)	approx. 16 cm

Seam allowances

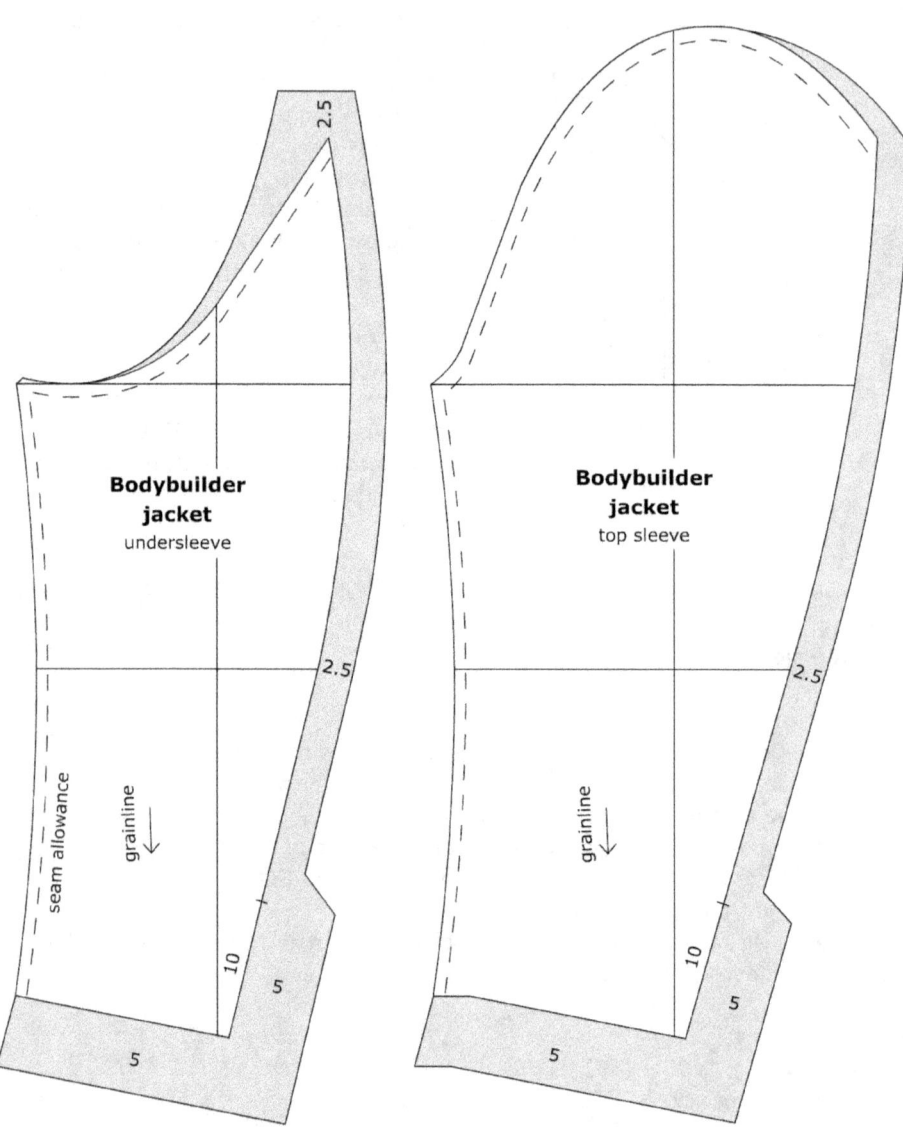

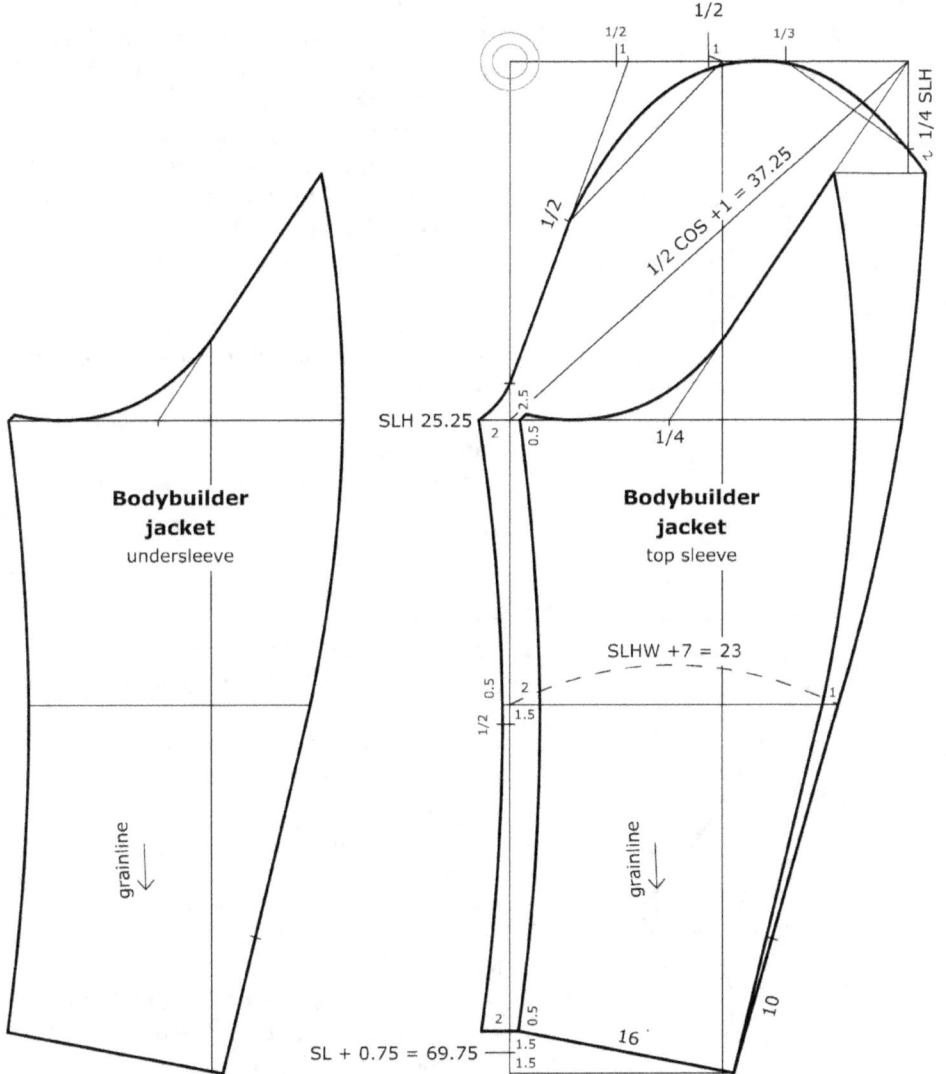

Manual for the Bodybuilder jacket collar

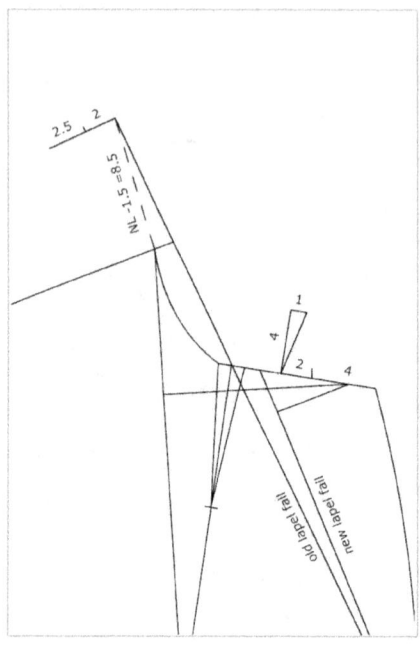

Start
- extend the line of the old lapel-fall (attention: not the new lapel-fall)
- from tip of shoulder/neckline: mark up neckline NL (1/6 NE + 1.5 = 10 cm) - 1.5 (seam allowances of front and back shoulder, see also pages 136 and 137) = 8.5 cm touching the extended lapel-fall
- from this point: square to the left using the extended lapel-fall-line
- on this line: first mark to the left 2 cm and then mark 2.5 cm as shown
- from lapel-tip: mark to the left 4 cm + 2 cm (size of the chest-dart) and square up
- on this line, mark up 4 cm, square right and mark 1 cm
- connect both previous points as shown

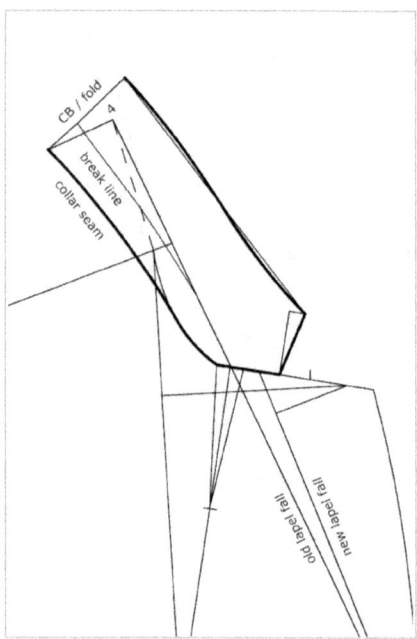

Finish collar
- draw curved line for neckline-seam
- at center back CB/fold: square right from collar seam
- draw curved line for collar-break-line
- at CB from collar-break-line: mark to the right 4 cm
- connect previous point with point at collar-tip
- shape collar nicely as shown

Note
The processing of the under- and top collar can be found in our book 'Guide to Men's Tailoring Volume 2' (see p. 162).

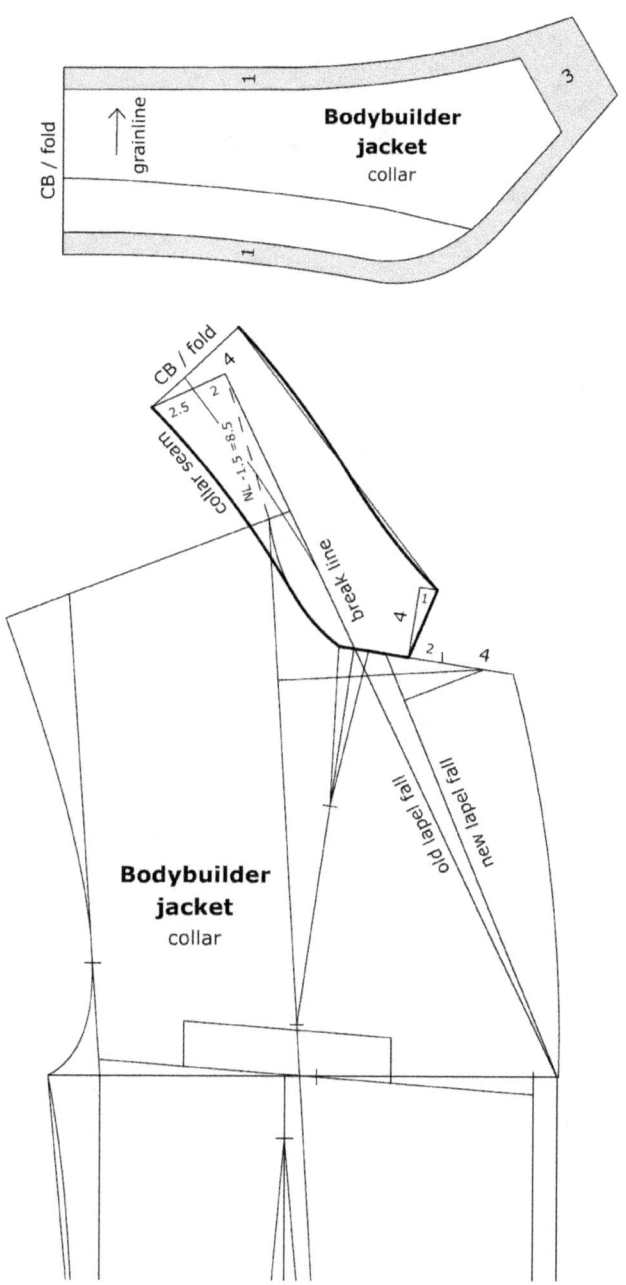

More pattern variations

Pants for straight shapes

Pants front

- 1/4 WB + 3 (pleat) = 24.5
- 0.5
- 1.5 / 1.5
- 1/20 HIP = 5.1
- INL 82
- 1/4 HIP +0.75 (1/4 pleat) = 26.25
- 1/2 | 1/2
- front break line
- 1/4 WOL 11.5 | 1/4 WOL 11.5
- 6.5
- 1/2
- OUTL 104
- 1/4 WOL-1 = 10.5 | 1/4 WOL-1 = 10.5
- 8 | 8

Pants back

- 1/4 WB + 4 (darts) = 25.5
- 1/2 | 0.8 | 1.2 | 1/2-1
- 1/4 HIP +2.5 fullness = 28
- 1/20 HIP +1 = 6.1
- T | 1 | M
- back break line
- T1 | M1 | M2 | T2 | M3 | T3
- 2 | 2
- 8 | 8
- 2 | 2

149

Jacket for straight shapes

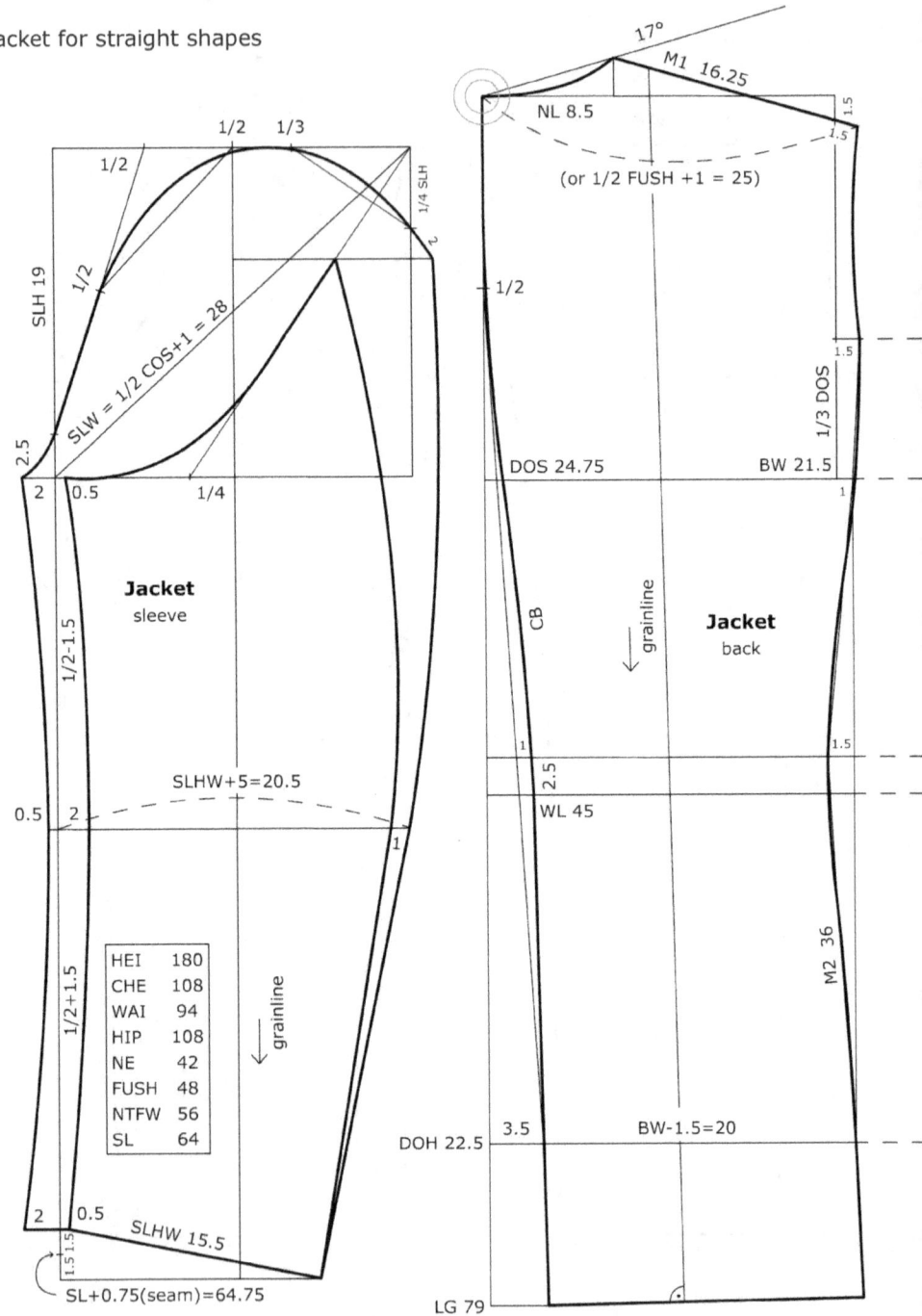

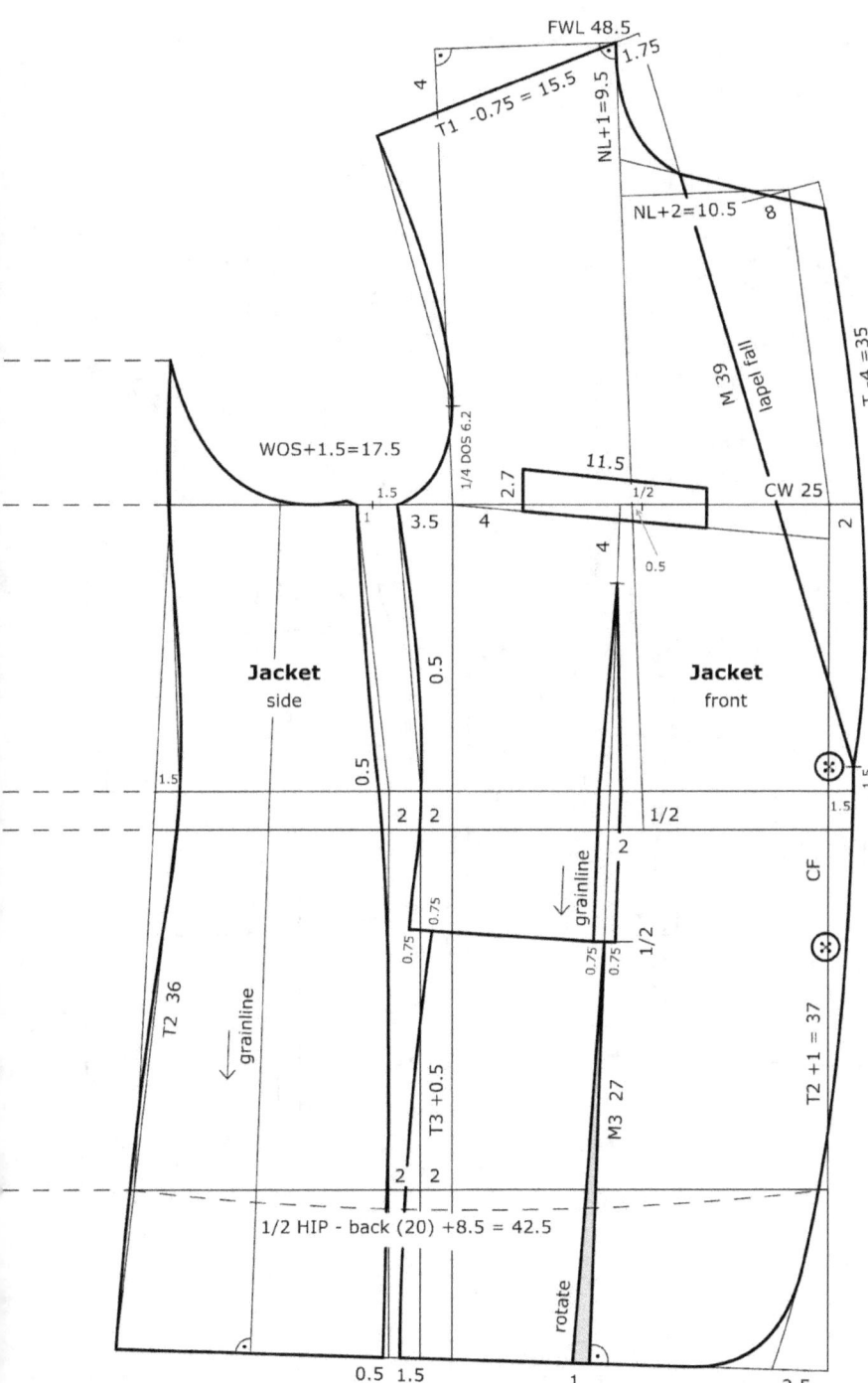

Vest for straight shapes

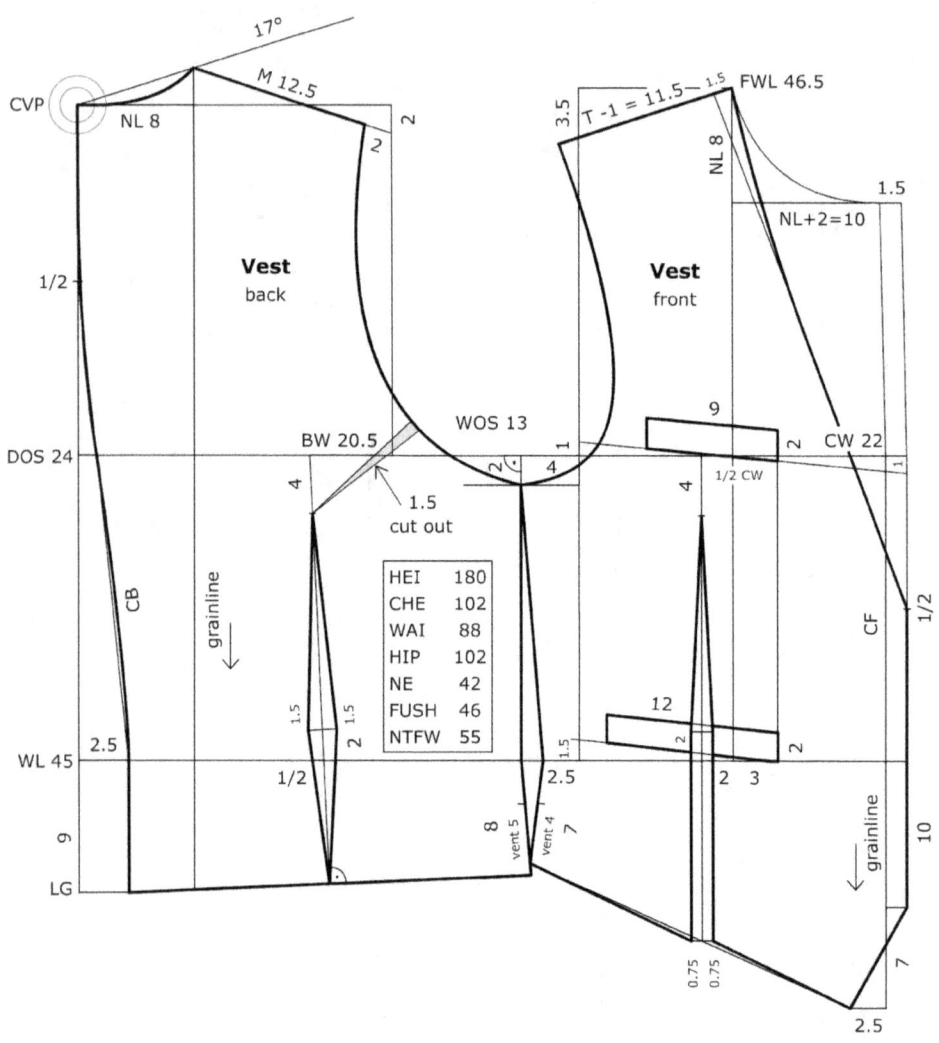

Pants for strong hips

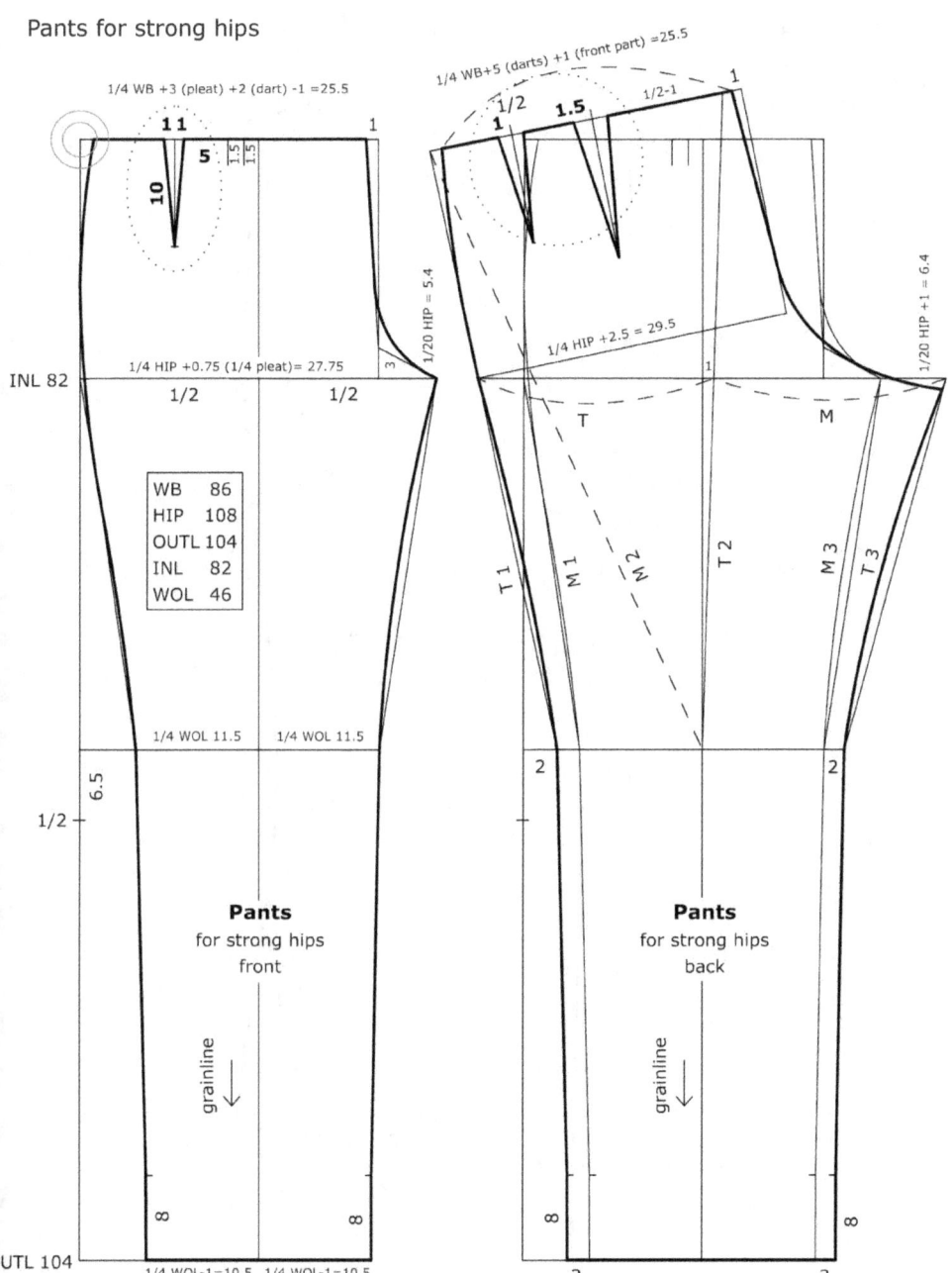

Jacket for strong hips

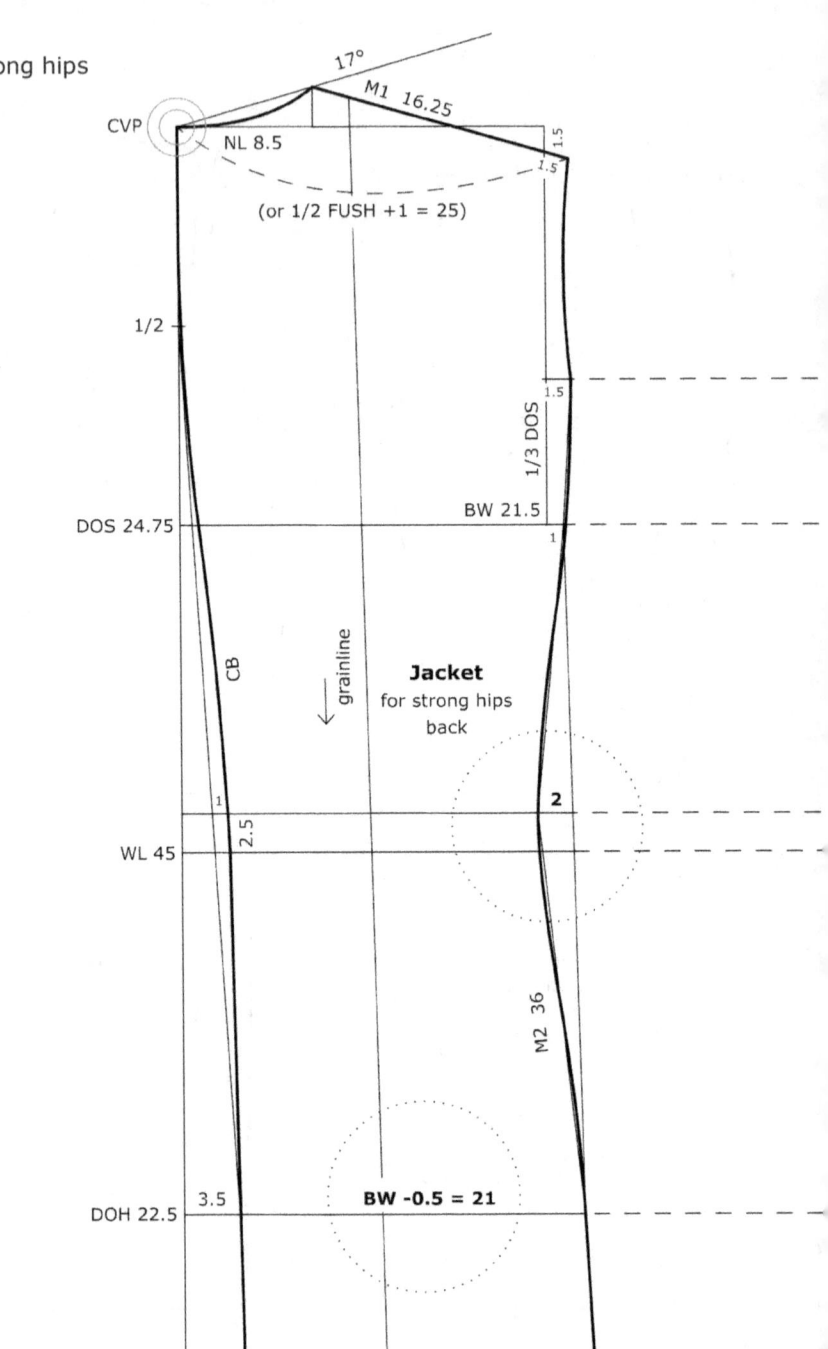

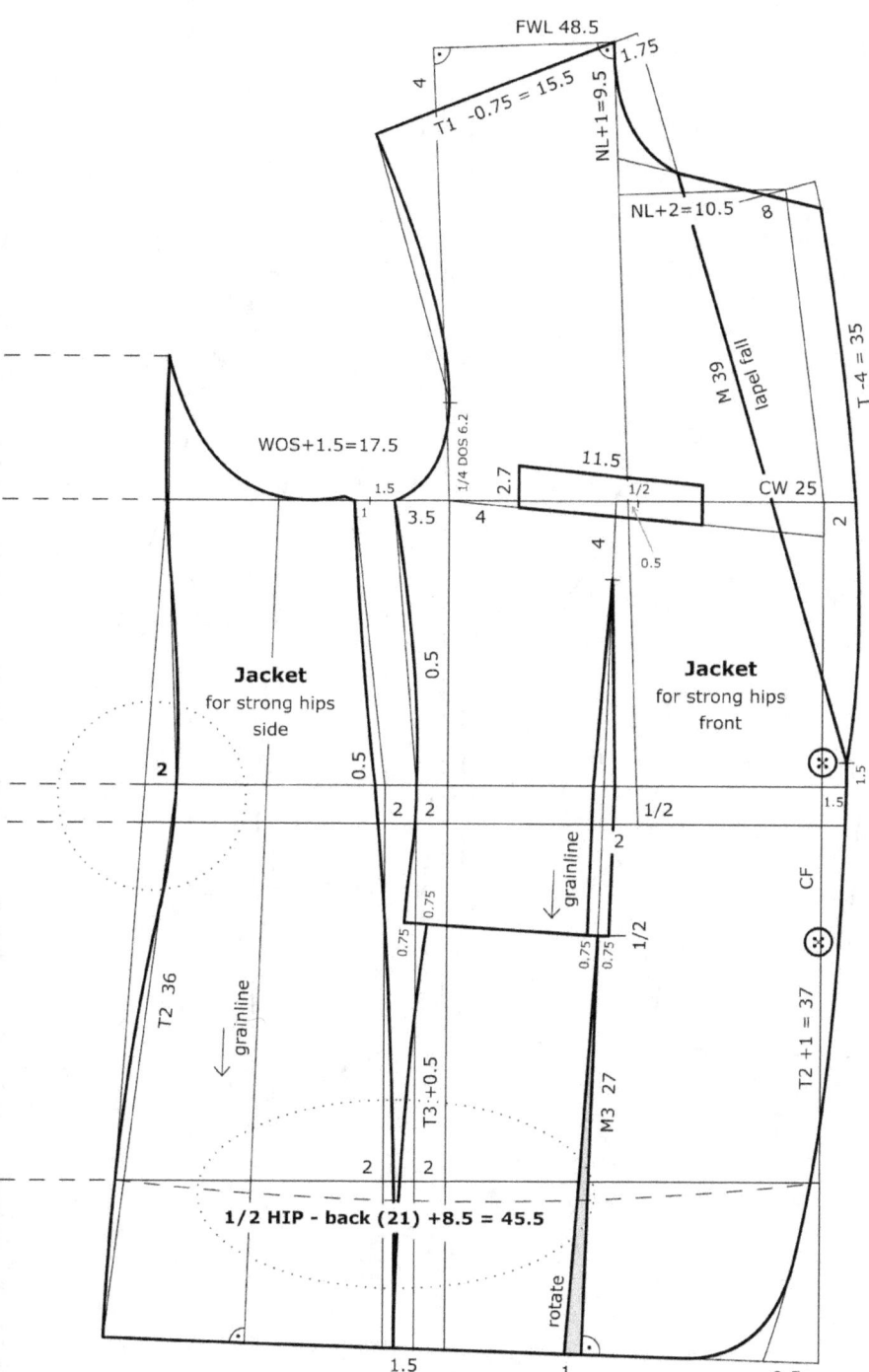

Vest for strong hips

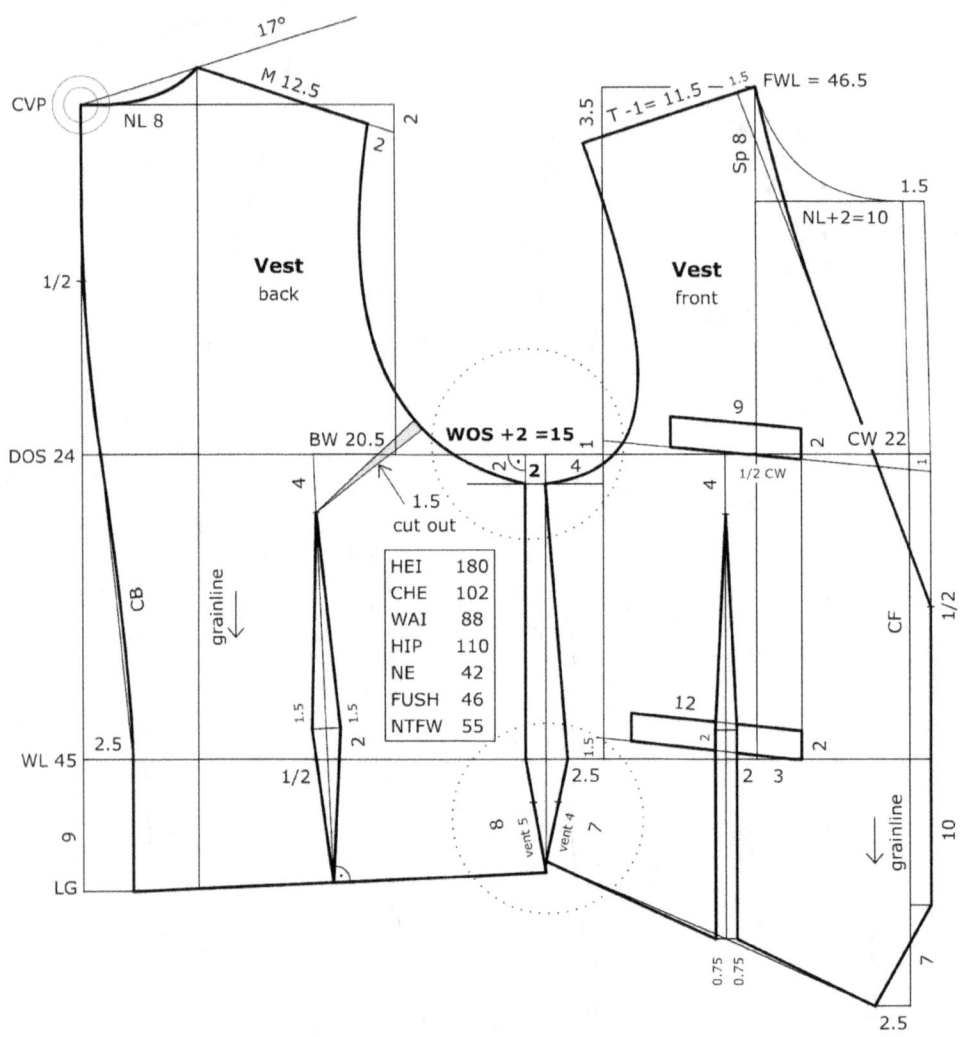

Appendix

Belly		47	49	51	53	55	57	59	61	63	65	67	69
Heigth	HEI	166	168	170	172	174	176	178	180	182	183	184	184
Chest	CHE	94	98	102	106	110	114	118	122	126	130	134	138
Waist	WAI	96	100	104	108	114	118	122	126	132	136	140	144
Hips	HIP	100	104	108	112	116	120	124	128	132	136	140	144
Neck	NE	40	40	42	42	44	44	46	46	48	48	50	50
Depth of scye	DOS	21.1	21.8	22.4	23	23.6	24.2	24.9	25.5	26.2	26.7	27.3	28.3
Waist lenght	WL	41.5	42	42.5	43	43.5	44	44.5	45	45.5	45.8	46	46
Depth of hips	DOH	20.8	21	21.3	21.5	21.8	22	22.3	22.5	22.8	22.9	23	23
Neckline	NE	8.2	8.2	8.5	8.5	8.8	8.8	9.2	9.2	9.5	9.5	9.8	9.8
Back width	BW	19.9	20.3	20.7	21.1	21.5	21.9	22.3	22.7	23.1	23.5	23.9	24.3
Width of scye	WOS	12.8	13.3	13.8	14.3	14.8	15.3	15.8	16.3	16.8	17.3	17.8	18.3
Chest width	CW	20.8	21.6	22.4	23.2	24	24.8	25.6	26.4	27.2	28	28.8	29.6
Belly width	BEW	23	24	25	26	27.5	28.5	29.5	30.5	32	33	34	35
Sleeve lenght	SL	60	61	62	63	64	65	66	67	68	68.5	69	69.5
Outside leg	OUTL	97	98	99	100	101	102	103	104	105	105.5	106	106
Inside leg	INL	73	74	75	76	77	78	79	80	81	81.5	82	82
Width of length	WOL	40	40	41	41	42	42	43	43	44	44	45	45

Abbreviations

B
BD	Belly difference
BEW	Belly width
BPL	Back pants length
BW	Back width

C
CB	Center back
CF	Center front
CHE	Chest
COS	Circumference of scye
CVP	Cervical vertebra point
CW	Chest width

D
DIFF	Difference
DOB	Depth of breast (NTB minus back neckline)
DOH	Depth of hip
DOS	Depth of scye

F
FPL	Front pants length
FS	Front shoulder
FUSH	Full shoulder
FWL	Front waist length (NTFW minus back neckline)

H
HEI	Height
HIP	Hip
HOS	Height of scye

I
INL	Inside leg

L
LG	Length

M
M	Measure

N
NE	Neck
NL	Neckline
NTB	Nape to breast
NTBE	Nape to belly
NTFW	Nape to front waist
NTK	Nape to knee

O
OUTL	Outside leg

S
SH	Shoulder width
SL	Sleeve length
SLH	Sleeve head
SLHW	Sleeve hem width
SLW	Sleeve width

T
T	Transfer
TH	Thigh

U
UPA	Upper arm

W
WAI	Waistline
WB	Waistband
WL	Waist length
WOC	Width of cuff
WOL	Width of leg
WOS	Width of scye
WR	Width of wrist

Sven Jungclaus

completed his training as a bespoke lady's and men's tailor in the 1990s with *Heinz-Josef Radermacher* in Dusseldorf. Already at that time, he worked for musical productions like *Grease* and *Forever Plaid* in Dusseldorf as well as *The Beauty and the Beast* and *The Fearless Vampire Killers* in Stuttgart.

After eight years at the *Bavarian State Opera* in Munich as a master tailor and head of men's costume, he has deepened his expertise at the *Royal Shakespeare Company* in Stratford upon Avon, the *Deutsche Oper am Rhein* in Dusseldorf and the *Salzburg Festival*.

Since 2013, he has been producing bespoke clothing for men and women in his tailor shop *Gewandmanufaktur* in Salzburg. In addition, the versatile tailor works again and again for the costume workshop *Das Gewand* in Dusseldorf and is requested for operas or musical productions - e.g., the *Metropolitan Opera* in New York, the *Nasjonale Opera* in Bergen, the *Theater Basel*, the Musical *Chicago* in Stuttgart and Berlin, *Het Muziektheater* in Amsterdam, the *Salzburg Festival* or the *Theater of Nations in Moscow*.

Another project of Sven Jungclaus is *Become-a-tailor*, an internet presence with professional tips on workmanship, patterns and instructions as well as other know-how for many costume epochs.

www.becomeatailor.com

You can find more information about our books as well as sewing patterns and video instructions for the tailoring process on our website
www.becomeatailor.com

Index

A
Abbreviations	159

B
Back pants	21
Back pants length	16
Become a tailor	163
Belly dart	43
- relocate	44
Belly jacket	66
- back armhole	68
- belly dart	73
- center back seam	68
- chest width	70
- front armhole	72
- front edge	72
- grainline	74
- lapel fall	72
- lower front edge	72
- pattern	76
- pockets	74
- sleeve	80
- sleeve pattern	84
- width of scye	70
Belly shirt	50
- pattern	56
- sleeve	60
- sleeve head	61
- back width	51
- chest	51
- front edge	54
- side seam	51
Belly sizes	158
Belly vest	38
- pattern	47
- armhole, back	40
- cut out armhole	45
- grainline	41
- length	39
- lower front edge	43
- neckline, front	42

B
Belly vest opening	43
- pockets	44
- shoulder, front	42
- side seam	40
Biceps width	14
Biografie	160
Body shapes	8
Bodybuilder shirt sleeve	122
Bodybuilder shirt, front edge	116
Bodybuilder jacket	126
- back armhole	128
- center back seam	128
- chest dart	133
- chest width	130
- front armhole	131
- grainline	134
- lapel fall, new	132
- lower front edge	132
- pattern	136
- pockets	134
- width of scye	130
Bodybuilder shirt	112
- pattern	118
- back width	113
- chest width	113
- side seam	115
- sleeve head	123
Bodybuilder sleeve	140
Bodybuilder sleeve pattern	144
Bodybuilder vest	100
- armhole, back	102
- dart	103
- lower front edge	105
- neckline, front	104
- opening	105
- pattern	108
- pockets	106
- side seam	102
Bodybuilder jacket front edge	132

C

Cervical vertebra point	13
Chest	12
Chest width	14
Circumference of scye	80
Circle, body shape	9
Collar, jacket	86
Cuffs	61

D

Dart pants back	24
Depth of breast	15
Depth of scye	13
Difference	55

E

Elbow line	81

F

Fly	20
Fold center back, belly shirt	52
Front pants	19
Front pants length	16
Front waist length	15
Full shoulder width	14

H

Height of scye	80
Height	13
Hüftweite	12

I

Inclination, seat seam	22
Inside leg	16

J

Jacket collar	86

M

Measurements belly jacket	75
- belly shirt	55
- belly vest	46
- bodybuilder jacket	135
- bodybuilder shirt	117
- over belly pants	35
- sleeve belly jacket	83
- sleeve bodybuilder jacket	143
- under belly pants	25
- bodybuilder pants	95
- bodybuilder vest	107
Modern ladies' tailoring	161
Modern men's tailoring	161
More books	161

N

Nape to breast	15
Nape to belly	15
Nape to front waist	15
Nape to knee	13
Neck	12

O

Outside leg	16
Oval body shape	9
Over belly pants	29
Over belly pants pattern	36

P

Pants for muscular thighs	88
Pattern alteration of pants	98

Index

P
Pattern for a belly jacket	76
- belly jacket sleeve	84
- belly shirt	56
- belly shirt sleeve	62
- belly vest	47
- bodybuilder jacket sleeve	144
- bodybuilder shirt	118
- bodybuilder shirt sleeve	124
- bodybuilder vest	108
- bodybuilder jacket	136
Pattern shirt collar	65
- for regular sizes	150
- for prominent hips	153
- jacket collar	87
- over belly pants	36
- under belly pants	26
- regular	149
Pleat	20

R
Regular pattern	149
Rise	16

S
Seat seam	24
Shirt collar	64
Shoulder width	14
Sleeve head jacket	82
Sleeve length	12
Sleeve notch	83
Sleeve width	81
Straight body shape	8

T
Taking measurements	11
Thigh width	17
Top sleeve	82
Trapeze body shape	9
Triangle body shape	9

U
Under belly pants	19
- pattern	26
Under sleeve	82
Upside down triangle	9

W
Waist	12
Waist length	13
Waistband back pants	23
Waistband line	21
Width of back pants	22
Width of length	17
Width of sleeve length	81
Width of waistband	12
Width of wrist	17

Y
Yoke, belly figure	51
Yoke, bodybuilder	113

www.ingramcontent.com/pod-product-compliance
Lightning Source LLC
Chambersburg PA
CBHW070239240426
43673CB00044B/1851